BLACK ZION

David Jenkins

BLACK ZION

Africa, Imagined and Real,
as Seen by Today's Blacks

HARCOURT BRACE JOVANOVICH
NEW YORK AND LONDON

Printed in the United States of America

The author and publishers gratefully acknowledge permission to reprint
the following material: extract from 'Heritage' by Countee Cullen,
in *On These I Stand*, copyright 1925 by Harper & Row Publishers,
copyright renewed 1953 by Ida M. Cullen; 'I've Known Rivers' by
Langston Hughes, in *The Weary Blues*, Alfred A. Knopf; 'Outcast' by
Claude McKay, in *Selected Poems of Claude McKay*, Twayne Publishers;
'The New Ships' by Edward Brathwaite, in *Masks*, Oxford University Press,
London; 'Guinea' by Jacques Roumain, in *Anthology of Contemporary
Latin-American Poetry*, edited by Dudley Fitts, copyright 1942 by New
Directions Publishing Corporation.

Library of Congress Cataloging in Publication Data

Jenkins, David, 1943–
Black Zion.

Bibliography: p.
1. Americans in West Africa. 2. Back to Africa
movement. 3. Negroes—Colonization—Africa. 4. Africa,
West—Foreign population. I. Title.
DT474.5.J46   325'.273'096   75-2174
ISBN 0-15-113193-7

First American edition

B C D E

CONTENTS

FOR MARIE DUMAS

'The Lord shall cause thee to be smitten before thine enemies: thou shalt go out one way against them and flee seven ways before them; and shalt be removed into all the kingdoms of the earth.'

(Deuteronomy, xxviii 25)

'Oh I'm bound to go to Africa,
I'm bound to go there soon.
I'm bound to go to Africa,
To wear those golden shoes.'

> (Traditional song adopted as hymn, circa
> 1900, by Southern Negroes who followed Bishop
> Henry Turner)

INTRODUCTION

From the first day on which an African was captured, then blessed by some swaggering fifteenth-century Portuguese cleric and consigned to the terrible Atlantic crossing, there have been two distinct Africas. There is the geographical entity, with its millions of social realities, and there is the Africa of the exiled Negro's mind, an Africa compounded of centuries of waning memories and vanquished hopes, translated into myth. Over the centuries — and in particular over the last two — a very special notion has come into being: Black Zionism, the ideal held by millions of blacks in America and the Caribbean of returning to the land from which their forefathers were wrenched. In this book I have attempted to show what happened to those who, since 1787, have attained that ideal and have actually gone back.

I have begun with the growth of the semi-poetic, semi-political, abstract idea of Africa in the New World. Africa? 'So long, so far away', said Langston Hughes. Africa, though, was a land of growth and freedom and ancestry and redemption and purity and deliverance, a land of giants, of the darkest and lightest shades of the soul, the signal for the end of the Diaspora and all suffering. In short, an antithesis of the plantations of the Southern United States and the Caribbean, a place where the spirit could roam free. This imagined Africa became a fountainhead of inspiration and pride for the downtrodden blacks in the Southern cotton areas, and later in the exploitative industrial North of America. It became a salve for the massive disappointment that followed the promises of freedom. It became the focus of literary movements, but also of mass political mobilization of working-class New World blacks. The Back-to-Africa movements that periodically sprang up in America — movements such as those of Bishop Turner and the amazing Marcus Garvey — had little to do with the Africa of the day, but had enormous significance for

9

the exiled black proletariat. Interestingly (and here we see one of the many parallels to Jewish Zionism) concepts such as Pan-Africanism were products of this Diaspora. Just as the State of Israel was born in Central Europe and out of the sufferings of the exiled Hebrews, so many modern independence movements in Africa drew their existence from ideologues from the West Indies and the United States.

But these movements are conspicuous by their almost total failure to send anyone at all back to Africa. Those who returned have done so as individuals. It is an incidental irony that the successful Back-to-Africa movements, which led to the setting up of Sierra Leone and Liberia, were conducted under the aegis of commercial or political colonialism, or of the dubious philanthropy of white people. I have looked at the development of these two strange communities, and especially at the relationship between the settlers from the New World and the Africans they met on the coast.

The Africa of the mind flourished with little reference to the realities of life in Sierra Leone and Liberia, where the settlers very rapidly set about reducing the Africans they found to a state of virtual slavery. Indeed, a country such as Liberia still manages to attract black Americans who are fired by a sort of Zionistic zeal.

The remainder of the book concerns the reactions, impressions and opinions of modern American or West Indian blacks who have gone to live in Africa. These make an intriguing comparison with those of their forebears. I have recorded the very first pungent impressions of the returnees, then looked at the way these sophisticated Westerners have adjusted to the African societies they have chosen. In all, I interviewed a hundred people in Ghana, Sierra Leone and Liberia during the first half of 1973. I chose these three countries because of the widely differing symbolism each contains, and also because, although all three are close neighbours, the social conditions to which the outsider must adapt are very different in each one.

Overall conclusions were difficult, mainly because of the enormous range of the people with whom I talked. People who contributed views were 7 years old and 86; they had been in Africa from between 1 hour and up to 80 years. Therefore — and this turned out to be a crucial point — they had left either America or the West Indies in very different eras. It rapidly became clear that those who had left the United States in the 1950s were very different from those who had left in the early 1960s. And those who had left in the early 'sixties were different again from those who left in the late 'sixties. In addition, they came from very distinct areas, from Brazil, from large and small Caribbean islands and from all areas, rural and urban, of the United States. Their reactions ranged from complete desolation to almost complete contentment.

So, instead of trying to put forward generalizations, I have tried to record as honestly as possible this range of reactions, to reflect the result of the collision between the expectation of Africa and the reality people found and to answer the question: What happens when a myth is confronted by facts?

I have tried — probably unsuccessfully — not to intrude my own reactions. I must, however, confess to an Africa of my own mind. It is a land as irrationally formed, I dare say, as that of any black American. It is a private land of terrors and ineffable beauties, overwhelming in their unexpectedness. It is the home of a certain kind of sceptical wisdom, dignity and style, of a wittiness that can make one smile in memory, of sadness and tiredness, and of gaiety and elegance — all wrapped up in the stench of the most dreadful climate on earth. The elegance of Africa is, for me, its supreme quality. Whenever I ask myself, 'Well, what is Africa to *me*?' I always think of Ada, a small town of no importance on the Volta estuary. There sits Madame Dumas, descended from the black novelist Alexandre Dumas, running a small, dilapidated hotel. Her own essential chic only barely diminishes with advancing years. She tells fortunes with splendid inaccuracy while her hotel is slowly seeping back to Africa (the room I stayed in actually collapsed into the floor below in the 1973 rainy season). As we sit drinking the foulest red-eye on benches on the sand outside, the wind off the Gulf of Guinea slurps up breakers in the dark distance, and continually spills the cards. Madame Dumas, her eyes watering with the wind, her dark cheeks ever so slightly rouged, her ample body in repose, looks up at each of my two companions and me.

I shall never forget the expression of battered majesty on her face in the light of the oil lamp. It is to this great lady that my book is dedicated.

Many people extended their friendship and hospitality to me. None more than Rajat Neogy el Amin, former editor of *Transition* magazine, whose thoughtfulness and companionship place me in a debt I can never repay. I must also thank the poet Syl Cheyney-Coker, who offered me a roof and, indeed, his own bed, in Freetown. Others who gave me their time and energy were: in Accra, Rose Odamtten, of the Ghana Broadcasting Corporation and Fred Agyemang, director of the Ghana Institute of Journalism; in Akropong-Akwapim, the Rev. E.T. Koramoa, who told me much of the early West Indian missionaries in the Gold Coast; in Kumasi, several members of the staff of the University of Science and Technology, and in particular Professor Bob Barclay. I would like to acknowledge also the help of the staffs of the Institutes of African Studies in Legon, University of Ghana, and at Fourah Bay College, University of Sierra Leone.

Mrs G.M. Sheriff and her staff in the library at Fourah Bay College were especially helpful. I also thank Royston Wright, of the Sierra Leone Broadcasting Service, who guided me round Freetown and starved with me in Makeni. In London I was given introductions (not least of which was to the writing of Ayi Kwei Armah) by Ilsa Yardley, and also invaluable research help from Mary James. From New York I received a deluge of material from Phil Fleet, New York editor of I.P.C. Magazines Ltd, and his ever-resourceful assistant, Elizabeth Ann Holzer.

Scores of people in West Africa gave up their time to answer impertinent questions and, although I promised not to name most of them, I do extend my gratitude to each one. This is in many ways more their book than mine. I am also grateful to *Nova* magazine for allowing me leave of absence.

None of the above are in any way responsible for the accuracy of the material in this book, or for the views expressed by me.

London, December 1973   DAVID JENKİNS

PROLOGUE

Whatever — or wherever — they came to think Africa was, many early slaves were convinced they would return to it in their own lifetimes.

The principle of religious freedom for the white man and the institution of slavery for the black man had both been established in the British American colonies at about the same time. In 1620, the year of the Pilgrim Fathers' landing at Plymouth Rock, a previous settler in America noted, 'about the last of August came in a Dutch man of warre that sold us twenty negars.'[1] Almost from the start, slavery was one of the foundations of the white man's economic system, perpetuated and justified by political cowardice and religious hypocrisy. For the black man it was a Diaspora, and a Return from it became a notion of great political and religious significance.

During the long years of the slave trade between Africa and the Americas, the captains of some slave vessels reported that certain vexatious captives jumped overboard, even when secured in irons, and tried to swim home.[2] Africans viewed slavery with a logic different from that of their masters. They were, of course, used to slavery being the natural fate of a prisoner of war in Africa, as a deal entered into between a family and a chief who needed menial servants to enhance his status, or as a level in the household hierarchy. They regarded the *sale* and export of human beings as an aberration and believed that, despite all the evidence, their servitude could only be for a fixed term. Their deliverance was not a vague possibility or something equally vaguely desired. It was inevitable. Only later, when they realised that the mass exportations were permanent, did the idea of deliverance become confused with the Christian idea of heaven. At first their masters' heaven was a living reality, mingled with their own animistic beliefs. As time went by, it became clear to them that their deliverance was through death, and that only after death could heaven, and therefore Africa, be reached.

'Lord, I want to cross over into camp ground,' went one

early slave song. 'Oh when I get to heav'n, I'll walk all a-bout. There's nobody there for to turn me out.'[3] And, 'We'll land on Canaan's shore.'[4] The earliest songs stress the 'we shall' of a definite return rather than the 'we hope' of a more orthodox religious aspiration.

A minority, however, clung to the belief that, after all, Africa was a real place, that no superhuman power had transplanted them in the New World, and that they could employ human, physical means to return. One such was Job ben Solomon, a Muslim Fulani who had been captured on the banks of the Gambia in 1731 and sold into slavery. From Maryland he wrote to his father, pleading with him to ransom him. The letter was intercepted in London, and Solomon came to the attention of the philanthropist James Oglethorpe. Oglethorpe redeemed Solomon for forty-five pounds and brought him to England, where he gained a reputation as an Arabic scholar, and was even presented at Court to Queen Caroline. Solomon was sent back to his village of Bondou, his sponsors believing him to be a useful means of encouraging British trade in the growing French–British trade rivalry on the coast. He arrived back in 1736. 'I must leave you to guess . . . the Raptures and pleasures I enjoy'd', he wrote, with disappointing lack of detail, to a friend. 'Floods of Tears burst their way . . . '[5] Little more was heard of Solomon. It is unlikely that he did anything to satisfy the greed of his sponsors.

Other attempts were made in the eighteenth century to harness this potentially dangerous desire of a few to return. Missionary societies variously tried to recruit Negroes for their African outposts since, they reasoned, the best people to proselytize among black folk were their own kind. Similarly, in the next century the American Colonization Society, founded in 1816 as a vehicle for black repatriation to Africa, was seen as a means to be rid of such nuisances by packing them off to Liberia.

There had been anti-slavery agitation, notably from the Quakers, in America and Britain for some years. As early as 1671, the founder of the Society of Friends in Britain, George Fox, said in Barbados, 'Consider with yourselves if you were in the same condition as the poor Africans are — who came as strangers to you and were sold to you as slaves. I say, if this should be the condition of you and yours, you would think it a hard measure — yea, a very great bondage and cruelty.'[6] Fox merely suggested, however, that the slaves' lot might be improved by conversion to Christianity — not by release. Arguments centred on the evil of the slave trade rather than that of slavery itself.

Towards the end of the eighteenth century there was growing awareness on both sides of the Atlantic, too, that slavery was not entirely the convenience it had originally been perfected as; perhaps its greatest flaw was that some slaves maintained this dogged belief in a return to Africa.

Some of the anti-slavery pressure was, to say the least, equivocal. In his *Notes on Virginia,* written a mere five years after the Declaration of Independence, the slave-owner Thomas Jefferson wrote that he believed slavery to be a 'blot in this country'. But, he went on, 'I advance it . . . as a suspicion only, that the blacks, whether originally a distinct race, or made distinct by time and circumstances, are inferior to the whites in the endowments of both body and mind.' He remarked on a 'very strong and disagreeable odour' and the capacity to live on less sleep than whites, and suggested the removal of these malodorous creatures to a faraway place.[7] As much as anything else, he was concerned about divine retribution. 'I tremble for my country when I reflect that God is just . . . that his justice cannot sleep forever.'[8]

Others lent their support to repatriation movements, less through even this dubious philanthropy and apocalyptic guilt than through fear for their own skins. In 1790, Ferdinando Fairfax, later a charter member of the American Colonization Society, utterly discounted the possibility of inter-racial harmony and warned that the presence of a distinct social and racial group within a society promised only 'to endanger the peace of society'. Fairfax strongly recommended transportation of at least the freed Negroes 'to a distance from this country', and Africa appeared to be the logical place.[9]

It would be unjust to attribute the worst of motives uniformly to those who eventually made it possible for descendants of Africans to achieve their forefathers' dreams. It would be equally wrong, however, to suppose that they were motivated by unalloyed altruism. Anti-slavery pressure in the United States

15

was largely preceded by pressure to repatriate freed slaves. In Britain, the opposite was the case. Agitation had been mounting in Britain during the latter part of the eighteenth century. Most vocal of the critics of slavery was a perhaps over-pious but nonetheless effective group known as the Clapham Sect, or the Evangelicals. The leading figures of the Sect included not only prudes such as Thomas Bowdler, but also conscientious and courageous men such as William Wilberforce, Thomas Clarkson and Granville Sharp.

It was Granville Sharp, grandson of the Archbishop of York, who led the fight that resulted in the Mansfield Decision of 1772. The judgment of Chief Justice Mansfield outlawed the traffic of slaves from England to the New World. This was by no means the revolutionary decision it was later held to be and, in fact, it was very limited in its application. Although economics and not philanthropy eventually brought down the slave trade, the Mansfield Decision was in many ways a factor that led to the English abolition of slavery in 1807. But it was Granville Sharp also who was to put into effect the first major scheme to repatriate black people to Africa.

For some time there had been black people in Britain. Most had originally been brought as personal slaves. Some became status symbols for the rich, and it was not unusual to see a black flunkey accompanying his mistress to the opera. But some, who did not belong to a parish, and were not eligible for relief, fell into destitution and congregated in various cities, but mainly in the East End of London. They were the object of occasional scurrilous attacks in the broadsheets, but were largely ignored.[10]

In the 1780s England was faced with the embarrassment of what to do with the Negroes who had fought on the British side in the American War of Independence. Under the terms of the Independence Treaty, Britain was bound to return to the Americans all captured property, including slaves. Those in authority may have been guided by the Mansfield Decision, but were more likely aware of what the fate of such slaves might be, and were, just possibly, grateful for the war service many Negroes had given in the Navy and in the Rangers. At all events, former slaves were given a kind of sanctuary in Canada and Britain. Those who settled in Britain — and they numbered several thousand — joined the destitute in the major cities, mainly

London. The newcomers were soon known as the 'indigent blacks', or, more usually, the Black Poor of London.

As usual in these matters, a committee was formed, the Committee for the Black Poor. In 1786 it was approached by a raddled gentleman named Henry Smeathman who, although the committee was not to know it, was making his last pitch for a fortune that had always eluded him.

Between 1771 and 1774 Smeathman had sailed extensively round the coast of what is now Sierra Leone. Based on the Banana Islands, he collected botanical specimens on commission for Kew Gardens and developed a great interest in the manifold insects of the region. Known by the local Temne people as the 'Flycatcher', his knowledge, for a white man, was considerable. According to one unkind historian, 'If he has any fame now it will be because he was the originator of a new table delicacy, a worm about the size of a man's thumb found in the crown of decaying palm-trees, fried in palm-oil and seasoned with pepper and salt and lime-juice.'[11]

Though endowed with such expertise in the natural history of western Africa, Smeathman had somehow never developed a parallel talent for making money, one of his main intentions. From his island the coast looked a land of promise. At its western extreme, the land rose sharply to lush hills, over which, in the rainy season, great clouds swarmed, purple and spectacular, to the coastal strip below. The natives seemed relatively friendly, although not especially profitable, at least to him. Smeathman also knew, however, that this land, so beautiful from a distance, was both dangerous and destructive. He knew that yellow jack, malaria and typhoid were endemic and that the soil, certainly on the coast, was not very fertile. In 1785, Smeathman told a House of Commons committee investigating the chances of setting up a penal colony in Sierra Leone that if convicts were sent in any numbers to the coast, not two would still be alive in six months. He may, of course, have purposely exaggerated the ghastliness of conditions with his eye on the main chance of greater profit to be derived by other means. At any rate, by the next year he presented a diametrically opposing view of the area in his *Plan of a Settlement* which was published in 1786 and formed a series of proposals to the Committee for the Black Poor. As a prospectus it is effulgent: Sierra Leone would be ideal for crops of cotton, rice, sugar and tobacco, was healthy and pleasant, and would admirably settle the problem of what to do with the Black Poor.

Smeathman offered to take the Committee's charges to West Africa for £4 a head. Being also something of an enthusiast for balloons, he offered — perhaps desperately — to advertise the scheme by means of sponsored balloon ascents. The scheme proved to be very attractive to the black domestics of London, as well as to former soldiers and sailors. It was this immediate appeal that was the decisive factor. Later in 1786 Smeathman died and the Committee began to lose interest in his scheme and toyed with thoughts of other areas for repatriation. Granville Sharp had been convinced for some years that West Africa was the proper venue for a return, but the issue was solved by a number of black people sending a petition to the Committee, favouring 'Mr Smeathman's humane plan'.

So it was that 411 people, including about 70 white women, set sail from Plymouth on April 8th, 1787. The departure itself was not without hazard. There was a delay of several months, during which about 50 of the emigrants died of fever aboard ship, still within sight of England. Their instructions, as the first-ever organized group of black people to be repatriated to Africa, were to behave in a manner appropriate to the spirit that had prompted their benefactors, to act as a model for those who were to follow, and to found the Province of Freedom. Said Sharp, 'They must be careful not to adopt any regulations that are at all inconsistent with the fundamental principles of the Common Law of England . . . [and] they must be careful also not to establish any Religion that is inconsistent with the Religious Establishment of England.'[12] A bizarre civil code was evolved by Sharp, derived from 'the Israelitish commonwealth under the Theocracy, purified and improved by the precepts of the Gospel, and the examples of congregational government among the primitive Christians who decided their own temporal controversies as well as ecclesiastical questions'.[13]

This patchwork of Mosaic Law and the Saxon system of *frankpledge* may be said to have been the model of the first representative self-government that any West African colony was to see for 170 years. On the other hand, it was an excessively cumbersome system, involving a renunciation of money and investing authority in people who were used to total authority being exercised over them, or to none. It was

18

agriculture-based, on the assumption that skills and usages their forefathers knew would surely still reside in them. The community was to be divided into households; each head of a household would be known as a *tythingman*. Ninety-six *tythingmen*, together with an elected chief or *hundredor*, two lieutenants and a municipal officer, would form the basic unit of legislature of 100 people. These units would also have a military function, with the *hundredors* acting as captains.

Further pious advice, and the promise of a tax on the idle, sped the settlers on their way. By the time they reached Tenerife, 14 were dead of shipboard diseases. But just over a month after they had left Plymouth, they arrived at the mouth of the Sierra Leone river. A party landed, climbed an escarpment — to the spot now occupied by the offices of the President of the Republic of Sierra Leone — planted the British flag, and named their huddling settlement Granville Town.

There is, regrettably, scant reliable record of these pilgrims' first impressions. But we do know that they arrived at precisely the worst time of the year. In mid May — they arrived on May 15th — begin the rains. On that part of the West African coast they are astonishingly violent. In the space of three or four months, upwards of a hundred and thirty inches of rain fall. (While I was there, the equivalent of one quarter of the annual rainfall of London fell in one night.) The settlers had arrived too late to plant their rice, and when the rains struck with their full force, they were still only in tents and other temporary dwellings. On the other hand, they had measured out a settlement of several hundred acres, and negotiated a piece of land about twenty miles square from King Tom, overlord of the Bulom coast, a sub-chief under King Naimbana. For their land, the settlers paid £59 1s. 5d. worth of muskets, gunpowder, shot, swords, laced hats, cotton goods, beads, iron bars (later a major item of currency), rum and tobacco.

Within three months, about one third of the colony were dead of fever and dysentery. Among the dead was the agent and also the gardener; in fact he was one of the first to die. The seeds that had been taken perished; in any case it was soon discovered that nothing but bush would flourish on the hill. The pastoral harmony envisaged by Granville Sharp was confounded by the reality of the fever-ridden, half-starved, soaking wet and bickering misery of the Province's early months. The elaborate system of *frankpledge,* designed to foster a sturdy breed of inter-reliant yeomen, dissolved into petty squabbling and total indiscipline.

In despair of becoming self-reliant, the settlers began bartering their stores, weapons and clothes to the Temne. By the fall of 1787, Sharp recorded, 'I have had but melancholy accounts of my poor little ill-thriven swarthy daughter, the unfortunate colony of Sierra Leone.' He tried to see the bright side. 'They have . . . purchased twenty miles square of the finest and most beautiful country (they all allow) that was ever seen! The hills are not steeper than Shooter's Hill; and fine streams of fresh water run down the hill on each side of the new township; and in the front is a noble bay, where the river is about three leagues wide: the woods and groves are beautiful beyond description, and the soil very fine.'[14] A general gloom had settled on the wretched colonists, however. They seemed scarcely able to know where to begin in listing their complaints. One morose settler, named Elliot, wrote to Sharp:

> I am sorry, and very sorry indeed, to inform you, dear Sir, that this country does not agree with us at all; and, without a very sudden change, I do not think there will be one of us left at the end of a twelvemonth. Neither can the people be brought to any rule or regulation, they are so very obstinate in their tempers. It was really a very great pity ever we came to the country . . . for we are settled upon the very worst part. There is not a thing, which is put into the ground, will grow more than a foot out of it. We are situated on a very high hill, where nothing will come forth at all . . . The natives die very fast: it is quite a plague seems to reign among us. I have been dangerously ill myself, but it pleased the Almighty to restore me to health again; and the first opportunity I have, I shall embark for the West Indies.[15]

More melancholy news was to follow. Not the least of it was that Henry Demane, whom Sharp himself had rescued from a slave ship in the Thames two years before, had entered the slave trade. (He was to continue as a successful slaver for twelve years.) Several others also found more profit to be gained in the trade. Sharp tried hard to vindicate the scheme and castigated the moral incompetence of the settlers. 'The greatest blame', he wrote early in 1788, 'is to be charged on the intemperance of the people themselves; for most of them (both Whites and Blacks) became so besotted during the voyage that they were totally unfit for business when they landed, and could hardly be prevailed on to assist in erecting their own huts . . . the climate of Africa is by no means chargeable with the mortality.'[16]

But the state of the colony was fast approaching that of anarchy. James Reid, designated head of the colony — who had been accused in a letter to Sharp of absconding with the stores — wrote:

> There was sixty-three muskets stolen by our people, by whom I knew not . . . After that Mr Weaver and Mr Johnson held with the people, and told them that I had made away with them myself, and got them under arms against me; and they rised on me, and seized my house, and took it from me, and all what little I had in the world . . . After they broke me, they thought to have God's blessing, as they said. The first thing was a young lad found shot, lying in the woods, but never found who was the person that did it. The second was, they got in a little trouble with King Tom, and he catched two of them, and sold them on board a Frenchman bound for the West Indies. The third was, five of them went up to Bance Island, and broke open a factory belonging to one Captain Boys, and stole a number of things; but they were detected, and Captain Boys sold the whole five of them.[17]

By March 1788, only one hundred and thirty were left alive, or at any rate within the Province as settlers. The colony soon came to understand the nature of land tenure in Africa. Among the Temne, indeed, among most tribes in West Africa,* land is not owned in any proprietorial sense; it is held on trust from the local chief. According to tribal law, the settlers were never there except as a favour granted by King Tom. The understanding of the settlers had been that they had bought a deed to their

---

* Settlers ancient and modern in Africa have frequently been confused by the tribal law of land tenure. But an Ashanti proverb goes, *'Tumi nyina wo asase so'* — 'all power is in land', and this power is indivisible with outsiders.

land. The understanding of the Temne was that they had not. The chief was frequently tempted to remind the settlers of this, and that involved several skirmishes between his people and the better-armed settlers.

When King Tom died later in 1788, King Naimbana gave the colonists notice to quit. With a great deal of grit, considering their woe-begone state, they defied him, and were joined by a group of thirty-nine more settlers, sent in June 1788 by Granville Sharp as reinforcements from Europe. Further trade goods, to the value of £85, were paid over to Naimbana, and a completely unenforceable treaty signed. This illegal treaty — never ratified by the British Government — was signed on August 22nd, 1788, and is regarded as the legal birth of the Sierra Leone colony.

Two years after the first settlers had landed, the colony still numbered fewer than two hundred people, and was struggling. There was the threat from within as the system of government disintegrated. And there was a growing threat from without, as Naimbana, undoubtedly encouraged by disgruntled slavers who naturally resented the little colony, continued his pressure, with the new sub-chief, King Jimmy, as catspaw, acting as his instrument of agression.

In November 1789, H.M.S. *Pomona,* commanded by Captain Henry Savage, anchored off shore. Captain Savage was asked to intercede by the settlers, who felt that King Jimmy was unreasonably refusing to honour the treaty of the year before. Savage summoned King Jimmy to appear before him. King Jimmy declined, so Savage sent a party of marines ashore. He later reported that he next heard firing from the shore, and that he saw a Temne town on fire. More general and heavier fighting broke out between the marines and the Temne, so Savage withdrew his men to the ship. He was certainly alarmed at the extent to which, as a representative of His Majesty's Navy, he was about to enforce an illegal treaty. He concluded the engagement by firing a 9lb. gun at any native who showed himself on shore. Then, without more ado, he sailed away.

Under the circumstances, it was a calm ultimatum which King Jimmy then presented to the settlers. He gave them three days to quit Granville Town. In that time, the pilgrims fled to the bush and scattered all over the western part of the promontory of Sierra Leone, most of them never to re-emerge. On the third day,

King Jimmy's men went into the still-pitiful straggle of huts and tents and burnt it to the ground. Thus, in the words of Christopher Fyfe, Sierra Leone's greatest historian, 'perished the first Granville Town, capital of the Province of Freedom'.

CHAPTER 1
A Phantom Land

What is Africa to me:
Copper sun or scarlet sea,
Jungle star or jungle track,
Strong bronzed men, or regal black
Women from whose loins I sprang
When the birds of Eden sang?
One three centuries removed
From the scenes his fathers loved.
Spicy grove, cinnamon tree,
What is Africa to me?

(From 'Heritage' by Countee Cullen[1])

Richard Wright once wrote: 'One does not react to Africa as Africa is . . . One reacts to Africa as one is, as one lives; one's reaction to Africa is one's life, one's ultimate sense of things.'[2] Wright was partially explaining his own failure, as a black American intellectual, to respond with total sympathy to the physical reality of the Africa he visited in the early 1950s. His truism probably holds for any traveller — black or white — in Africa. Yet uniquely embedded in the individual black American are historical, political and cultural phantasms of Africa, a special sensitivity that is at the same time a heightened awareness and an impediment to awareness. For the black American the curiously blended myth of Africa is a broad social phenomenon and yet also a highly personalized mesh of images.

In *Black Orpheus*, Jean-Paul Sartre described this image as an 'Africa beyond reach, imaginary continent'. Sartre wrote that modern black poetry in the Americas reflected in the writer, as in all black people,

> Africa, the last circle, navel of the world, pole of all black poetry; Africa, dazzling, incendiary, oily as the serpent's skin; Africa of the fire and the rain, torrid and suffocating, phantom Africa, vacillating as a flame, between being and non-being . . . the black soul is an Africa from which the Negro is exiled in the midst of the cold buildings of the white culture and the white techniques.[3]

This phantom is not, of course, purely a lyrical metaphor in an isolated literary sense; but neither has it imbued Negro culture with a constant intensity down all the years. It is a spark that has periodically sprung to life in literary and political forms; it is a subjective value, a wayward thing, part of the complex psychological luggage that the individual

27

black New Worlder takes with him to the actual Africa. It is a myth that is fed or repudiated — perhaps even simultaneously, as in Wright's case — at deeply personal levels.

The phantom Africa has surfaced in the bold rhythms and strident images of poetry and song all over the New World, from Brazil, by way of Haiti, Cuba and the formerly British West Indies, to Harlem. The imaginary continent has been the pivot of political upheavals in the Caribbean, the rural South and the urban North of America, in ghettoes right across the United States. The name of Africa has been a watchword for rebellion, race pride, separate heritage, exclusivity, religious or social assertion, cultural accomplishment and escapist fantasy; although frequently serving as the ensign of deliverance from the injustices of American society, it has often played the equally important part of solidifying a fragmented ethnic minority into a political grouping within the United States, demonstrating its considerable presence in' American society.

The forces that have shaped this mythical Africa are many. The myth often amounts to an intimate and personally perceived ideal and so may not always be ascribed to historical or objective causes. However, at critical times for American blacks Africa was conjured up by leaders with intuition, showing that at a time of domestic crisis a certain deep psycho-political well was there to be tapped.

There is a strong claim that the real Africa never fully faded for the captives who were brought in their hundreds of thousands across the Middle Passage. The claim is most strongly put by Melville Herskovits, a painstaking and influential researcher into African retentions in the New World. Part of the evidence consists of the notable retentions that have been found in language, religious custom and social organization all over the New World. It would be absurd to suppose that Africa was suddenly blotted out by the crossing of the Atlantic: marriage and burial ceremonies, for instance, frequently reflected African traditions. One striking case in the very early nineteenth century was child burials. Into the grave were put various symbolic objects, including a miniature canoe, in which the spirit of the child could sail back to Africa.[4]

Linguisitic retentions have also been well researched. One researcher found no fewer than 4,000 words of West African origin in the Gullah dialect on the coast of South Carolina and Georgia.*5 Whole communities shaped along West African patterns have been examined in Bahia, Brazil, and the religious ceremonial and beliefs of the macumbas, candomblés and shangos of Brazil and the Caribbean show clear relation to an animistic heritage such as is found in West Africa. Even on the smaller plantations of North America, where the Negroes were placed in lesser concentrations, there was evidence of linguistic and musical retention.

But when considering Herskovits's evidences (published in 1941)it is as well to remember his reasons for advancing them. In *The Myth of the Negro Past*, he set out to disprove certain myths: that Negroes were naturally of childlike character and adjusted easily to the most unsatisfactory social conditions, that only the poorer stock of Africa was enslaved, that tribal identities were immediately submerged in slavery, that the African cultures were so inherently weak that faced with the superior culture of white America they capitulated, and that the Negro was thus a man without a past. Herskovits pointed out that these myths were primarily used to validate the concept of Negro inferiority, and essentially they were used by whites. African-ness was used as a weapon of scorn by whites in some American states and in the West Indies. It is to be expected then that black Americans should, as products of many generations of shame in African-ness, feel themselves to have lost their connection with Africa. While the retentions may be

---

* In general, the linguistic retentions are stronger the further south you go in the Americas. From virtually non-existent influences in the Northern cities in the United States, they develop into strong and undeniable forces in the Caribbean. Brazil has been described by Jose Honorio Rodrigues in 'The Influence of Africa on Brazil and of Brazil on Africa' in the *Journal of African History*, III, 1 [1962] pp. 49-67, as a demographically changed nation. Words in Brazilian Portuguese that have African roots number many hundreds. Notable are the Kimbundu and Yoruba influences, as in *bangue* (stretcher, wheelbarrow), *banze* (row, rumpus), *banzeiro* (wave, swell), *baturai* (to hammer on the piano), *bengala* (walking stick), *cambada* (bandy-legged), *carcunda* (hunchback), *inhame* (yam), *mulambo* (cloth, rag) and, of course, *samba*.

validly provable they are rarely felt to be present by modern blacks. Certainly very few I spoke to in Africa felt any such common roots when confronted by them. Assertions of African-ness turned out as often to be reactions against white scorn as spontaneous expressions of a true Africa-within.

The single area in which whites came to feel no threat, no dispute, and indeed a certain amused admiration, was music and dance, and it remains the sole area in which the retentions are both evident *and* perceived, with no inherited guilt and little ambivalence.

Most slaves who were shipped to the United States came from an area that stretches in a band two or three hundred miles wide that runs down the African coast, roughly from the Gambia River to the Cameroons (much later to the Congo and Angola). Herskovits identified a 'core area' of influence, an area of West Africa from which he said that the most culturally developed slaves were taken: Ashanti, Dahomey and Yoruba lands, the Akan, Fon, Ewe and Twi speaking peoples.[6] The basic features that the black American and West African musical traditions share are: a distinctive metronomic sense, a dominance of percussion, polymeter, an off-beat phrasing of melodic accents, and an overlapping of call and response. All of which may be a lofty way of expressing what most New Worlders said to me: that they felt the rhythm and function of African music were familiar to them, and that this, as we shall see, was one of the very few things that set black Americans inside the same culture camp as Africans in West Africa itself, a camp that excludes Europeans.

However, in other areas of culture black Americans, together with the Europeans, were irretrievably outside the culture camp. This can be a most painful experience for the black American in Africa. Music is perhaps the only subjective evidence of Africa-within that black Americans know they have before they travel to Africa, and that survives once they get there.

Too much of the theory of African retentions depends on ingenious explanations of phenomena that can equally be explained otherwise. It has been suggested, for instance, that the success of the Baptist preachers in converting slaves in the South lay in the folk-memories the total immersion evoked of the river cults of West Africa. Yet whites also fell under the spell of the aggressively proselytizing Baptists (and Methodists), whose message was one of deliverance from an earthly condition that was mean and degrading. Similarly, the high incidence of illegitimacy and common-law marriage among the early slaves has been interpreted as a diluted form of African marriage customs. In fact it may prove the opposite: the destruction of the African family structure rather than its retention.[7]

Residues of the real Africa still feature inconsistently in black American culture, but the phantom Africa chiefly derives not from a clearly articulate race memory but from ideas and reactions on American soil. The moulding of this symbolic Africa falls roughly into three main phases:

1.   The period from the turn of the eighteenth century (when the primacy of cotton expanded the plantation system, and hence slavery, into an organized social order) up to the outbreak of the Civil War. This was a time when the numbers of Africans who had actually made the Atlantic crossing were gradually being far outnumbered by those who had been born in America. During this time the condition of Southern blacks was one of bondage. In the North, freed blacks were forming into working-class communities, harassed but socially organized in their churches and friendly societies. The cultural expression of Africa was, in the South, a folk-oral one. In the North, where the repatriation movement was to be based, it was also oral, but channelled through the sermons of high pietism by black preachers. The literature of the Negroes, North and South, was almost entirely involved in the anti-slavery campaign.

2.   The period from the end of the Civil War, through the violent years of the Reconstruction in the South and the humiliating 'accommodations' of the Negroes to a white supremacist society which returned them to a state of near-slavery, up to the mass migrations to the North at the beginning of the twentieth century. Here, amid the turmoil of a social revolution, Africa was most significant as a political stimulant. White-organized repatriation had tailed off (only about 13,000 had gone back to Africa). But some blacks who had returned to Africa had become eloquent spokesmen of the new colonization by blacks of their own homeland, and were encouragement, albeit faint, in the general desperation of those post-war years. These spokesmen eventually paved the way for black leaders in America itself to advocate a mass return.

31

3.   Finally, the period beginning immediately before the
First World War, with the enormous influx of blacks into the
Northern cities, the subsequent growth of this black urban
proletariat in the North, and the emergence of a truly Africa-
oriented mass movement, and leading to the excitement of the
'forties and 'fifties, with the constant news of independence
struggles in colonial Africa. During this period references to
Africa began to form a major part of the black literary
revolution that swept urban America. From this period stem
the modern movements, such as the Black Muslims, that speak
of the commonality of the Third World peoples with American
blacks.

Only comparatively recently can Africa-awareness be said to
have become a mass awareness. It was always a simmering
cultural factor in black life, but those who boldly and
specifically invoked Africa were a minority, and usually
appealed to minorities. Only in this century, with the rapid
development of sophisticated information and propaganda
media — not least of which was the Negro press — has this myth
been accessible to a majority. Even so, that majority has
invariably, and rightly, preferred not to take refuge in an
illusory Afro-American nationalism, but to use it as a means to
assert their rights as Americans.

In theory slavery is a uniform atrocity; in practice it is an
experience of enormous variation in mood and effect. While
large numbers of slaves were gathered in relatively stable
'African' communities on the sugar plantations of the
Caribbean and Brazil, the slave population of the United
States was shifted, and sometimes convulsed, by events.
Slavery had radiated from Virginia and Maryland as the
cultivation of rice, tobacco and indigo had spread during the
eighteenth century. The great cotton years of the nineteenth
century saw a massive increase in the slave population — from
around 700,000 in 1790 to nearly 4 million in 1860 — but also
a geographical movement. In the first 60 years of the nineteenth
century an estimated three-quarters of a million slaves were sold
from the border states of Delaware, Maryland, Virginia, the
District of Columbia and North Carolina to plantations in the
Mississippi Valley and the Gulf States. At the same time, many

'plantations' were in reality small farms that owned only one or two slaves. By 1860 at least half of all the slaves in the South were on plantations with fewer than 50 slaves. Although perhaps a quarter of a million slaves were smuggled into the United States after the abolition of slavery, the greatest element of growth in the slave population was natural increase, so that a very high proportion of the slaves in America by the mid-nineteenth century had been born in America.[8] It is therefore most likely that the movement and mix of the slaves helped to diminish the real memories of Africa while it enriched an idealized, but by no means uniform, apocrypha of Africa.

The treatment shown the slaves was also a variable. It was in no way a stark alternative between brutal oppression and cosy paternalism. It was 'a curious blend of force and concession, of arbitrary disposal by the master and self-direction by the slave, of tyranny and benevolence, of antipathy and affection.'[9] Slavery provoked extreme inhumanity, extreme rebellion and extreme intolerance, but there was also a complex middle ground of dependency, fear, and perhaps even mutual respect.

The consciousness of Africa that was kept alive after the establishment of the slave era was, then, correspondingly variable. It grew from the beginning of the realization early slaves had that they might not, after all, be returned to Africa while they lived. There was a further compound of religious myth, a singular mixture of white fundamentalist Christianity and race memory, and a lack of reliable information from Africa itself. There was also a feeling of vacuum created by the deprivation of a true identity, and a definite hope for a personal deliverance. Africa was seen as a place of natural, universal justice.

Early slave songs, which survive selectively in written form, illustrate the clandestine infancy of an American image of Africa. Direct references to slavery and to the real Africa were disguised in Biblical terms, which in turn might be believed literally by illiterate slaves. Thus the Atlantic became the Red Sea or, more often, the Jordan.

Deep River, my home is over the Jordan, Deep River,
Lord I want to cross over into camp ground . . .[10]

And, of course, Africa became heaven:

I cannot stay in hell one day,
Heav'n shall-a be my home;
I'll sing and pray my soul away,
Heav'n shall-a be my home.[11]

Or, alternatively, the Promised Land:

I asked my Lord, shall I ever be the one
(I asked my Lord) shall I ever be the one,
    shall I ever be the one,
(I asked my Lord I be),
To go sailin', sailin', sailin', sailin',
Gwine over to the Promised Land?[12]

Or, simply, 'the kingdom':

No more backbiting in de kingdom,
Hallelu, hallelu,
No more backbiting in de kingdom,
Hallelujah.[13]

When florid accounts later came back to America of the
progress of the repatriates who returned to Africa in the early
nineteenth century, these accounts were forced in turn to the
service of the further glory of what lay in store.

De trumpet sound in de oder bright land [or world]
    And I yearde from heaven today,
De trumpet sound in de oder bright land,
    And I yearde from heaven today.[14]

Had the singers and listeners had access to dispassionate news
from the new African settlements they would have found it far
from assuring. (See Chapter 2) But instead, they were treated
to inspirational poems and accounts, such as were published in
the *African Repository and Colonial Journal* — organ of those
who sponsored the repatriation — or were retailed from the
pulpits of Southern chapels. In any case, even if they had known
the worst, they might well have transformed the bad news into
hymns about nobility in adversity.

An indication of the minimal politcal pull of Africa is that, at
any rate among the Southern slaves, individual or organized
rebellion was almost entirely concerned with freedom rather

than any thought in going home. It is true that after the
abortive rebellion led by the slave Gabriel in Richmond,
Virginia, in 1800, the state of Maryland adopted a policy of
repatriating to Africa certain freed slaves, and indeed
subsequently of freeing troublesome slaves in order that they
might be sent back.[15] But Gabriel, like so many leaders of
organized slave rebellions, was more inspired by the idea of
throwing off the yoke than by the possibility of leading his
people to a promised land. Nat Turner, a Baptist mystic, led a
revolt in 1831, but, instead of fleeing, his band set about
murdering whites where they were, on the farms, killing
fifty-five. Turner had only the vaguest idea of where
precisely his deliverance might lead. The Underground Railroad,
which ferried countless hundreds of fugitive slaves from the
South during the first part of the nineteenth century, led to that
other more immediate Canaan in the North, to the cities, and
eventually to Canada.

Practical attempts at repatriation perhaps dwindled because of
the fact that, once freed, the Negro had a reasonable chance —
at least in the early part of the nineteenth century — of
establishing himself in a skilled trade or in a small enterprise in
one of the large Southern cities in, for example, New Orleans or
Charleston.

In the Northern cities, where the repatriation movement was
based from 1816, the situation was different. Slavery had existed
only as a form of domestic service, so the proportion of freed
Negroes to slaves was very much greater. Here, where the free
Negroes were often in economic competition with whites,
relations between the races were poor and sometimes violent.
Reaction to prejudice, or segregation, was frequently the
raising of a symbolic 'African' banner.

For instance, in the closing years of the eighteenth century
blacks were beginning to be excluded from white churches. Two
blacks, Richard Allen and Absolom Jones, were said to have
been forcibly ejected while on their knees praying in their church,
St George's in Philadelphia. Allen and Jones formed what they
called The Free African Society, and this became the basis of
the first independent black church. This was also the first use of
the term 'African' to denote a black institution set up in America
to defy white institutions. Allen went on to found his own church,
the Bethel African Methodist Episcopal Church. Several other

black leaders in Delaware, Maryland, New Jersey and
Pennsylvania followed suit. In 1816, the disparate group of
black churches was formed into the African Methodist Episcopal
Church, with Richard Allen as its first bishop. Further 'African'
churches sprang up in the early part of the nineteenth century,
the Abyssinian Baptist Church of New York and the African
Baptist Church of Philadelphia, for instance. The primary aim of
the churches was to allow black people to identify with each
other, rather than with Africa, in promoting a united front
against segregation. The churches chose to stress the very aspect
that attracted white supremacists' contempt, and they drew
great numbers of worshippers from the growing communities of
semi-skilled and unskilled workers in the cities. [16]

The use of the term 'African' in this development was purely
symbolic; Bishop Allen was later to take a very firm stand
against the black repatriation movement, being convinced of the
need to obtain rights in America itself. The symbol of Africa
was to remain a factor in creating solidarity and political muscle
among blacks in the American cities, much as the Black Muslim
movement today has infinitely more relevance to reality in
Oakland or Harlem, say, than to conditions in Cairo or Damascus.

Direct competition with whites in the North forced blacks
into their own institutions and on to the political defensive; the
plantation system in the South, though not a static regime,
formed the basis of relations between the races there. Culturally
the blacks were saddled with singularly insulting stereotypes.
By the beginning of the nineteenth century there were troupes
of Nigger Minstrels, itinerant whites blacked up with burnt cork.
In the shows performed by these minstrels the stock black
characters were the maladroit half-wit and the pretentious
dandy. Cheap comic effects were brought about by silly
imitations of accents and mannerisms. Minstrel groups were
appearing all over America through the middle years of the
century. The extravaganzas staged would end with a huge song-
and-dance chorus, known as the 'breakdown'. It might be said,
however, that some positive function was served by these
extravaganzas. Janheinz Jahn, one of the most distinguished
historians of African and neo-African literature, says: 'For the
first time white Americans were being influenced by Afro-
American folklore, even though a travesty of it. Their ear was
sharpened in advance for when they met the real thing.'[17]

36

The established culture of the United States, as elsewhere in the New World, was white; to achieve any hearing at all, such black artists as there were had to conform to white, indeed European, models. It is not evident that much African style survived in nineteenth-century black literature. Even in Haiti, independent from 1804, black writers took European contemporaries, Lamartine, Victor Hugo, Goethe, as models. Only in Brazil, where to have an African grandmother was the mark of the complete Brazilian, were there a few exceptions to this trend. Tobias Barreto de Menezes asked in mid-century: 'Neither a pure Aryan nor a pure African nor a pure American — what am I then? An individual of a race of a sub-race, which is still evolving?'[18] The Brazilian writers seemed to be aware of a new racial identity, an essential part of which was African. João da Cruz e Sousa, who may be said to be a direct precursor of the Negritude school, was very early writing of blackness being a positive, a definite quality. It was, he said, lust, fetishism and pain, but also life, fertility, creative power. To be black and African was the same thing.[19]

In the United States incalculable African influences survived in black folk culture, largely unsanctioned by whites (and therefore now unrecorded), in dance and extempore music. Much of nineteenth-century black American literature took the form of accounts by escaped slaves, somewhat passionless works, emasculated of vivid expression by white editors anxious to subordinate style to political objectives. Preachers in many 'African' churches developed a wild melodious style — an oral art form not unlike the *hwyl* of the nineteenth-century Welsh preachers.

During the years immediately preceding the Civil War, the slave songs evolved into the spiritual, the result of the American and African cultures mingling at a deeper folk level than they did in the published sermons and poetry. The slave songs developed into more organized musical forms as they increasingly commanded white audiences. The spirituals took white America by surprise. One contemporary writer felt obliged to notice that

they are never 'composed' after the manner of ordinary music, but spring to life, ready made, from the white heat of religious fervour during some protracted meeting in church or camp. They come from no musical cultivation whatever, but as the simp e ecstatic utterances of wholly untutored minds . . . The child-like, receptive minds of these unfortunates were wrought upon with a true inspiration, and . . . the gift was bestowed upon them by an ever-watchful Father . . . to keep them from the hopeless apathy into which they were in danger of falling.[20]

The Negro spiritual was variously misinterpreted as this kind of inspiration, or, by abolitionists, as a sad longing for freedom. While by now the descent from Africa was very extended, the spiritual possibly contained as much African philosophy as white non-conformism. Jahn has claimed that slavery was even now still seen through African eyes, and that it was thought to be

a rather protracted initiation process leading towards rebirth as a new personality; its unpleasantness, however, made rebirth certain. So they carried out the work demanded of them, while doing everything they could to shorten the initiation period using the most effective means in their culture: they invoked the future in a magical way. The Spirituals were the songs of invocation which originated from this need and with this purpose.[21]

Although the Civil War failed in almost every particular materially to improve the lot of Southern blacks, its aftermath was to prove crucial to the political development of American Negroes and to trigger a totally new brand of Africa-consciousness. Emancipation was only a secondary consideration in the overall purpose of the war. Lincoln's principal aim was simply to save the Union, and his championship of the slaves was dependent on that aim. The Emancipation Proclamation of 1863 was seen by articulate blacks of the Northern lower middle classes as a concrete achievement. For them it was a confirmation of the race pride that was gaining in confidence, a race pride that was being continually bolstered by word from Africa itself.

Prominent among the champions of the race in Africa was Edward Wilmot Blyden, an early philosopher of black

nationalism and the recognized father of Pan-Africanism — a
native of the Virgin Islands who had emigrated to Liberia in
1850. He became an early ideologue for American blacks; his
oratory tended to emphasize the potential of Africa rather
than the reality he must have known. In *A Voice from Bleeding
Africa on behalf of her Exiled Children*, he wrote:

> Africa! There is no heart beating under a covering of
> sable hue, which does not throb with emotion at the sound
> of this word. To the exile from these shores labouring under
> the burning, though congenial, sun of South America, or
> shivering under the influence of Northern snows, it brings
> comfort, consolation and hope. It tells him of a country,
> a home given to him by that Almighty Being who
> "Drove asunder and assigned their lot
> To all the nations."
> It assured him that, though an outcast among strangers, whose
> bearing towards him is haughty, insulting and cruel, he has a
> country of his own, where his own race, being lords of the soil,
> exercise uncontrolled sway.[22]

Blyden's intention was not merely to attract blacks to Africa
from the New World. It was to inspire them to 'honour and love
your Race. Be yourselves . . . If you are not yourself, if you
surrender your personality, you have nothing left to give the
world. You have no pleasure, no use, nothing which will
attract and charm men . . .' This concept of race became what
Sartre in a different context described as 'anti-racist racism',
which was regrettably racism nonetheless. Its extreme expression
was: 'One of the melancholy results of the enslavement of the
Africans by the European is the introduction on a very large
scale of the blood of the oppressors among their victims . . . '[23]

This then developed into a fixed prejudice against any product
of miscegenation, and in particular a hatred for and a mistrust
of mulattoes, a hatred Blyden shared with many other pure-
black leaders. He and others contributed in very large measure
to the fostering of the imaginary Africa — certainly in the North —
and indeed was a major academic and political figure in the
real Africa too. He simply chose to retail his hopes and
expectations and oratory to the New World rather than to

explain the real hazards and conditions that faced the person who actually emigrated.

For Southern blacks, without much direct access to such sturdy promotion of their race, the end of the Civil War merely brought the disruption of the plantation system, which was for better or worse the prevailing economic system in the South, and the only one where they played a part. Instead of the promised instant freedom, there was instant confusion and disturbance. In some cases the transfer from slave status to that of employee was made with little fuss, depending on the attitude and benevolence of the planters. But in many instances slaves were abandoned, forced finally to wander back to the plantations to beg for work. The Reconstruction governments — in which many blacks found themselves for the first time holding legislative positions — gained a reputation for graft and chicanery. However, the Reconstruction governments were not dominated by blacks — they were in the majority in only one state, South Carolina — and such graft as there was, was certainly encouraged by Northern plunderers and carpetbaggers; in any case it never approached in dimension the fortunes being collected by Northern capitalists. Nevertheless the planter class felt it had learned the lesson of allowing the Negro to get out of his place. When Federal military rule substantially failed to enforce Negroes' rights and was abandoned in 1876, the Southern blacks found themselves caught in the growing class war between the old planter class and the rising class of industrial entrepreneurs who were gaining footholds in the Southern cities. Unable to identify with either side, despised and distrusted by both and unprotected from both, the blacks quickly found themselves forced back into a state that very nearly resembled their former condition. President Andrew Jackson had himself been the champion of the lower middle class, of the small (white) farmer, and had had little sympathy with the blacks, so what momentum towards emancipation there had been soon evaporated. The 14th and 15th Amendments — which respectively recognized blacks as citizens and gave them the vote — proved to be unenforceable in the South. The traditional safeguards of the old system having been removed, the situation became outright racial conflict. The passage of the 14th Amendment had been accompanied by race riots in which hundreds were killed. The Jim Crow railroad car for blacks had been established in Mississippi in 1865; further legislation on segregation on transport systems, in educational and penal establishments followed in other states as they drafted their new constitutions. The Ku Klux Klan made its appearance in Tennessee. Very soon, those Negroes who refused to accept the new situation of white supremacy were being openly assaulted, intimidated and liquidated.

About 50 blacks were lynched in the South in 1882; an estimated 162 in 1890.[24] The 'race riots' that became a regular feature of those years were very much one-sided terrorism perpetrated by whites on blacks for the most arbitrary or imagined offences. Even the Populist movement, in which whites recognized for apparently the first time that the economic forces that enslaved the blacks also oppressed them, collapsed. Indeed, one of the great Populist leaders, Tom Watson, who had proclaimed: 'This race antagonism perpetuates a monetary system which beggars both (races)', turned on his black followers with the words: 'In the South, we have to lynch him (the Negro) occasionally, and flog him, now and then, to keep him from blaspheming the Almighty.'[25]

These years were catastrophic for Southern blacks, yet somehow there was a determination among them to survive, and, if possible, escape. From this seedbed of hope grew a number of exodus movements, playing on the image of the lost and oppressed tribe. One of these was that of 'Pap' Singleton, a self-styled 'Moses of the Colored Exodus' who promised his 'Exodusters' a Canaan in Kansas, where they could be proud and self-reliant. He led several thousand followers to Kansas in the early 1880s. But coming from the Deep South, mostly from Alabama, Georgia, Mississippi and Texas, the pilgrims were unprepared for the bleakness they found. Only about a third of the Exodusters stayed.

Once again Africa was to become a beacon stoked this time by a furious black demagogue, Bishop Henry Turner. Exclaiming that the Constitution was a 'dirty rag' that had cheated and insulted black people, he tried several times to organize ship-loads of emigrants and to return his people to Africa. Turner was the first black leader in the South to urge a mass return to Africa, and was the first to have his message heard by substantial numbers of poor Southern blacks. He wrenched the emigration platform from under the urbane, but financially tottering, American Colonization Society. That his enterprises mostly failed is almost irrelevant: his was one of the loudest voices challenging the new humiliation into which Negroes had been crushed and his was the voice that invoked Africa.

Meanwhile, however, other migrations were taking shape. By the end of the nineteenth century, in fact as late as 1910, about 90 per cent of the black population of the United States was still in the South. The conditions and atmosphere in the South — constant crop failure, the ravages of boll weevil and flood, disastrous race relations — were such that many Negroes felt they were being economically propelled from the area. Turner and Singleton offered dramatic escapes, full of heroic possibility. But the lure of the industrial North by the first decade of the twentieth century was even greater.

The mass migrations by blacks in the early part of the twentieth century to New York, Chicago, Philadelphia and Detroit are among the most impressive movements of population anywhere. In many ways the migration was simply another symptom of the forces that were shaping American society as a whole Between 1900 and 1940 the proportion of white Americans living in towns and cities increased from 43 per cent to 57.8 per cent. Mechanization and rationalization were forcing people off the land, but those same forces were attracting them to the cities as industries expanded. In the same 40 years, however, the proportion of blacks living in urban areas increased from 22.7 per cent to 48.2 per cent.

Although large numbers of rural blacks were moving into Southern cities — between 1900 and 1930 perhaps a million did so — the increases in the Northern cities were colossal. In one twelve month period in the early 'twenties, half a million blacks left the 13 Southern states. In just ten years, from 1910 to 1920, the population of the 4 major Northern cities increased by three-quarters of a million. In that period, the black population of Detroit increased by 611.3 per cent; that of Chicago increased by 148.2 per cent. Smaller towns felt the impact too: one town — Gary, Indiana — found its Negro population increased by 1,283.6 per cent. The black population of Akron, Ohio, went up by 749.3 per cent. [26]

Many Negroes undoubtedly felt that moving to the North was

a positive personal solution. In fact they were being driven by economic forces: as migration from Europe had tailed off during the war years, their services were needed as unskilled workers in the growing industries. Rapid peace-time industrialization soon replaced the temporary demands of the war machine, so the urban migration continued through the first half of the twentieth century.

Those who had journeyed North found that although their relative affluence had increased there was no parallel enhancement of their dignity. They were still at the bottom of the economic and social pyramid, their homes assembled in the new-born ghettoes, 'across the tracks' or 'back of the hill'. At the close of the First World War, black soldiers who had fought alongside whites — and indeed, against whites — returned. In Europe they had found that the racial situation, while by no means ideal, was much more relaxed than at home. Back in the United States they found society still ossified, even reinforced by working-class competition between the races, in its prejudices. The democratic ideals propounded by President Wilson had failed to materialize.

A turbulent groundswell of social frustration and acrimony grew, and once again the clamour for recognition of the dignity of black people took the form of an appeal to mythical Africa. Into the starring role of prophet and redeemer strutted Marcus Garvey,* the most extraordinary urban black leader of them all. His slogan was 'One Aim! One God! One Destiny!', the ephemeral destiny being, once more, the return of all blacks to Africa. His movement failed to send anyone back to Africa, but it expanded race consciousness and mobilized the black masses in America in the most tremendous demonstration of unity and purpose of any black movement before or since.

In these post-war years, mythical Africa saw its finest hours. The burgeoning black press carried the myth to ever greater numbers; the energy of Garvey's raucous personality implanted the name of Africa in the hearts of millions of urban blacks. But it would be an exaggeration to claim that Africa-orientated movements dominated black consciousness in America; nor can it be said that the invocation of the name of Africa invariably worked to the Negro people's benefit. At the same time, the

---

* See Chapter 3.

Garvey years of the 1920s set in motion a new dimension of black consciousness, the reverberations of which are still being felt.

At around the same time, and against the same social background, there arose the literary Negro renaissance, based in Harlem, a movement that was to be the richest literary flowering of Imagined Africa. Parallel movements appeared in the Caribbean, and from these movements grew new literary forms and ideas of liberation for the black man. Politically the Negro had long since liberated the back-to-Africa movements from white sponsorship; now he was freeing himself from the intellectual patterns of white models in his literature. Although the forms of the poetry were still primarily Euro-American, the renaissance poets looked to African rhythms and themes for their inspiration. They absorbed current white American forms and went far beyond them. The literary renaissance extended the appeal of Africa to the articulate literary classes.

The movement had emerged as a reaction to a stereotype of Africa and the Afro-American. The last straw in this process of sterotyping was a wicked poem by (the white) Vachel Lindsay, published in 1914, called 'The Congo', subtitled 'A Study of the Negro Race'. Lindsay looked at 'fat black bucks in a wine-barrel room' and had discovered in them the heritage of 'tattooed cannibals'. He saw 'wild crap shooters', and 'then I saw the Congo, creeping through the black.'

> Then I heard the boom of the blood-lust song
> And a thigh-bone beating on a tin-pan gong.[27]

A group of poets reacted to this claptrap. Poets such as Countee Cullen and Langston Hughes showed that the 'talented tenth', as well as the dispossessed nine-tenths from whom Garvey drew his support, could be inspired in a positive way by Africa. Both Cullen and Hughes — and the group of poets loosely gathered around *The New Negro*, published by Alain Locke in 1925 — asserted their blackness as a mark of nobility. Hughes wrote:

> I built my hut near the Congo and it lulled me to sleep . . .
> I've known rivers:
> Ancient dusty rivers.
> My soul has grown deep like the rivers.[28]

The passionate identification with Africa was echoed in the Caribbean, in the *negrismo* movement in Cuba and in the indigenism movement in Haiti, as expressed in Jacques Roumain's poem, 'Guinea':

> It's the long road to Guinea
> No bright welcome will be made for you
> In the dark land of dark men:
> Under the smoky sky pierced by the cry of birds
> Around the eye of the river
>   the eyelashes of the trees open a decaying light
> There, there awaits you beside the water a quiet village
> And the hut of your fathers, and the hard ancestral stone
>   where your head will rest at last.[29]

As a literary symbol, Africa represented long-felt anguishes: the reticence to accept or discuss the artist's own African background, the dispossession and the exile. The myth of Africa was reinforced by an idea of some kind of golden age before slavery, a strident sensuality, a refuge from humiliation in a place where blackness was not only accepted, but vaunted, where what Aimé Césaire was the first to call *négritude* might even be worshipped. It carried the myth further.

Claude McKay, a Jamaican from Clarendon, was a gentler poet than his Caribbean precursors who often used frenetic rhythms and clashing phrases in an attempt to re-create a syncopated African-ness. McKay best expresses the wistful subtlety of the literary African myth:

> For the dim regions whence my fathers came
> My spirit, bondaged by the body, longs.
> Words felt, but never heard, my lips would frame;
> My soul would sing forgotten jungle songs.
> I would go back to darkness and to peace,
> But the great western world holds me in fee,
> And I may never hope for full release
> While to its alien gods I bend my knee.
> Something in me is lost, forever lost,
> Some vital thing has gone out of my heart,
> And I must walk the way of life a ghost
> Among the sons of earth, a thing apart.

For I was born, far from my native clime,
Under the white man's menace, out of time.[30]

Such sentiments were not always welcome in Africa itself.
Intellectual anglophones felt that too great a burden of
symbolism was being placed upon the Africa they knew. Later,
when the slightly dotty quasi-biological theories of the
Negritude movement were properly debunked, the Nigerian
playwright Wole Soyinka remarked: 'I don't think a tiger has
to go around proclaiming his tigritude.' (Leopold Senghor —
later president of Senegal — who shared the nominal
leadership of the Negritude school with Césaire, was to
adumbrate the idea that the black man had a special type of
nervous and glandular system.) But in the 1920s, while
Garvey — who never himself visited Africa — was giving
political voice to the myth, Imagined Africa was also being
enshrined in memorable verse.

The symbol had by now become too strong to uproot. It had
been forged in suffering, and had come to a mass maturity, of
which the poetry of the 1920s was one manifestation. It grew
out of a basic absence of factual knowledge. Remarkably little
encouragement or contribution to the myth had come from
Africans. In fact, Africans who were being educated were
gaining instruction from Europeans, so were gaining only broad
information about America or about black American history
and culture. Similarly, few black Americans were aware of real
events in Africa until news began appearing in black American
newspapers of independence struggles in colonial Africa.

Through the 1930s and 1940s a powerful interaction of
black American and African ideas began to gather speed.
African leaders, such as Nkrumah and Azikiwe, were beginning
to appear at American universities. They were excited by the
mythical Africa many black Americans dreamed of, and in turn
excited their listeners with what seemed only marginally more
realistic myths: those of a free decolonized Africa. There is no
doubt that subsequent leaders of African nations were
influenced by the ideas they encountered among black
Americans, and that black Americans, though still physically
distant from Africa, absorbed much of the African spirit of
independence.

Since the Second World War Africa in the New World has become this synthesis of political awareness that so influenced a section of American blacks that they uprooted and settled in Africa. One businessman in Accra quoted to me Kwame Nkrumah's declaration of 1958: 'Long may the links between Africa and the peoples of African descent continue to hold us together in fraternity.' This, he said, had accelerated his decision to emigrate. Nkrumah certainly found an exultant echo for his sentiments in the United States. Stokely Carmichael, who later moved to Guinea to dedicate his life 'to armed struggle leading to the reinstatement of Kwame Nkrumah', declared: 'We are all an African people.'[31] I was somewhat taken aback in Monrovia, of all places, to find a prosperous American businessman quoting to me: 'You cannot understand what is going on in Mississippi if you don't understand what is going on in the Congo . . . The same schemes are at work in the Congo that are at work in Mississippi. The same stake — no difference whatsoever.' The words were those of Malcolm X.

Huey Newton, the Black Panther leader, said in an interview in 1968 when he was in prison: 'We believe that it's important for us to recognize our origins and identify with the revolutionary black people of Africa and the people of colour throughout the world.'[32]

It may well be true that this political awareness of emerging Africa has formed itself into cogent pressure on the United States government from black people over matters such as South Africa, and perhaps the anti-Portuguese movements in West, Central and Eastern Africa, and anti-colonialist struggles everywhere. As we have seen, black Americans often used Africa as a banner to give their demands more political weight. The effectiveness of this is debatable, but it might be argued that concern shown by white American politicians in African affairs was motivated by awareness of the black American electorate as much as of Africa. Arthur Schlesinger, Jnr., recorded that in the 1960 presidential election campaign, John Kennedy made 479 references to Africa, and that this was the first time Africa had become prominent in such a campaign.[33]

The most startling evidence of this new and political Africa awareness among a section of young American blacks came on February 15th, 1961.

The United Nations headquarters in New York were invaded by a group of young blacks, protesting at U.N. policy in the Congo and at the murder of Patrice Lumumba. As Adlai Stevenson was giving his first speech as United States representative, fighting broke out in the gallery between U.N. guards and a group of about sixty blacks. This was followed by a march to Times Square, the women wearing black veils, the men wearing black arm-bands. They were said to belong to the United African Nationalist Movement, the Liberation Committee for Africa and On Guard, organizations that took the *New York Times*, for one, by surprise.[34] As a protest, the demonstration was certainly valid and timely. Concern about U.N. involvement in the Congo and the death of Lumumba was undoubtedly widespread in many countries. But it was the first time overt identification with African affairs by black Americans had been seen on such a scale on the streets of New York.

The demonstration was another stage in the development of imaginary Africa. In the death of Lumumba the myth found a perfect confluence: a dramatic event overtaking a very real figure, in a place that by its name and history fell into the context of Ideal Africa.

Melville Herskovits says that there has been significant progress in the image of Africa in the United States in recent years. (Even Herskovits does not, though, underestimate the power of Hollywood, travel brochures and magazines sustaining a range of white myths that are also believed by blacks.) The factors promoting change of attitude are, he says: firstly, the drive to self-government in the post-war years ('The sheer drama of the ending of the era of colonialism . . . has brought about a re-examination of earlier views and a re-orientation of attitudes'[35]); secondly, the growth in the numbers of African students studying in America, being a kind of cultural ambassadorial service; thirdly, the spectacle of heads of independent African states entering the arena of world politics; and finally there is the growth in the black studies programmes and a greater integration of black culture into general educational programmes. To these, one might also add the function of the news media.

But the fact is that these influences have probably produced no fundamental change in the attitudes of American and West Indian blacks to Africa; they have merely been submerged in the greater myth. Perhaps only the Hollywood image of Africa, and its dissemination through television, is strong enough to dislodge the older myths. (It should also be said that those who make the greatest claims for the impact of educational programmes are themselves invariably concerned with black studies programmes.)

To take Herskovits's points in greater detail:

In the first place, the drive to self-government produced figures of undeniable charisma, Nkrumah and Jomo Kenyatta, for example. Nkrumah was by no means the first international figure to urge the involvement of Afro-Americans and Africans in a common struggle. In 1903, Dr. W.E. Burghardt Du Bois, the most powerful Negro intellectual of this century, said in *Souls of Black Folk:* * 'The problem of the twentieth century is the problem of the colour-line — the relation of the darker to the lighter races of men in Asia and Africa, in America and the islands of the seas.'[36] When the Gold Coast became, in 1957, an independent Ghana — a deliberate reference to a noble ancient African empire — black Americans chose to focus their attention on Nkrumah himself, to disregard the reality of what subsequently took place in Ghana. The importance of the Osagyefo was just this: that he symbolically put Africa on the world political map and emphasized its potential. He acted as a lens rather than a mirror — focusing attention on to certain points rather than giving an accurate reflection. Thus Nkrumah — who attracted intellectual black Americans to Ghana in great

---

* Du Bois was a very good example of a moral and political black leader who did *not* base his appeal on any illusions about Africa. Throughout his life (which lasted almost a hundred years) this scholarly and immensely able man fought stolidly for the rights of the American Negro with rational and erudite skill. Yet oddly, he ended his days in Nkrumah's Ghana, having been invited there to compile an Encyclopedia Africana. No man would have been better suited to the job, now, however, sadly unfinished. Incidentally, the review of *Souls of Black Folk* that appeared in the London *Times* on August 14th, 1903, said, prophetically: 'In America it [colour prejudice] seems destined to become a question of the first importance, as it will be in South Africa some day.'

49

numbers, and at times trusted them to a greater degree than he did Ghanaian civil servants *because* they shared his vision — himself became a part of the pantheon of imaginary Africa.

Secondly, a great many black Americans and West Indians in Africa told me that their first contact with what they would describe as a real Africa was when they met African students in the United States or in Britain. But a common complaint, among the expatriate blacks, and particularly among their wives, was that African students abroad tend to be very conscious of their role as roving ambassadors. Being outstanding themselves, and exceptional in their own countries, even alienated from them in the classic 'been to' manner, they gave a necessarily subjective view. Blacks frequently regarded them as quasi-heroic figures in the early 1960s. Africans that I met who had been in this position often talked of the difficulties of breaking down the romantic expectations their colleagues had of them.

Thirdly, it may be said that the number of influential or charismatic African heads of state active on the international political scene has actually decreased since the *belle époque* of independence in the late 1950s and early 1960s. The enormity of the economic problems of post-colonial Africa has turned individual governmental attention inwards. National unity, indeed national survival, has become a much greater imperative than international public relations exercises. The number of those political leaders who rose through early independence struggles and still survive today as heads of state has sharply diminished, as the regrettable tendency towards military rule has spread. In black Africa south of the Sahara there can be said to be only a handful of internationally recognizable (recognized, that is, by the majority of black people in the New World) statesmen: Gowon, Kenyatta, Senghor, Nyerere, Amin. Of these, perhaps only Nyerere can be said to attract the undiluted admiration of politically motivated black Americans.

Finally, although black studies programmes have certainly provided more factual and historical material to students than ever before available, it would be a rash teacher who claimed that these studies therefore gave a rounded portrait of Africa to black youngsters in the United States. The first official programme of African studies in the United States was inaugurated in 1927 at Northwestern University by Melville

Herskovits, and the growth of such studies has been enormous. Their effectiveness in replacing myths with objective analysis has yet to be thoroughly assessed. But even recent arrivals in Africa told me that they could remember little of relevance from such studies. The courses were in no way a preparation for Africa as they found it (although admittedly that was not their function); nor did they form a meaningful background against which they could relate to Africa. Nearly all said that it would take a great deal more than a course at school to dislodge the years of myth formed in a white society, an essentially informal myth that was perceived on many levels, only one of which was susceptible to challenge by facts.

On the question of the press, Stanley Meisler of the *New York Times* wrote in 1964: 'U.S. press coverage of Africa is small in volume, spotty, and tends to focus on crisis situations.'[37] The same may be held to be true of the British Press, and of the early 1970s. The year 1973 was conspicuous for its coverage of the massive droughts in Ethiopia and West Africa (belated, however – the first reports appeared in British newspapers about nine months after the first declaration of a state of emergency in June 1972), the murder of Dr Amilcar Cabral, the border dispute between Ethiopa and Somalia, the tribal massacres in Burundi, and and the incursions of guerrillas into Smith's Rhodesia, together with the latest activities of that odious regime. Otherwise, news from Africa was dominated by General Idi Amin.* (At the same time, Amin was the most often quoted African head of state in Ghanaian newspapers while I was there; he was beaten in terms of coverage only by Ghana's own head of state.)

---

* Another recurring story in the American news media has dealt with the presence of Afro-Americans in Africa and their reactions. These, on the whole, have stressed the negative aspects. A typical extract, from *Newsweek*, September 4th, 1972: 'For [black] Americans . . . Ghana holds a case of culture shock. Its relatively Spartan hotels disappoint some tourists and the spicy diet upsets some U.S. stomachs. "The only thing I can't hack is the food," admits Mrs Eleanor Charles of Spring Valley, N.Y., who hopes to start a program to bring U.S. ghetto youngsters to Ghana. "I love the people here, but *fu-fu* [pounded yam] and *kenkey* [balls of fermented corn dough] just aren't my style." '

Moving from the general to the particular, how in fact has Cullen's question: 'What is Africa to me?' been answered, and what preconceptions were held by those black Americans and West Indians who went back to Africa?

Du Bois, always a vigorous opponent of repatriation, did himself travel to Africa. But not before he had asked himself that same question. He wrote:

> Once I should have answered the question simply: I should have said 'fatherland' or perhaps better 'motherland' because I was born in the century when the walls of race were clear and straight; when the world consisted of mutually exclusive races; and even though the edges might be blurred, there was no question of exact definition and understanding of the meaning of the word – As I face Africa I ask myself: What is it between us that constitutes a tie which I can feel better than I can explain? Africa is, of course, my fatherland. Yet neither my father nor my father's father ever saw Africa or knew its meaning or cared overmuch for it . . .[38]

More recently a younger, more angry black, Charles J. Patterson, wrote in *Transition* magazine:

> As it probably did to most Negroes in America, this powerful question, in all its full and threatening might possessed me during the tender years of childhood, unreason and eager repression. My answer, of course, in screaming silence, was nothing, nothing, nothing! For Africa was the place of the savage, the natural abode of evil, the banquet hall of the cannibal, and the pit of blackness itself.[39]

Images on pages of geography books were no help. 'There among the handsome Nordics, the noble Indian, the dignified Oriental, and the sinewy Polynesian, stood the naked African, with a bone in his nose, an elongated head, and prognathous jaw.'

When I put the same question to scores of black Americans and West Indians all over West Africa, it was clear that they had little conception of Africa before they arrived. What they did appear to have known about the reality of Africa was selective and interleaved with many other issues, their own experience of racial segregation-or prejudice, for instance, or a desire to leave the United States. It was not surprising that their knowledge should be selective, but the extent to which popular white media concepts had colonized the reality and image of Africa in the New World was unexpected. The British seemed to have done a thorough job in the West Indies of over-riding the natural links with Africa. Serious and accurate information was difficult to come by, and encouragement to seek it was slight; one woman from St Lucia told me of reading a copy of Frobenius' *Voice of Africa* that was chained to a desk in the United Nations Trusteeship Library reading room.

The myth of Africa, the lyrical phantom, is one that has operated on many strata of culture and has played an important part in motivating people to return to the land of their ancestors. And yet educated, articulate people I met were often as ignorant of the phantom as they were of the reality. Many spoke of their preconceptions as featuring vague white clichés: jungles, primitiveness, mud huts, nakedness and Tarzan, as if Hollywood images were somehow even easier to believe than the myths of their own culture.

'I believed people were running wild here,' said a black American businessman in Accra. A dentist, Dr Robert Lee, who was floating a scheme to encourage black repatriation to Ghana, recalled:

> I gathered that it was mostly an underpopulated, mostly forest area, except for the large deserts, of course, and that the people were backward and primitive. And disorganized. I must admit that as a young boy growing up there was a kind of mental wall I created whenever we got to the subject of Africa in class-rooms. This was the kind of reaction we all had as young blacks in the South: you didn't believe anything your white teacher told you about blacks in Africa, anything about Africa. But maybe this just left a large gap in my knowledge which I still sort of filled with the crap the teacher was putting out: that Africa was far, far away and very primitive and nothing at all to be proud of.

A black girl employed by the U.S. Government in West
Africa said:

I have known the word Africa since I first knew words,
I guess, but I can't say it meant anything to me until I
came here. As a kid, around twelve or thirteen, I was a
great fan of *Reader's Digest*. That was around the time of
the coming to independence of a lot of African countries,
and they used to run a lot of articles about how we were
providing foreign aid to these countries, and they were
taking our money yet they were going non-aligned and
socialist. That made me mad as a kid. Actually I remember
being startled later that I had had that attitude. I grew up
pretty ignorant. I have one aunt that said I would go to
Africa over her dead body. We had a terrible row. I
announced that I was going whether she lived or died.
'*Africky?* All them people in the jungle? What d'ya wanna
go ter Africky fer? You should get a job teaching school
with your education.' I'd be really ashamed if I admitted
how much I might have agreed with her, even when I was
about to come.

And a Jamaican woman in Freetown said: 'I had a very dull
impression. I couldn't conceive of there being a modern way of
life here. All I thought of was bad sanitation and grass skirts. I
had my impression by word of mouth, and the word — yes, and
the mouth — were all Englishmen's.'
On to this basic lack of practical knowledge, some people had
grafted very personal myths. One old gentleman, originally from
Georgia, who emigrated in 1951 and now lives in Bong County
in the Liberian interior, said:

What was Africa to me? Why, man . . . *man.* I was brought
up by an old blind man, an uncle, his name was Uncle Merrill,
and he had this bugle, a long straight bugle. It had six joints,
and my uncle always said that each joint carried the music
one mile. I always remember he would take me out on
starlit nights into the fields. And he would play this bugle,
and he'd sing . . . 'Oh, I'm bound to go to Africa . . . to
wear those *golden shoes,*' see? And he'd say you can maybe —
maybe — get a mule and forty acres in America, but in *Africa,*

man, in Africa you can get a water-buffalo and six hundred acres! I moved to Chicago and I was cleaning in the slaughterhouses. I was doing all right, you know, I was the first black man to get to clean out the sliced bacon department. Now I lived in Morgan Park, in the black section, and every morning I'd come down that main street, and if I was on time, there'd be a long, long, freight train crossing the road. I used to look at it, and I'd think to myself, and well, play little games, like saying it's worth five million dollars today. And always, at the front, the engineer would be a white guy. And it would pass by, and when it came to the back, to the caboose, the conductor would always be a black guy. I said to myself, well, doggone, I'm going to carry my kids away from here, and they'll have a whole train to operate if they should so desire. And we'll *build* the train and the railroad if they don't have one in Africa. Every child that came along, we'd say we dedicate this child to *Africa*. We had seven children, and I was forty-seven when we came.

For other people too, a memorable relative played a part in nurturing a heavily symbolic idea of Africa, which had much more to do with the America of the particular period than with Africa. For instance, Garvey's movement is recalled with the misty quality of early childhood encounter. The American wife of a Ghanaian academic said:

I had a cousin called Eldridge, who, incidentally, also taught me to play the guitar. He was a staunch believer in the Back-to-Africa movement. He would come to our house in New York every Saturday. He called me Hagar, which I guessed was a sort of Biblical or African name, and we would go down to a place on Lenox Avenue, I think between 115th and 116th Streets. It was a kind of store-front church, and they sang, hymns and anthems, and there'd be speeches. I was too young to know what they were talking about mostly, but I do know it was a lot of stuff about going back to Africa. Then I had an aunt who insisted that when I finished school and university, I *must* go to Africa. When I got married to an African, she was the happiest woman in the world, and when I went back to the States, she opened up her trunk and showed me this brownish old uniform, with buttons all down the front, and that had been her Garvey uniform, the uniform all the Garvey legions wore, and she was finally showing it to me.

A gracious and beautiful black American businesswoman in Accra said to me:

My parents were from St Kitts and my father was a Garveyite. In the 'twenties I remember him going on these great parades through New York. I would be only six or seven, but this was the first time I ever heard about Africa, and it shaped a lot of what I later thought. I remember those parades, oh my, the colour, the uniforms and the flags, so many flags. And everything was so gay and everybody was so proud, not at all like the dismal affairs my father also used to go to with the Masons and the Odd Fellows. But most of all I remember the music, which in all the gaiety had a sort of funeral air to it, the kind of slow marching jazz they played at funerals. When I play, let's see, King Oliver's Creole Jazz Band, or Charles A. Matson's Creole Serenaders, or Freddie Kippard's Jazz Cardinals, those old records, it all comes back to me. It's gay, but it's also kinda sad.

Some people were surprised at how African they had been without knowing it. A Guyanan woman I met in Ghana found that the dish she knew as *mettege* (vegetables cooked in coconut milk) had in fact originated in eastern Nigeria; that the *Nanse* stories she heard as a child were the very same as the *Ananse* spider stories of western Ghana; and that the spell known as *Sense* back home was actually *Asense*, the curly-feathered chicken that is supposed to root up spells and harmful charms that may have been buried by your door.

Du Bois recognized very little of Africa in himself:

With Africa I had only one direct cultural connection and that was the African melody which my great-grand-mother Violet used to sing . . . she shivered and shrank

in the harsh north winds, looked longingly at the hills
and often crooned a heathen melody to the child
between her knees, thus:

Do bana coba, gene me, gene me!
Do bana coba, gene me, gene me!
Ben d'nuli, nuli, nuli, nuli, ben d'le.[40]

A black American from South Carolina told me he now
recognized that the small houses on the islands off the coast of
the Carolinas had definite structural similarities to certain
West African huts. And others to whom I spoke, when
prompted by exposure to Africa, could recall recognized
African 'ways' in elderly relatives.

But the sense of retentions was not strong, at least in serious
settlers in West Africa, and was sometimes forced. (These
alleged retentions may, on occasion, reach absurd proportions.
In Accra I met a young Afro who had been in Ghana for two
days. He told me he was the chief of the Yorubas in New Jersey.
He had reached this conclusion after he had died and come to
life again. 'You mean, in some kind of dream?' I asked. No, he
insisted, he actually died, and came back to life as a full-blown
Yoruba. I said that apart from the fact that the Yorubas were
situated in Nigeria, the territory the tribe occupied was very
extensive indeed. Where precisely did he come from? He said
he didn't know exactly. More importantly, I said, which
village did he come from, since the term Yoruba would be
meaningless to most Yorubas without reference to a
particular village. 'I have no idea,' he replied. 'But if it takes
two years, five years, ten years, I shall find it.' I said he
would be regarded as a very bereaved Yoruba, since to have no
village was far worse than having no family. He said he'd apply
for a visa all the same. For all I know, he, like myself, is still
waiting for his Nigerian visa.)

It is worth noting in passing that the duality of the black
American personality, the African and the exile, while it may
haunt a number of individuals who are finally driven to settling
it by removing themselves to Africa, does not occur
frequently as a subject for fiction. There have been a number
of non-fictional works by blacks on their reactions to Africa,
and there is a large body of contemporary poetry. But James

Baldwin, in *Notes of a Native Son*, remarked that the slave history had obliterated the African-ness in at least his kind. Writing of meeting Francophone Africans in Paris in the 1950s, he said:

> They face each other, the Negro and the African, over a gulf of three hundred years — an alienation too vast to be conquered in an evening's good-will, too heavy and too double-edged even to be trapped in speech. This alienation causes the Negro to recognize that he is a hybrid. Not a physical hybrid merely: in every aspect of his living he betrays the memory of the auction block and the impact of the happy ending — The American Negro cannot explain to the African what surely seems in himself to be a want of manliness, of racial pride, a maudlin ability to forgive. It is difficult to make clear that he is not seeking to forfeit his birthright as a black man, but that, on the contrary, it is precisely this birthright which he is struggling to recognize and make articulate. Perhaps it now occurs to him that in this need to establish himself in relation to his past he is most American, that this depthless alienation from oneself and one's people is, in sum, the American experience.[41]

One outstanding novel stands virtually alone in this area. It is *Other Leopards*, by the Guyanan novelist Denis Williams. The hero-narrator says:

> It began, way back, with those two names: the one (Lionel) on my birth certificate, on my black-Frank-Sinatra face; and the one (Lobo) I carried like a pregnant load waiting to be freed and to take itself with every despatch back to the swamps and forests and vaguely felt darknesses of my South American home . . . All along, since I'd grown up, I'd been Lionel looking for Lobo, I'd felt I ought to become this chap, this *alter ego* of ancestral times that I was sure quietly slumbered behind the cultivated mask.[42]

Lionel feels he is 'trying hard to feel — how shall I say? — this mystic union, this ineffable what's it, this identity.'[43]
    As we shall also see, those who try the hardest to feel this

'mystic union' fail the most dismally.

One irony in the situation is that many Africans and black Americans see each other's lands as Canaan. One of the shocks for an Afro-American in Africa is the unseemly eagerness with which Africans appear to grasp opportunities to go to the United States. The blandishments of Afros about its not being a material paradise, a land of affluence and justice for all, go unheeded in the scramble to join the ranks of the 'been-tos' (those who have travelled to America or Europe). A black American member of one Ghanaian university faculty wrote to his university magazine recently:

> None of the bloody ghetto insurrections, recurring "ripoffs", police shoot-outs, Indian uprisings or dollar devaluations can convince the "never-been-to" that U.S. streets are not paved with gold, lined by trees growing dollar bills. And the new influx of U.S. educated Ghanaians with four to six letters behind their names, driving mighty petrol-drinking automobiles is not helping to destroy the myth.[44]

Even while the Ideal Africa myths were developing in the United States, and to some extent in the Caribbean too, blacks were actually going back to Africa, sometimes themselves feeding the old myths and creating new ones. Over the past 160 years or so, several thousand American blacks have tried in a personal way to reverse their race's history. The conditions they met and the communities they formed could hardly have been more different from those their cultures would have led them to expect. The significance of those who did go back is not in their numbers; rather, it is that they were putting into effect an urge that was sporadically felt by millions of blacks in the New World. Thus, their sometimes intense experiences have a significance beyond the individual. For with them they carried not only their own hopes and confusions and courage, but those of a whole race.

CHAPTER 2

The Black Man's Grave

'Great is my trials now on the right hand and on the left. My family are now Sold to the traders and gone; But this does not go So hard with me as the Being deprive of going and Preaching the Gospel to the down trodden Sons and Daughters of Africa. Great is my zeal for their souls and Great is my philanthropy for that Country at large.'

> (Letter written in early 1849 by Bureel W. Mann
> to the American Colonization Society; an inquiry
> for a place aboard a Liberia bound ship.[1])

'You are, perhaps, anxious to know how I like Africa. I am very much pleased with it so far. It is a noble country. I am also pleased with the people . . . They have the manly bearing of high minded and intelligent freemen! They look and act like men who know and have no superior but their maker!'

> (Letter in the *African Repository and Colonial Journal*,
> December, 1865[2])

'What do you do in Sierra Leone? We *work, work, work;* sleep sleep; eat and drink, drink, drink and take quinine — and die. — Yours faithfully,'

> (Letter in the *Sierra Leone Weekly News*, January 11th,
> 1896[3])

If it is astonishing that people actually journeyed back to Africa, it is even more astonishing that any of them survived once they got there.

Back-to-Africa movements under the guidance of both philanthropist-merchants, bigoted puritans, occasional altruists, and also blackguards, demagogues and strange visionaries, did a comparatively healthy business during the nineteenth century and the early part of the twentieth. Over the years, thousands of blacks reversed the Middle Passage and returned to West Africa. Many hundreds died of the diseases in the swamps. A fair number were killed by African tribesmen. Some gave up and staggered back to the United States. Many were totally disillusioned. But the majority stayed and, against the most terrible odds, survived. By fair means or foul they created two nations, Sierra Leone and Liberia, and founded two curious societies, each unique on the coast, in the Freetown Creoles and the Americo–Liberians of Monrovia. The histories of these two communities are different but complementary, and each of the present-day countries presents its own historical conditions, conditions of a special kind that must be adjusted to by the modern resettler.

Out of Sierra Leone has come a slightly embittered community, overtaken by African events, and indeed by the African people. Creole society in Freetown evolved from a band of pilgrims into a group of haughty despots, and when the privilege was wrested from it, the Creoles settled into areas of the professions that they could still control and lived on a set idea of their past. Freetown still contains reminders of the various New World and African pasts that founded it. At one time, up to ninety different African languages were spoken there. When its confused cultural head stops spinning and has to decide in which direction it should point, it points to England, but to an England of eighty years ago, eclectically influenced by Africa.

In Monrovia, the settlers eventually made the wise decision to intermarry with the natives. An oligarchy of Americo - Liberians, or what appeared to be Americo-Liberians, developed, but hardly any families remain that could trace their ancestry back directly to the early settlers. The exclusive Creoles lost political control of Sierra Leone in 1951, but their equivalents — the Americo-Liberians — are still firmly in the saddle in Liberia and are likely to remain so.

In comparison with Liberia, Sierra Leone diminished in importance for those New Worlders who looked towards Africa for inspiration. Liberia, despite the reality of the true activities of the oligarchy in charge there, continued to act as a brilliant star beckoning some black Americans. This odd little country * was made the beloved object of those who had never seen it and became a lasting symbol of Africa. To the succession of Back-to-Africa orators who emerged after the eclipse of the American Colonization Society, it was Home.

In 1791, it was decided to revive the shattered colony of Sierra Leone. A new agent was appointed, Alexander Falconbridge, a tiresome drunkard, who had, however, displayed excellent judgment in his choice of wife, Anna Maria. It is to this acerbic and highly intelligent woman that we owe firsthand accounts of the re-establishment of the colony.

At the end of the American War of Independence, a group of former slaves who had fought on the British side were given sanctuary in Nova Scotia. But of the 3,000 or so who were taken there, only about 10 per cent actually achieved what they were promised in land and a means to earn a proper living. Slavery was still legal there; there was undoubtedly racial discrimination shown in the allocation of land; the weather was cruelly cold and the former slaves were frequently so poverty-stricken that, as their miserable plots of land gave out, they were either forced back into slavery or, probably an even worse fate, were left to

---

* Anyone inclined to be condescending towards Liberia should remember Du Bois' remark in 1933 that Liberia's 'chief crime is to be black and poor in a rich, white world'.[4] The remark was made, however, after charges of forced labour and feudalism in Liberia had been substantially proved by a League of Nations Commission, and the Vice-Predident, Allen Yancy, implicated.

fend for themselves. One of their number, a barely literate millwright named Thomas Peters, sailed from Canada to London, where he petitioned the Sierra Leone Company to make arrangements for the Nova Scotians in Africa. He took the journey at great personal risk: he might well have been recaptured and resold, or have been the object of reprisals from the Nova Scotian administration. It was duly arranged that 1,190 former slaves should sail from Canada to Sierra Leone in January 1792. There was very great excitement at the prospect of resuscitating the colony. Four men walked three hundred miles through the wintry forests to join the convoy.

Meanwhile, the Falconbridges had gone to reconnoitre the land. What they found of the original settlers was distressing. Wrote Mrs Falconbridge, 'I never did, and God grant I never may again, witness so much misery as I was forced to be a spectator of here: Among the outcasts were seven of our country women, decrepid with disease, and so disguised with filth and dirt, that I should never have supposed they were born white.'5   There were, in all, fifty survivors who had remained in the neighbourhood. Once *in situ*, Mrs Falconbridge was appalled at the prospect of more than a thousand new settlers joining them. 'It was surely a premature, hare-brained and ill-digested scheme, to think of sending such a number of people all at once, to a rude, barbarous and unhealthy country ... I very much fear [it] will terminate in disappointment — if not disgrace to the authors.'6

But the Nova Scotians arrived. Another account shows a repetition of the earlier disastrous decision to land in what elsewhere is regarded as late spring.

They arrived . . . at the most trying and sickly season of the year . . . without the least shelter being afforded them, many being very sick at their time of landing. The Colony . . . was then quite a forest, thickly populated with wild and ferocious animals, without any passage of approach to the now beautiful and principal town 'Freetown'. Pioneers . . . were despatched on shore . . . to make road-way for their landing, which being done they all disembarked and marched towards the thick forest, with the Holy Bible and their preachers (all coloured men)

before them, singing the hymn taken from the late
Countess'* Hymn Book commencing

'Awake! and sing the song
Of Moses and the Lamb,
Wake! every heart and every tongue
To praise the Saviour's name.'[7]

Inevitably, very soon the fevers began. In the following
extract from her letter Mrs Falconbridge sounded the keynote
to the reputation this stretch of coast was to enjoy for many
years:

'Alass! alass! in place of growing better, we seem daily
advancing towards destruction . . .' Only two hundred
of the seven hundred stricken with fever could crawl about, she
wrote. Each day half a dozen died and were 'buried with as
little ceremony as so many dogs or cats'. Then, 'It is customary
of a morning to ask "how many died last night?" Death is viewed
with the same indifference as if people were only taking a short
journey, to return in a few days.'[8]

One slightly bizarre journal kept by an agent a little later lists
day after day the stores and the deaths with equal lack of passion.
This agent, George Ross, was disturbed by the amount of rum
consumed at funerals, although he appears to have been not
averse to its consumption himself. At times, his writing becomes
shaky and uncertain. Occasionally he interrupts his own narrative
wildly, in this way doing more than most other descriptions to
illustrate the Sierra Leone of the day. One evening he is evidently
writing and becoming listless with his endless counting of stores
and cadavers. He breaks out, 'Bless my bonny eyes! — What's
this I see? — Nothing less than two white ladies in the
Government House of Sierra Leone — let me look — it's Mrs and
Miss B [name indecipherable] — Ah — no great things after all —
but they're *white* — 'Here he tails off. But at some later date he
has apparently gone back to the page, for in a different ink and
steadier hand he records:' . . . died last night or this morning'.[9]

---

* The Countess of Huntingdon's Connexion, a break-away Anglica
sect dating from the eighteenth century, was especially popular in
the American colonies. There are still a number of Huntingdonian
chapels in the Freetown area of Sierra Leone.

Nearly a hundred of the Nova Scotians died in the first rainy season. But the town was re-established, this time in an undisputed spot, an old deserted village abandoned because it was alleged to be haunted. Tents made of sails and spars were rigged up as houses and chapels. A prefabricated canvas house from England was fitted out as a church and legislature, much to the chagrin of Mrs Falconbridge, who had hoped that it might serve as her residence. In fact, all the European wives stayed on the ships, back-biting and grumbling.

Mrs Falconbridge had little time for the company representatives. They were 'men of little worth and much insignificance unfit to be guardians and stewards of the immense property required . . . [they] are men, whose heads are too shallow to support a little vicissitude and unexpected *imaginary* aggrandizement, whose weak minds delude them with wrong notions of their nominal rank, and whose whole time is occupied with contemplating their fancied consequence, in place of attending to the real and interesting designs of their mission.'[10] Those in London did not appear to be much more competent. Instead of sending stores or seed, the sponsors sent a cargo of garden watering pots, she reports. They also sent bulky implements for dressing cotton, taking up valuable hold space, when in fact none had been planted. The colony was indeed ill-served by its sponsors. Flour was sent in sacks, instead of casks, and was consequently ruined by the time it reached the coast and so, too, was the molasses, packed in leaking barrels.

In any event, the Nova Scotians appeared as disinclined to do agricultural work as their predecessors. They proved to be just as adept at factionalism and bickering as the earlier settlers, too. Accusations ranged from embezzlement by company representatives to watering the rum. Although gardens were laid out, hogs raised and a dozen fishing boats built, the practice of agriculture was virtually abandoned, and the colony was to develop into a trading community, later acting as a kind of entrepôt for European goods en route to other areas of British Africa.

In 1793 a new governor was installed, Zachary Macaulay (father of the historian), a stiff and humourless prig, who had been a plantation manager in the West Indies. A woman in Sierra Leone caught in adultery was ordered by him to be flogged. (Her lover was fined £5.) But Macaulay's journal does record how, for many of the settlers, it was indeed a home-coming. Some were of the Koranko, of Bance Island; one man apparently found his long-lost mother, a slave to a Temne chief, and another man met the Mandingo who had sold him. According to Macaulay, he promptly gave the man a present and thanked him handsomely for having unwittingly been the means of his deliverance from paganism to Christianity.[11]

Once again there were threats to the stability of the colony from within. Dissension and rebellion arose, mainly over the shilling-an-acre quit rents which were imposed, contrary to promises made in Nova Scotia. Even William Wilberforce was exasperated. He wrote: 'They have made the worst possible subjects, as thorough Jacobins as if they had been trained and educated in Paris.'[12] But real Jacobins threatened from without. Numbers of them were roaming the seas on free-booting missions after the conclusion of the French Revolution. In 1794 seven of their ships arrived and their crews looted the colony.

In 1800 some new blood arrived in Sierra Leone. These were Maroons, originally from Jamaica. In the mid seventeenth century English soldiers had driven the Spanish from Jamaica, and the slaves had taken to the mountains, where they set up an almost autonomous region. These *montagnards* were joined latter by a group known as the Koromantees, a group that gained a reputation for intractability all over the New World. The Koromantees were without doubt Ashanti and Fanti who had been shipped from West Africa via Fort Abandze at Cormantine (remnants of the Twi language are still heard in the Jamaican interior). Together with the Maroons they formed an effective guerrilla band, harassing the British. They waged sporadic war for many years, and only when threatened with dogs did they capitulate, in 1795. Most were removed to Nova Scotia under pain of death should they return to Jamaica. In 1800 some 550 of them were taken to Sierra Leone to augment the population of the colony. The Maroons were not as patently grateful for their repatriation as the previous settlers had been, and many nursed a desire to return to the West Indies. The Nova Scotians were, in fact, terrified of them. They were described as 'not easy to be governed, and to be brought into that state which would best promote the civilization of Africa'.[13]

The fourth group that added to the colony began arriving after the abolition of slavery in 1807. A maritime court was set up in Freetown — the building is now occupied by the famous City Hotel, the crumbling yet hilarious place immortalized as the Bedford Hotel in Graham Greene's *The Heart of the Matter* — ships carrying slaves were tried there and the slaves set free in Sierra Leone.

In the following years, the expatriate ingredients were mixed, with a constant influx of 'recaptives' (slaves liberated by the Royal Navy), into what was to become Creoledom. In all, 40,000 liberated Africans were landed at Freetown between 1807 and 1850. The Sierra Leone Company failed from incompetence and an almost total lack of income, and yet the community itself survived. In 1807 the area become a Crown Colony, and remained so for 154 years. By 1850, Creole society had melded and gathered in the western end of Sierra Leone, around Freetown, and in the hills behind, in the recaptive towns, Regent, Gloucester and Leicester.

Although Creole society today has many essential African qualities in custom and tradition, the early recaptives did not form themselves into African-style villages. They came from Senegal and the Gambia in the north, and from Angola and the Congo in the south, and practically everywhere in between, but apart from certain individual tribal groups, such as the Yorubas and the Congos, they kept only fragments of their individual cultures, despite the fact that they had been removed from them only a comparatively short time. They formed themselves into distinctly Creole communities, with an architecture and set of traditions uniquely Creole. In place of single-storey hut compounds they built stone and wooden houses of several floors (the Maroons introduced the verandah) and were soon gathered socially round the chapels. Some aspects of tribal religion and law survived — trial by ordeal, for example — but the chapels were an important focus for the communities.

The process of settlement for the recaptives entailed their having to assimilate to the hybrid community in the villages on the coast. There was no suggestion that they should go back to Africa. A social hierarchy was established, with the recaptives at the bottom. They were apprenticed to the Creoles, and often this apprenticeship was criticized as being indistinguishable from slavery. (Indeed, a number of apprentices were resold.) They were taught market gardening, carpentry and masonry, and were brought under a form of English Common Law. In time they moved out of the coastal villages and into Freetown — by now an increasingly important and prosperous commercial centre — where they were hawkers, pedlars, tailors, barbers and petty traders. Slowly, in the Victorian manner, they used their profit to buy upward social mobility into Creole society proper.[14] Some went back to Nigeria: a group of five hundred were successfully repatriated in 1839. This in part accounted for the new colony beginning to look outwards and along the coast, rather than towards the interior. Contacts with the African tribes of the interior, the Temne, Mende and Limbas, were minimal. By the mid nineteenth century, inter-marriage with the recaptives had begun, and this newly-merged class of Creoles engaged in coastal trade. A number of Sierra Leoneans also came to be much in demand as clerks in the Gold Coast and Nigeria.

During the later nineteenth century, Freetown had all the appearance of a successful and dynamic community. The reluctance to farm had paid dividends, in that the trade in which the Creoles engaged provided a wealth that was unusual for black West Africa. But the Creoles were socially introverted. They went back to Africa, but they did not go back *into* Africa. In addition, they were in a state of at least nominal subjection, under British colonial rule, although they did materially rather better as a society then did many other nations and tribes. They were encouraged by the British to believe that they were a form of élite, which their literacy certainly made them. The sons and grandsons of the repatriates were, however, raised to believe in their marks of superiority, yet were scorned for the pretentiousness that this naturally created. This 'side' caused fury among other people on the coast. Sir Richard Burton had some acid things to say about the worst of the Creole popinjays: 'There are portentous studs upon a glorious breadth of shirt, a small investment of cheap, gawdy, tawdry rings set off the chimpanzee-like fingers, and when in the open air, lemon-coloured gloves invest the hands, whose horny reticulated skin reminds me of the cranes which pace at ease over the burning sand.'[15] (The man Burton was describing was the son of Samuel Crowther, later to become a bishop.)

By 1870 the assimilation of all the immigrant groups with each other was virtually total and the Creoles unashamedly lorded it over the natives of the interior. It became the practice of educated natives to call themselves Creoles. A trade slump in the 1880s was attributed by the Creoles to lack of control over the hinterland, and finally the British Government was pressured into declaring the hinterland a Protectorate. The divisions between the Creoles and Africans became entrenched by events in the 1890s. The British decided to raise a hut tax to pay for facilities and utilities. This, together with the natives' strong resentment and mistrust of the Creoles as instruments of colonialism, led to the vicious Hut Tax War of 1898. The natives were quelled, and Creoles were installed in the Protectorate as agents. The apparent perfidy of the Creoles was never forgiven and the division was irretrievable. The present-day contempt which many educated Africans have for the decaying Creole society can be said to date from the Hut Tax War.

Even so, Africans did see a kind of *cachet* in having their children fostered by the richer Creoles. It was not unusual for a native child to perform menial household tasks, leaving the Creole children to more effete pursuits.

The Creoles came to see themselves exclusively as 'professionals' and this led to their loss of economic power. Prosperous Creole traders began putting their children into professions, such as medicine, the law and engineering, leaving a hiatus in the succession in the business community. This vacuum was filled there, and to a much lesser extent all along the coast, by Lebanese and Syrians. (Levantines still substantially control the trade of Sierra Leone. It is quite usual to walk into a tiny village of a dozen or so houses and find that one of these buildings is actually Khallil's or Aziz's emporium. Occasional campaigns, which remind one of pre-war German anti-Semitic propaganda, sputter into life and the Lebanese are accused of everything, from illegal profiteering to child-selling.[16] But the main odium is still attached to Indian traders.) Almost in exchange for their economic control, the Creoles maintained political power, and they still do maintain a grip on the professions, especially the Church and the civil service.

The repatriation of New World blacks to Africa was

successfully achieved. The early unruliness of the settlers was probably caused in part by their being expected to fulfil an agricultural role which they were reluctant to accept. Prosperity followed only when this role was abandoned and their energies were channelled into trading. In place of the failed expectations of their sponsors, the settlers substituted expectations of their own. Instead of participating at the deepest level in Africa, they participated in those expectations. The New World graft stuck to Africa, and some African life flowed into it. It was successful in so far as the community survived and flourished and developed a strange identity of its own. The literacy, favoured status, varied history of suffering, Christian religion and experience of the New World in themselves all set the early settlers aside from Africans from the beginning. In addition, the settlers evolved their own ways of dealing with their environment, an almost technological approach, compared with the natives' ease of familiarity with it.

This division between Africans and Creoles was greatly supported for expediency's sake by the British colonial administration. At the same time, it would be wrong, as Professor Eldred Jones of the University of Sierra Leone has pointed out, to describe Creole society as rootless: 'This is how Freetown often strikes people who look at it from the outside. Those who are part of the society, however, as they celebrate their weddings with *gumbe* music, or dance in evening dress to the strains of western-style bands, or talk to their dead during an *awujo* feast, or sing Bach in the choir on Sundays, seem quite unaware of their "rootlessness" and display a surprising self-confidence which is perhaps the source of outside irritation.'[17] Creole society, he says, is designed rather like the structure of a golf ball. 'Outside there is the Bach and the well-cut English suit, while inside there is the *awujo*, the complaints at the grave of dead relations, the extended family with all its commitments, all of which are at the heart of the society, and bring Freetown very close indeed to . . . African concepts of being.'

Close it may be, but distinct none the less. Succeeding generations have brought Creole society closer to Africa, but the present-day community still bears the unmistakable mark of the outsider when viewed in relation to the rest of West Africa.

Throughout this century, Creole society has declined. But during the decline natives have increased their apeing of Creole mannerisms; foreign-educated natives still will join the ranks of the Creoles. And at the same time, many Creoles went fashionably native, taking African names, advocating polygamy, and in some cases — after a century of separateness and haughty disdain for the hinterland — repudiating their Creole backgrounds and vaunting their African kinship. The political decline was completed in 1951, so that after independence in 1961, the country was left in the hands of an essentially African government.* Relations between Creoles and Africans in present-day Sierra Leone are relatively good; the Creoles have their illusions, their past, control of the professions and a kind of decayed elegance. The Africans rule the country.

The use of the term 'Creole' is different in Sierra Leone from in the Caribbean and the southern United States. In this particular case, it means, as I have shown, the descendents of the very first settlers from England, the former slaves from Nova Scotia, the Maroons, and the recaptives.

The organized repatriation of freed blacks from the United States to Liberia has been described as an unparalleled swindle and a vicious, hypocritical plot by the Southern 'slavocracy' to buttress the institution of slavery by ridding the U.S. of its freed slaves.[18] This is partly true. But the pressure for repatriation came not only from the South. Subsidized emigration was also seen as a convenient means of clearing out from the Northern cities a class that had only a vague legal status and was a potential threat of friction. The numbers of freed slaves in America were increasing at a phenomenal rate from the end of the eighteenth century. In 1800 they numbered 52,190. By 1830, there were 160,063. The census of 1860 shows there were 230,958 freed slaves in the United States.[19] As early as 1796, St George Tucker, professor of law at William

---

* In the elections of 1973, the 105-seat assembly was divided thus: 61 Christian, 36 Muslim and 8 Creoles. This, despite the obvious and violent rigging of the election itself, does represent at least the socio-religious structure of Sierra Leone. In 1973 Sierra Leone became the newest *de facto* one-party state in black Africa. Its nextdoor neighbour, Liberia, is the oldest.

and Mary College — although he was a fierce critic of slavery — warned that free Negroes would become 'the caterpillars of the earth and the tigers of the human race'. [20] Governor James Sullivan of Massachusetts said: 'We have in history but one picture of a similar experience, and there we see it was necessary not only to open the sea by a miracle for them to pass, but more necessary to close it again, in order to prevent their return.'[21] In the euphoria that followed Independence, enemies of slavery were very evidently to be seen as the enemies of the Negro race as well. But to this hypocrisy should be added two further driving forces behind the formation of the American Colonization Society. The first was the vision of Liberia as a base from which to launch the conversion of the heathen continent of Africa. The second was an undoubtedly genuine conviction that although slaves and their descendents might never achieve full participatory rights in the United States, they were still capable of governing themselves in some other place.

Some people managed to combine all of these motives. The Rev. Robert Finley, of Basking Ridge, New Jersey, a vigorous anti-slavery campaigner, believed that America might be rid of a troublesome minority, but that Africa would receive 'partially civilized and Christianized settlers', settlers who would enjoy, quite simply, a 'better situation'. It was his habit to call Negroes 'Africans' anyway, and his convictions sometimes led him into memorable nonsense: for example, he pictured the repatriated African returning to a place where his 'sable hands will strike the lyre, and weave the silken web'.[22]

Even before the American Revolution there had been projects to train freed Negroes to become missionaries, to atone for the abomination of slavery. Several schemes had been abortive, but there was at least an awareness among certain white groups, especially the Quakers, that Negroes had some desire to return to Africa. The established colony of Sierra Leone served as a pivot for the less fanciful schemes. In 1811, one Paul Cuffee, a half-Negro, half-Indian Quaker from Cuttyhunk Island, Mass., visited Sierra Leone. Cuffee had been a whaler, a merchant trading in plaster of Paris and wheat, and was a successful trading captain. He had earlier, with his brother, unsuccessfully petitioned for the right to vote and other civil rights; when he and his brother refused to pay their taxes, a

suit ensued, and new laws were passed. As a sea captain and
trader, he had become anxious to develop his African market.
'The travail of my soul is that Africa's inhabitants may be
favoured with reformation', he said.23 In 1816 Cuffee took
the first group of American Negroes to Africa. At a cost of
4,000 dollars he landed 38 at Freetown.
Support grew for the idea of repatriation, and federal funds
were sought. The plan was not universally accepted by Negroes,
however, many seeing through the more blatantly cynical
motives of the movers of the Colonization Society. They not only
felt that they were now entitled to some of the fruits of the earth
which their blood and sweat had drenched, but they also
resented being cast as a useless and dangerous sector of society.
The plans proceeded, however. An envoy sent to scout out
Sierra Leone returned with the view that 'the time is coming
when the dwellers in those vales and on these mountains will
sing hosannas to the Son of David.'24 So an expedition of freed
slaves was made up. It was denied direct federal funds, but the
U.S. Government contributed about 33,000 dollars for items
of equipment — which included wagons, ploughs, iron work for
a saw mill and a grist mill, a couple of cannon, 100 muskets, a
fishing seine and a four-oared barge — and provided a naval
escort for the emigration ship, the *Elizabeth*. Those who went
on the expedition were thus rather better equipped than the
early Sierra Leoneans had been. They were, however, as laden
with pious advice as the earlier emigrants. 'Habits of industry
should be particularly inculcated, and if necessary enforced
by authority. No drones ought to be permitted to live among
you', wrote E.B. Caldwell, secretary to the board of managers
of the Society.25
The party numbered 88, 40 of whom came from New York,
and 33 from Pennsylvania. They were 33 men — mechanics
and labourers, and 18 women — seamstresses, cooks, nurses and
washerwomen. There were also 37 children.26 A press of several
thousand excited people saw the *Elizabeth* sail from New York
at the end of January 1820. The first week saw her proceed
approximately half a mile. She became stuck fast in the ice in
the harbour. One account runs:

> The farewell spoken, it was painful for the emigrants to
> linger within sight of those shores which they never

expected again to behold, and almost within sound of those scenes, now doubly dear to their hearts, in which they could never again mingle . . . Some grew faint-hearted, and murmured, 'Wherefore are we brought here, with our wives and our little ones, to be a prey?' Those who had counted the cost, and made up their minds to look every difficulty in the face with a steady eye and a brave heart, stood firm and unmoved, rejoicing even that they were accounted worthy to be pioneers in an enterprise, whose far-off yet glorious results already seem to gild the dark mountain-tops of Africa with the beams of the Sun of Righteousness.[27]

Eventually, the ship was freed from the ice, and with the official blessing of President James Monroe, headed for Sherbro Island, down the coast from Freetown.

A curious point about all these early expeditions is that nobody seems to have learned anything from anybody else about the experience. For, sure enough, the party landed at Sherbro just before the beginning of the rainy season. The colonists were thankful to have landed and, unsuspecting, they prepared for their first impressions:

> That evening the voice of praise and thanksgiving ascended from this little band of African Christians in the palm-groves of their fatherland, with a savour sweeter than spices, and a token of the planting of that tree whose leaves shall be for the healing of the nations. Their naked countrymen, wild, dirty, and savage, came lounging through the thickets with curiosity and wonder, trying to hold intercourse with them through the medium of the few English words already familiar to their ears. Alas! those English words were little more than oaths and curses, learned from the slaver's crew. How striking was the contrast between them and the new comers, clean, orderly, well dressed, sober, Christian men and women. It was a happy evening.[28]

It was a short-lived happiness. The new colonists had trusted a villainous local contact, John Kizell, to negotiate a piece of land. When they had landed at Campelar on the eastern side of the island, towards the coast of what is now Sierra Leone, they found that it was a foetid swamp, with no drinking water, and thirty miserable huts, surrounded by dense thicket. The pilgrims began complaining of burning headaches and inflamed eyes, and soon half of them were delirious. Since the doctor was away, trying to negotiate for a better piece of land, the settlers began to die. By the beginning of the rainy season, just two months after they landed, there were only a couple of men who could be described as fit. Kizell was brazenly profiteering by selling the stores to the Sherbro kings. At the beginning of May, there was no hope left. Somehow, under the able leadership of Daniel Coker, himself a freed slave, the little colony lurched on until the October, by which time they had had enough. In the same month, the band left the island and took refuge at Freetown. Thus, another province of freedom perished.

In 1819, the Federal Government of the United States had passed a bill, instructing the American Navy to seize any American vessel engaged in the slave trade. Although not eager to embark on colonialism itself, it needed a station, similar to Freetown, where recaptives could be landed. The American Colonization Society therefore received at least the tacit backing of the Government in its efforts to refound the Liberian settlement. (The Government later accepted the Society's agent as its own in Liberia.) So in 1821 a further party of four white agents and thirty-three Negroes were sent aboard the vessel *Nautilus* to arrange the colony anew. Three of the agents went under (two died, and the third fled in terror), leaving the group in the charge of Dr Eli Ayres, a Baltimore physician. This time, the Society refused to accept the answer No from the natives.

Eli Ayres, under the protection of Lieutenant Robert Field Stockton of the U.S. Navy, took British advice and sailed further down the coast to Cape Mesurado, two hundred miles from Freetown. There the group entered into negotiations with a recalcitrant local king, King Peter. The king said he would not sell the land, since, as we have seen, he was in no position to do so. Whereupon Stockton took out a pistol and handed it to Ayres, ordering him to shoot if necessary. His other pistol he cocked and levelled at King Peter's head. With the customary delicacy of the American armed forces,

Stockton then told Peter that the party had come as benefactors, not as enemies. Just at that point, according to one account, Stockton raised his free hand to the sky and a ray of sunshine burst through the clouds.[29] Whether it was the pistol of a U.S. Navy lieutenant or the meteorological conditions that persuaded King Peter can only be guessed, but the king immediately signed a lease on a piece of land for something less than three hundred dollars a year.

And so the Republic of Liberia was founded.

The early years of the Republic followed what had become a familiar pattern: occasional skirmishes with the natives whose customs the former slaves neither respected nor, indeed, understood. (I once asked an aged Grebo from eastern Liberia what the oral tradition of the area was about the coming of the former slaves. 'They didn't ask the news', said the man. I thought that they'd hardly be interested in the 'news', but the old man went on, 'No, I mean they didn't try to find out what the customs were. They thought it was bad that the Grebo left their dead on a small island, not burying them, and they said we must bury them, and we said no, and there was a big palaver and then a big fight. They didn't ask.' I asked him what he thought of modern American blacks coming to Africa. He smiled and said, 'They don't ask the news, do they?') The early settlers squabbled among themselves on their spit of land on the Cape. The weather became humid, and then rainy. They had not enough food and equipment, and in fact still preferred an American diet based on pork and flour and coffee. But, although they were faced with utter poverty and suffered disastrously from fevers, there were still one hundred and fifty settlers huddled on Cape Mesurado by the next year.

Their survival was due in great part to the leadership of a new agent, Jehudi Ashmun, a failed doctor, failed lawyer, failed journalist, failed teacher and failed scholar. Ashmun, however, may be regarded as the true founder of Liberia. He cajoled and somehow unified the early settlers, while sending back hugely optimistic accounts for American consumption. 'From the ruins of human virtue and hope [God's] wisdom is displaying a new moral creation, and the exile, sufferings and degradation of the Africans may be succeeded by their return, felicity and honour.'[30] He bullied the settlers into building proper accommodation for themselves and tried to introduce rules, especially governing the trade of rum, as he feared the colony might otherwise swarm with 'tippling shops, tipplers and drunkards'.[31]

But lack of funds dogged the colony. It seemed that the liberal-minded rich were eager to contribute to the removal of the freed blacks, but less eager to help sustain them in their new colony. So many tales of disaster filtered back to the United States, despite Ashmun's propaganda, that alternative sites were considered for colonization. For a while Haiti was considered a possibility. That possibility, and a newly-formed Haitian Emigration Society, faded, but not before sorely needed funds were channelled away from the American Colonization Society.

In 1825, the *African Repository and Colonial Journal (A.R.C.J.)* was founded, partly to assure benefactors that all was well, and partly to drum up new funds. It was therefore a highly partisan organ, but was nevertheless the only place where the new settlers could publish their reactions, favourable or unfavourable. Naturally, the *Journal* printed the most favourable ones. It contained a fine mixture of articles such as 'Moral Qualities of the Africans', and 'Remarks on the Dromedary', and stirring accounts of the fighting in Ashanti, oddly enough reprinting accounts by white correspondents of the exploits of the British Army in their attempts to repress the Ashanti. But the *African Repository* also contained letters, poems and articles by the new settlers in Liberia, and it gives the few insights we have into the life of the pioneers.

Poems such as this were not infrequent:

I looked, and the coming of the day
Had dim'd that bright star in my eye;
And, afar in the distance, there lay,
At the meeting of the ocean and the sky,
A land, that, as nearer I drew,
Most enchantingly rose on my sight,
While the sun rose in glory, and threw
O'er its green woods his mantle of light.

The sun had far mounted the sky,
When my pathway on ocean was o'er
And none was so happy as I,
When delighted, I leaped on the shore.
In freedom and joy did I stand,

And pour forth my thanks to my God,
Who thus led me back to the land,
My fathers for ages had trod.[32]

Ashmun thundered to the A.C.S., 'You have . . . founded an
empire. Heaven help you to the means of sustaining the happy
beginnings.'[33] Ashmun was reassuring about the moral calibre
of the settlers: ' . . . [their] only philosophy had been acquired
from a series of disspiriting conflicts with every form of
physical and moral adversity . . . and [their] prospects, at that
moment, were as dark and appalling, as the memory of the
past was embittered — ejected from the land of their birth —
hostility, famine and destruction menacing them in that of
their adoption', and they were prevailing.[34]

Among the settlers' adversities was at least one attack of
a massive swarm of bees. The bees invaded eight or nine
building lots. People jumped into the river, to little avail. One
woman was stung three to five hundred times.[35] On another
occasion 'several Tigers of the Leopard species' destroyed a
number of dogs, ducks, goats and even bullocks.[36]

One of the settlers, Lott Carey, a Baptist preacher from
Richmond, Virginia, had said before departure, 'I am an
African. I wish to go to a country where I shall be estimated
by my merits, not by my complexion; and I feel bound to
labour for my suffering race.'[37] His labour for his suffering
race had involved his killing a fair number of them in wresting
the foothold from the Africans. But he writes in the *Journal*:
'There never has been an hour or a minute, no, not even when
the balls were flying around my head, when I could wish myself
again in America.'[38]

The *Journal* described how town lots had been set out, and
how people had constructed frame houses and cabins on them.
They were growing fruit and coffee, although, as now, there
were complaints about the food. One settler found the yams
'tough and tasteless and [bearing] much the same relation to
an excellent or common potato as codfish or shark meat does to
a well-dressed pike or trout'.[39]

The *Journal* also contained letters from satisfied immigrants
to former masters and mistresses. One reads: 'I am, Sir, much
pleased with the country, and have not the least desire to
return to Virginia; and I am under a thousand obligations to

the white people for sending me and my friends to the benighted land of Africa, and hope that God will bless every one that put in the least mite to assist us away.'[40] Another went, 'What my sensations were upon landing I can hardly describe . . . You here behold coloured men exercising all the duties of offices of which you can scarcely believe, many fulfill the important duties with much dignity. We have now a republic in miniature . . . I long to see young men, who are now wasting the best of their days in the United States, flocking to the land as the last asylum to the unfortunate.' [41]

And for the enormous number of settlers who died, there was the comfort of knowing that they had died, not only on their own lands, but in the arms of the Lord:

> Jesus can make a dying bed
> Feel soft as downy pillows are;
> While on his breast I lean my head,
> And breathe my life out sweetly there.[42]

This was, apparently, the dying address of one agent. But death was not only regarded as a repose in the Lord, or even as the commonplace it became. It was often thought to be the settlers' own fault. They 'owe their death to imprudent exposure during convalescence, and a free indulgence in the fruits of the place, particularly the pine-apple; than which nothing can be more deleterious; the oldest settlers not being able to use it freely without feeling its ill effects'.[43]

There was an air of public ebullience and enthusiasm. A number of citizens of Monrovia got together and composed a circular address to 'the coloured people of the United States':

> We know nothing of that debasing inferiority with
> which our very colour stamped us in America. It is this
> moral emancipation — this liberation of the mind from
> worse than iron fetters, that repays us, ten thousand
> times over, for all it has cost us . . . The burden is gone
> from our shoulders: we now breathe and move freely —
> and know not (in surveying your present state) for
> which to pity you most, the empty name of liberty,
> which you endeavour to content yourselves with in a
> country that is not yours; or the delusion which makes

you hope for ampler privileges in that country . . . We
have nearly all suffered from sickness, and of the earliest
emigrants, a large proportion fell in the arduous attempt
to lay the foundation of our Colony. But are they the
only persons whose lives have been lost in the cause of
human liberty . . .?[44]

What the *Journal* did not mention were the two bloody
defeats inflicted by the settlers on the local Vei in late 1822.
The cannon, paid for by the United States Government, had
proved to be extremely useful. On one occasion it was filled
with grapeshot and fired from a range of a few score yards at
a mass of natives. That was a bad year for native Liberians,
since the victories gave the settlers a new confidence in their
right to stay, and a confidence, too, in their cannon as a
reinforcement of that right.

Nor did the *Journal* record the petty squabbling that
resulted in a state of open insurrection, led, ironically, by Lott
Carey. In many ways like the Sierra Leoneans, the settlers
shared a repugnance for agriculture, and they too gravitated
towards trade instead. The trade brought them a relative
prosperity, so that by the early 1830s, Monrovia was in
reasonable shape. A visitor recorded: 'Their houses are well
built, ornamented with gardens and other pleasing decorations,
and in the inside are remarkably clean — the walls well white-
washed and the rooms neatly furnished. They are very
hospitable to strangers and many English naval officers in the
station have been invited to dine with them, and joined in
their meals, which were wholesome and good.'[45]

The just-so prosperity did not last long; the supporting
American Colonization Society found itself in the middle ground
between the pro- and anti-slavery vested interests, a situation that
led, of course, to the Civil War. But still the trickle of colonists
continued to arrive in Liberia, usually at a rate of one or two
hundred a year, but rising to peaks, such as 796 in 1832.
Agencies, too, spread all over the United States. Only about
fifty settlers had given up by 1834 and gone back to America,
where they raised a disproportionate amount of anti-Liberian
propaganda.

Liberia had its bitter enemies in America. There were
allegations of a grave problem of drink in the colony, and it

was frequently said that the country was awash with 'ardent spirits'.[46] At the same time, despite the settlers' confidence in their reports and letters to the A.R.C.J., there was widespread disease and several crop failures. Already, the Americo-Liberians, who had, as they said, lifted the burden of debasing inferiority from their shoulders, were in the process of replacing that same burden on the shoulders of the natives. Disliking agriculture, they developed a highly dubious system of people-pawning. This was later the source of much abuse. People who failed to repay debts were made to work for their creditor until the debt was paid off. But in at least one case, a man worked for an Americo-Liberian for nearly forty years before his debt was adjudged discharged.[47]

During the main period of immigration, from 1822 to 1867, some 18,958 settlers were landed in Liberia. Of these, 5,722 were recaptives freed by the U.S. Navy as a result of the law of 1819. Thus only one-tenth of the number of recaptives taken to Freetown were landed in Liberia. It followed, then, that the American backgrounds of the settlers were less diluted by Africans joining their community than were those of their counterparts in Sierra Leone. They did, however, maintain exactly the same disdainful superiority over their native brothers.

Their relationship with the United States itself was ambiguous. The U.S. Government never accepted that the Cape Mesurado colony was in fact their colony. While this was never tested in the early days, the relationship continued to be one resembling *de facto* colonialism. As soon as a serious challenge came the way of the Liberians, however, they were virtually abandoned by the Americans. In the 1840s, the British Government laid claim to certain parts of Liberia. The Americans, while expressing 'concern', preferred to leave the Americo-Liberians to sort out their own problems. The Liberians therefore declared their independence. Section 13 of the new Constitution — laid down in 1847 — stated: 'The great object of forming these Colonies being to provide a home for the dispersed children of Africa, and to regenerate and enlighten this benighted continent, none but Negroes or persons of Negro descent shall be eligible to citizenship in this Republic.'[48] Ironically, the British Government was the first to recognize the independent black Republic, the second, after Haiti, in the world. The United States did not recognize Liberia until 1862. America remained, however, a strong influence on Liberia, and did intercede on her behalf in 1909 when European colonial powers laid claim to Liberian territory in default of government loans.

The mid nineteenth century brought good years for Liberia. While struggling with its large debts and political problems, the Colonization Society still sent emigrants, and internally Liberia appeared to manage its own affairs with stability. It happened that an essential element of this stability was the deliberate withholding of resources from the interior. There were inordinate wage differentials between Americo-Liberians and the natives. There were widespread abuses of the apprentice system by farmers, who also abused their curious power to 'fine' dilatory workers.[49]

The decline in Liberia's fortunes is attributable to several developments: the more direct European involvement in Africa; the start of the European Scramble for Africa which got seriously under way in the 1880s; the competition from coffee from Brazil and sugar beet from Europe; the series of unwise foreign loans which all but bankrupted the country in the 1870s; developments within the United States, notably the Civil War, and the hopes of many Negroes that they would be freed when the North won.[50]

The American Colonization Society (A.C.S.), already operating with highly precarious finances, was hard hit by the announcements of the 14th and 15th Amendments, by the attendant legislation and the resultant hopes for an honourable' destiny in America felt by many blacks. The economic decline in Liberia which this helped to cause itself discouraged emigration. It is at this point that the two histories diverge: that of the internal development of Liberia itself, with the entrenchment of the Americo-Liberians, and that of the un-official — but unlike that of the A.C.S. — *mass* — Back-to-Africa movements.

In Liberia, the settlers had not repudiated the traditions, religion and criteria of the land that had repudiated them. Instead, they attempted to reproduce American culture on African soil. Often their views were parallel to those of nineteenth-century whites, just as American blacks visiting Africa frequently reflect white views. Their consciousness of the distinction between them and the savages grew even more, and in return the natives took to referring to them as 'white people'. (A distressing experience for the black American visitor today to, say, modern Ghana is the African custom of calling New World Negroes by the Twi word *abruni* or *obruni*. This means, in fact,'white man'. Europeans are also called *abruni*, or sometimes *abruni coco*: 'pink white man'.)

The abused apprentice system proved a way for natives to assimilate into Americo-Liberian society. On the other hand, it became a form of domestic slavery. The Americo-Liberians were aware of what they chose to call their 'Manifest Destiny' of civilizing the interior, but until comparatively recently, they did nothing about fulfilling it. Several large Americo-Liberian families came to dominate Liberian politics, and hence the economy.

The arrogance of the Americo-Liberians became legendary. They created rules for the natives on matters such as nudity, and they refused — until this century — to marry people from the interior, although liaisons were permitted. There was severe segregation in housing and education, no roads were provided in the hinterland, and precious few other utilities. In 1910, King Gyude and a group of chiefs of the Grebos wrote to the A.C.S.: 'Since the incorporation of the colony . . . we and our fathers have always befriended the Liberian Republic as a struggling nation of our race, but on the other hand, they, having established a government which bade fair to make some sort of showing, soon began to despise us, placing us in their room and they in their masters', just as in the same fashion as in their slavery days in America.'[51]

The fact that the Liberians have not been overtaken by the forces that toppled the Creoles of Sierra Leone from political power is possibly due to the Africans of the hinterland being even less educated than the Africans of the interior of Sierra Leone, and to power being concentrated in fewer hands. Political power rested in the hands of a group of families; economic power was virtually given away in 1926. In December of that year, the Liberians signed a contract with the Firestone Rubber Company, which gave the company a lease on one million acres of the country for ninety-nine years. The company thereby acquired control of almost the entire revenue of the country, and with it probably the real government of Liberia as well. Thus, the descendents of a particularly adventurous group of freed slaves found themselves once more in hock to the company store.

But the even greater humiliation was still to come. A first-generation black American, Thomas Faulkner — who had arrived in Liberia before the First World War — was twice an unsuccessful candidate in rigged presidential elections. He had a form of power base in Monrovia, in that he ran an ice-cream parlour, supplied much-welcomed ice to concerns and individuals about Monrovia, and had begun electrification work in the city. He could not compete, however, with an efficient ballot-rigging presidential machine. In 1927, after his second defeat against President Charles King, he went back to America, where he denounced members of the Liberian administration, and in particular accused a number of being implicated in the forced recruitment of labour for the cocoa and other plantations on the Spanish island of Fernando Po. The accusations spread to Firestone — who acknowledged that in the company's early years, certain chiefs had 'assisted' in the recruitment of labour — and further charges were levelled against Liberian soldiers that they went on midnight raids to kidnap likely labourers.

It was alleged — but never proved — that President King himself was involved in the forced labour recruitment. The payment for such labourers was allegedly 45 dollars a head up to 3,000 slaves, with a bonus of 5,000 dollars for every 1,500 thereafter. Cries of outrage followed Faulkner round the United States as he stumped the country belabouring the Liberian Government. The cries were soon taken up in Britain (the British had actually abolished domestic slavery in Sierra Leone only in 1928) and in France, whose colonial administration, notably under Governor Félix Eboué, a French Guyanan, was certainly not slow to recruit forced labour for its railway and road building programmes in Central Africa.

Liberia itself asked the League of Nations to investigate the allegations. The League's Commission reported in 1930 that: the state of slavery as defined by the Anti-Slavery Convention did not exist in the Republic; that domestic slavery was not participated in, nor encouraged by the Government; that leading citizens were not participating in slavery, although they did adopt aboriginals as bonded servants, according to African usage. But the Commission also found that:

1. The Republic *did* employ forced labour;

2. Shipment to Fernando Po was associated with slavery because it carried compulsion with it;

3. Labour for private purposes was forcibly impressed by the Government, and used in the Firestone plantations (the Commission expressed its doubts about Firestone, but allowed the finding to stand);

4. The Liberian Government had not at any time expressly given sanction or approval to the recruiting of labour with the aid of the Liberian Frontier Force . . . [but] . . . persons holding official positions had illegally misused their office in recruiting with the aid of the Force.

The Commission said: 'Vice President Yancy and other high officials of the Liberian Government as well as County Superintendents and District Commissioners have given their sanction for the compulsory recruitment of labour for road construction, for shipment abroad and other work.'[52]

Vice-President Yancy resigned, closely followed by the President. Somewhat exaggerated joy was expressed overseas; a stream of hypocritical abuse was poured on the little Republic from the colonial nations. The British Government first attempted to gain a League of Nations' mandate over Liberia, then applied to establish a protectorate over it. The attempts were resisted, but of course the opprobrium remained.

At the same time, it is doubtful that the revelations of aspects of Liberian political and social life made much difference among American blacks to the state of Imagined Africa. The colonial powers overplayed their hand in their denigration of Liberia. Soon the whole affair had the air of a contrived campaign by the greedy European colonials. (This is a belief that is still strongly held in certain areas of the black community in America.)

Organized emigration had tailed off by the beginning of this century. The pattern changed to one of individuals and occasional groups making their own way to Africa. A number of black American servicemen were posted to Liberia in the Second World War, and today one finds a few who stayed or returned. After the war, and with the growth of dynamic independence movements elsewhere in West Africa, attention moved away from

Liberia. The 1962 census showed that of 10,268 citizens of foreign birth in Liberia, only 231 had come from the United States.[53] The American Colonization Society had left the centre of the Back-to-Africa stage by the end of the nineteenth century.

It is one of the more remarkable aspects of the Back-to-Africa movements that their success at mobilizing black opinion and pride of race should have coincided precisely with the growth of sheer unpleasantness in the regime of the African country with which they were primarily concerned.

CHAPTER 3

'Our Armies Come Rushing to Thee...'

'I'm bound for the happy land.'

> (Hymn overheard by passing ship from the *Horsa* as
> she headed for Monrovia in March, 1895[1])

'The Negroes of the world say, "We are striking homewards
towards Africa to make her the big black republic." And in
the making of Africa a big black republic, what is the barrier?
The barrier is the white man; and we say to the white man who
now dominates Africa that it is in his interest to clear out of
Africa now, because we are coming not as in the time of Father
Abraham, 200,000 strong, but we are coming 400,000,000
strong, and we mean to retake every square inch of the
12,000,000 square miles of African territory belonging to us
by right Divine . . . We are out to get what has belonged to us
politically, socially, economically, and in every way. And what
15,000,000 of us cannot get we will call in 400,000,000 to
help us get.'

> (Marcus Garvey, September 1920[2])

Many American Negroes were always suspicious and critical of plans to repatriate them. Some clung to what they believed was evidence that the American nation might accommodate them comfortably, even handsomely. In 1833, James Forten, a wealthy sailmaker of Philadelphia, said:

> My great-grandfather was brought to this country a slave from Africa. My grandfather obtained his own freedom. My father never wore the yoke. He rendered valuable service to his country in the war of our Revolution; and I, though then a boy, was a drummer in that war. I was taken prisoner and was made to suffer not a little on board the Jersey prison-ship. I have since lived and laboured in a useful employment, have acquired property, and have paid taxes in this city. Here I dwelt until I am nearly sixty years of age, and have brought up and educated a family . . . yet some ingenious gentlemen have recently discovered that I am still an African; that a continent, three thousand miles, or more, from the place where I was born, is my native country . . .[3]

Others attacked the idea of repatriation as a form of cowardice. It was a potent charge, that of want of courage to participate in the great American adventure, and it was raised all through the nineteenth century. In 1901, a certain William Hannibal Thomas published a book, *The American Negro, What He Was, What He Is, and What He May Become.* In it he warns against what he called Chimerical Expatriation:

> To remove . . . social disabilities, he [the American Negro] is advised to shirk duty by cowardly flight, to stultify himself by exile, and to entail upon his children perpetual debasement. The freedman is urged to this

course, notwithstanding the fact that negro expatriation would be a confession of personal inferiority, an avowal of inherent servility, an acknowledgement that the race is not by nature, training, capacity, or possibility, the equal of other American citizens. If that be true, why go abroad? If wrongs exist here, exile will not right them. An African hut and a tropical sun will not create manhood, develop intelligence, impart industry, foster thrift, nor promote courage in illiterate, craven-hearted, shiftless people; nor will these physical agencies endue them with such transforming qualities of mind or character as will lift a confessedly inferior race to a plane of equality with American citizens. The plea is preposterous. No successful migration of a people was ever instituted by arrant cowardice. It must also be borne in mind that Africa is a far distant continent, whose inhabitants are savages, whose speech is barbarous, whose climate near the coast is execrable, whose plains are barren wastes, and whose forests are impenetrable jungles. It is to this wilderness that American negroes are invited to migrate — a land without houses or roadways, shops or stores, factories or mechanics, agriculture or railways, schools or churches, libraries or newspapers, scholars or history, but one to which negroes have gone, and are still going, empty-handed, without money or skilful industry, knowledge or power. For what? To combat savages, to war with nature, to struggle with poverty, to live in disappointment in a savage Eden and die in despair in a sensuous paradise.[4]

The A.C.S. was accused of failing to dispel the illusion that slaves were property, of failing to attack the institution vigorously enough, and by its actions increasing the value of slaves. A strong anti-emigration movement flourished all through the nineteenth century. But opposition came not only from thoughtful, or manipulated or eccentric,Negroes, who saw emigration as a Northern plot to get rid of them. Others looked at Liberia itself and thought, along with a Harvard-trained black physician, Martin Delany, that it was 'a poor miserable mockery . . . a burlesque on a government'.[5]

Looking for an alternative site and scheme which did not depend on Northern white liberals, Dr Delany and his assistant

Robert Campbell, a young Jamaican chemist, helped form the Niger Valley Exploring Party, and travelled to Africa in 1859. Said Delany, 'I had but one object in view — the Moral, Social and Political Elevation of Ourselves, and the Regeneration of Africa, for which I desired, as a preference, and indeed the only adequate and essential means by which it is to be accomplished, men of African descent, properly qualified and of pure and fixed principles.'

Delany visited Liberia on his way to Nigeria, and described what he saw there: 'How unsightly to a stranger, as he steps from the boat at the mouth of Stockton Creek, on the Mesurado River, is the rude and rugged steep, leading by simple pathways in true native style, from the warehouses up to the town, which if improved as it might and should be, would be one of the most pleasing as well as attractive approaches to any city in the world.'[6] Although he was disappointed with Liberia, even beyond his worst expectations, he recorded reactions to Africa which he was to share with many thousand other Negroes who have returned to this day.

He described how his feelings of gentle pleasure 'merge into feelings of almost intense excitement, not only mentally, but the entire physical system share largely in it, so that it might be termed a hilarity of feeling almost akin to approaching intoxication; or, as I imagine, like the sensation produced by the beverage of champagne wine. Never having enjoyed the taste of it, I cannot say from experience.' These first feelings were succeeded by a certain lassitude, a disposition to stretch, gape and yawn with fatigue. Then, actual febrile attacks, with nausea, chills and violent headaches, plus 'a feeling of regret that you left your native country for a strange one; an almost frantic desire to see friends and [land of] nativity; a despondency and loss of hope of ever seeing those you love at home again'. But then, 'When an entire recovery takes place, the love of the country is most ardent and abiding.'[7] I have a tape-recording of almost identical feelings expressed, rather less stiffly, by a young black American who had been in Ghana a few months.

The *Report of the Niger Valley Exploring Party*, and Campbell's own *Pilgrimage to My Motherland*, are classic mixtures of both pious outrage at native customs and the commercial fervour of the day. Among the Egba of western

93

Nigeria, Campbell noted that 'cases of adultery often occur, and must be expected until the natives are taught to abandon their disgusting system of polygamy.'[8] He had no doubt been somewhat shocked by his first sight of Africa. 'A disgusting spectacle presented itself at the entrance of the river: on the right margin stood two bodies transfixed by poles passing through their mouths.'[9]

But some fervid sympathy shone through: 'Not long since, and even now, there are not a few who regard the African to be like the snake or the alligator, a lazy creature whose life is spent basking in the sunshine, subsisting on roots and herbs, or whatever else of food is within reach of his arm . . . I assert and appeal to every one who has visited this section of Africa to verify any assertion, that there is not a more industrious people on the face of the earth.'[10] Campbell proposed to harness this industriousness:

> If, by the cheap labour of the teeming millions of Africa, cotton should be produced at a rate considerably lower than in America, not only will the looms of Lancashire be beneficially supplied and the consumers of cotton manufacturers be more reasonable clothed, but slavery will receive its severest wound . . . The destruction of the slave-market, through the depreciation of slave-labour, is a matter of dry calculation. It is simply a question of the price of cotton. If Africa can bring down cotton, Africa can bring down slavery. African industry may yet be God's means for annihilating African servitude! [11]

On December 27th, 1859, Campbell and Delany negotiated permission to settle skilled Afro-Americans on any part of the unoccupied lands of Abeokuta, the Egba city-state. Delany declared, 'Our policy must be . . . Africa for the African race, and black men to rule them.'[12] This may well be the first time that the phrase was used.

But the treaty with the chiefs of Abeokuta was never implemented. The American Civil War made the project irrelevant; Negroes were once again promised manumission in America. Delany himself was commissioned as a major in the 104th Regiment of the Unionist Army, and after the war he worked in the Freedmen's Bureau as a sub-assistant commissioner.

Campbell returned to Abeokuta and lived and travelled there for a number of years, but the main project was never completed. Delany had missed his chance. When he was disillusioned by the work of the Freedmen's Bureau and by the disappointments of the late 1870s, he launched, with a number of other Southern blacks, the Liberian Exodus Joint Stock Steamship Company. On the crest of a renewed Back-to-Africa wave in 1878, the company's ship, the *Azor*, made its single voyage to Africa. Of the 206 who sailed on the ship that April, 23 died at sea. The incompetence of the company landed the *Azor* in pawn to its creditors — later a familiar pattern — but at least Delany's new project had shifted the Back-to-Africa movement to where it truly belonged, the Southern agricultural states. It might also be said that the project was the first in a modern series of extraordinary — and connected — movements run by black people involving a return to Africa which was but rarely achieved.

The finances and support of the American Colonization Society always fell when black Americans were most deluded by hope for freedom. However, support was never fully recovered in the despair that followed disillusion. It was soon obvious that even the desperate support that existed in the increasingly violent South could not be matched by the Society's capability to do anything about it. The last great financial crisis for the A.C.S., in 1892, left hundreds of hopeful migrants stranded in the major cities. This created such terrible public relations for the Society that the white press took to attacking the raising of false hopes in the blacks. It printed vivid descriptions of the degredation in the impoverished encampments of stranded migrants.

Only poverty-stricken blacks were applying for emigration, whereas Liberia needed skilled artisans and the relatively better-off. Besides, Liberia could only offer much the same conditions as those that had greeted settlers in the early part of the century. If they were not immediately successful in trade, there was a grinding struggle against poverty and ill-health, years of subsistence farming.

Two forms of international migration were to re-inflame the emigration fever, however. The first was the mass movement of millions of Europeans across the Atlantic to chase the American dream. The other was the European

Scramble for Africa. It became clear that it might well be Europeans who were going to usurp the dream of New World riches, and reap vast profits in Africa, too.

In 1855, Alexander Crummell, who had emigrated from America to Liberia, made probably the most important speech in the nineteenth century to black Americans on the subject of emigration. Crummell was a black American missionary, an intellectual Episcopalian who was to become a close academic associate of Blyden's at Liberia College. In 'The Relations and Duties of Free Coloured Men in America to Africa' he said:

> Africa lies low and is wretched. She is the maimed and crippled arm of humanity. Her great powers are wasted. Dislocation and anguish have reached every joint. Her condition in every point calls for succour — moral, social, domestic, political, commercial, and intellectual. Whence shall flow aid, mercy, advantage to her? Here arises the call of duty and obligation to coloured men. Other people may, if they choose, forget the homes of their sires; for almost every European nation is now reaping the fruits of a thousand years' civilisation. Every one of them can spare thousands and even millions of their sons to build up civilisation in Australia, Canada, New Zealand, South Africa, or Victoria. But Africa is the victim of her heterogeneous idolatories. Africa is wasting away beneath the accretions of civil and moral miseries. Darkness covers the land, and gross darkness the people. Great social evils universally prevail. Confidence and security are destroyed. Licentiousness abounds everywhere. Moloch rules and reigns throughout the whole continent . . . [13]

Although Crummell eventually returned to America in 1873, one man directly influenced by this speech was Henry McNeal Turner, whom Crummell was later to call 'that turbulent, screeching and screaming creature'.[14]

Turner was a passionate demagogue, gifted with alarmingly picturesque oratorical powers, a forceful and tactless man. Entirely self-taught — Du Bois described him as the 'last of his clan: mighty men, physically and mentally, men who started at the bottom and hammered their way to the top

by sheer brute strength'[15] — Turner became a preacher at
the age of sixteen. He had plenty of personal experience
of white prejudice: he had been a chaplain until white
pressure forced him out of the ministry after the Civil War;
he had entered the Georgia state legislature but was thrown
out by the whites; he even at one time held a job as the only
black postmaster in the state of Georgia, until again prejudice
dislodged him.

From Crummell he gained a belief in the redemption of
heathen Africa, and began preaching about the 'voice of a
mysterious providence, saying, "Return to the land of your
Fathers."' He said: 'There is no more doubt in my mind that
we have ultimately to return to Africa than there is of the
existence of God.'[16] There is little doubt that Turner was
substantially motivated by personal bitterness. His ambition
for power and prestige had been thwarted by white men.
Many blacks of the time believed they could achieve progress
within the political system, but, unlike Turner, most had
never actually tried. His repudiation of the American system
grew in volume in succeeding years. As American Negroes also
became disenchanted with political developments, they lent
their support to him in swelling numbers.

Although nominally committed to the aims of the A.C.S,
Turner nevertheless pronounced his benediction on the sailing
of the *Azor*. In 1880, he became a bishop in the American
Methodist Episcopal (A.M.E.) Church. His theological view
was that 'the great Jehovah, in his allwise providence, had
made a distinction in the colour but not in the political or
social status of the human race.' Not unnaturally, this view was
not shared by Southern whites. Lynchings were becoming a
daily occurrence. As the atmosphere grew more violent and
wretched, Turner declared that it must all end in 'war, efforts
of extermination, anarchy, horror and a wail to heaven'.[17]

'Whoever the white race does not consort with, it will crush
out', he warned. Turner's contempt for America grew alongside
his African dream. 'We were born here, raised here, fought,
bled, and died here, and have a thousand times more right here
than hundreds of thousands of those who help snub, proscribe
and persecute us, and that is one of the reasons I almost
despise the land of my birth.'[18] He in time dropped the word
'almost'. 'Yes, I would make Africa a place of refuge, because

I see no other shelter from the stormy blast, from the red tide of persecution, from the horrors of American prejudice.'[19]

His message was built on a foundation of alluring and supportive exhortations that had come across the Atlantic from people like Crummell and Blyden. Blyden said: 'It ought to be clear to every thinking and impartial mind, that there can never occur [in the United States] an equality, social or political, between whites and blacks.'[20] He later said:

> I rejoice to know that . . . where the teachings of generations have been to disparage the race, there are men and women who will go, who have a restless sense of homelessness which will never be appeased until they stand in the great land where their forefathers lived; until they catch the glimpses of the old sun, and moon and stars, which still shine in their primitive brilliancy upon that vast domain; until from the deck of the ship which bears them back home they see visions of the hills rising from the white margin of the continent, and listen to the breaking music of the waves — the exhilarating laughter of the sea as it dashes against the beach.[21]

But millions of Negroes resolutely clung to the American dream. Turner was accused of being, at best, unduly pessimistic about the Negro's lot and, at worst, a coward. Conservative blacks were annoyed that he should reject the possibility of race harmony. (From this conservative stream eventually rose Booker T. Washington: see p 101) But Turner thundered on. He had, he said, seen men 'sit down and cry because they were compelled to hire out their daughters as chambermaids, after spending all they had to give them an education'.[22] He was in favour of creating an equivalent, in reverse, of the Middle Passage, and also of the flight from Europe to America, for his ideas of self-redemption and freedom from persecution were a direct reflection of the urges that brought the hordes of settlers from the Old World.

Turner tried various plans. The first was to demand payment of a debt of forty billion dollars which he reckoned the Federal Government owed the black people for services rendered. Failing that, he was confident that an emigration movement could be sufficiently well backed by a business world anxious to develop trade links with Liberia and the rest of Africa.

The last straw for Turner in his exasperation with America
came with the 1883 Supreme Court decision. The decision, he
said, absolved the Negro of his duty of allegiance, and 'makes
the American flag to him a rag of contempt instead of a symbol
of liberty'. The Constitution — with its suppressed 14th and
15th Amendments — had become 'a dirty rag, a cheat, a libel
and ought to be spit upon by every Negro in the land'.[23] Turner
denounced his conservative black opposition as 'scullion Negroes'
and urged all to 'Respect Black!'[24] Those who opposed him, he
said, were 'fighting the God of the universe, face to face'.[25]

When Turner finally travelled to Africa in 1891, he found
nothing to quell his ardour. Even Sierra Leone he found full of
inspiration. The natives he worshipped with were 'right from
the bush, with a mere cloth over them,' but they were 'full of
the Holy Ghost'.[26] In grandiloquent letters he described Africa
as being the land of true wisdom, full of proud-walking sons
of Nature. Above all, he said, what the black man had in Africa
was *manhood*. He blinded himself to the suffering and disease
and poverty, and permitted himself only to see a pleasant,
sanitary city. His month's travelling in Sierra Leone and Liberia
impressed him only with the dignity of the resettlers.

On his return to the United States he redoubled his thrashing
attacks on mean-spirited Negroes who failed to share his vision.
'We have been denounced and ridiculed a thousand times by a
number of these mushroom pimps who know how to scribble
a little on paper for the public press.' Such people were 'Northern
coons,' he scoffed, made up of either 'this young fungus class'
or 'those old fossils'.[27]

Turner made further visits to Africa in following years. He
noted disturbing increases in the numbers of white people there,
and warned that the whites would soon destroy all black men's
hopes of being able to set up self-governing nations there.
Turner also spoke to gatherings of Africans, especially in South
Africa, where his radical views seriously upset the whites and,
it should be added, had a profound effect on the blacks. Back-
to-Africa orators in succeeding years had significant influence
on black aspirations in Africa itself and strengthened the
nascent nationalist movements.

In America Turner's agitation gained him a sizeable and
fiercely loyal following, and it led to at least two voyages of

emigrants to Africa. Turner and a group of other prominent blacks formed the International Migration Society in 1894. From the start it suffered from inadequate financial resources, but it managed to acquire a ship, the *Horsa*, a small Danish fruit ship. The *Horsa* left with about two hundred emigrants and much reported hymn-singing from Savannah in the spring of 1895.

Unfortunately, the *Horsa* was not expected, so that when it arrived at Monrovia, the Liberians were at something of a loss to know what to do with the two hundred penniless immigrants. There had not been room on the small ship to take much in the way of provisions. The Liberians, however, welcomed these new immigrants. Official immigration had tailed off, so a new arrival, however poor, was a novelty. Local people took the new-comers into their homes and cared for them until land could be cleared and fevers had abated. With surprisingly little fuss, most of the immigrants settled well in rural areas, and generally appear to have made the project one of the most successful of its kind. Regrettably, a small number grew discouraged and made their way back to America, where the white press eagerly snapped up their harrowing stories — this time, at least, untypical.

Turner, of course, ignored the attacks of the white newspapers, and put in hand preparations for a second expedition. A second ship, the *Laurada,* left amid carnival-type celebrations in March 1896.

This time, however, the result was a disaster. The novelty of the first group had worn off for the Liberians. There is evidence, too, that apart from stores carried by the *Laurada* being even less than the *Horsa* had taken, the calibre of this second group was very different. Unlike their predecessors, they were grumbling even before they arrived. Given nominal amounts of land in Liberia, they were dispersed and left to fend for themselves. Yet again, a West African rainy season massacred a group of New World settlers. By the end of the first summer, it was reported that a hundred of these immigrants were dead of fever. A great many others were failing completely at farming, and were beginning to leave Liberia.

Back to the United States came pitiful survivors with well-publicized accounts of disaster. In Liberia the situation of those who stayed grew steadily worse. One group petitioned

President William McKinley for food. 'Not a hundred dollars
or a thousand dollars, just food,' they pleaded.[28] Of the 321
who had sailed on the *Laurada*, only a handful remained. This
episode attracted lasting and highly damaging publicity.
Turner's Society began to decline, as much through its failure
to send more than two ships as through the disastrous results
of the second sailing.

Between 1890 and 1910, about 1,000 American blacks
emigrated to Liberia, some on Bishop Turner's ships, and others
independently. Turner's scheme did not create mass migration.
He kept up his flow of oratory until his death in 1915, but his
central plans were unfulfilled. His failure was because he was
long on rhetoric and inspiration and short on funds and
organizational ability. Race relations at the turn of the century
were appalling. There was Jim Crow legislation, an undiminishing
recourse to the lynch mob, and even race riots, in New Orleans
for instance, in 1900. Turner failed to attract the more affluent
middle class and the intelligentsia to his movement. Thousands
of working-class blacks responded to his speeches, but
the leadership of the articulate blacks passed to Booker T.
Washington, founder of the Tuskegee Institute, Alabama, a
college for blacks.

Washington, who was to remain a leader until his death (also
in 1915), has often been held to be a betrayer of the black
movement. Cited as evidence is his famous 'Atlanta Compromise'
speech of 1895, in which he declared that 'the agitation of
questions of social equality is the extremest folly.' The
compromise stated: 'In all things that are purely social we can
be as separate as the fingers, yet one as the hand in all things
essential to mutual progress.'[29] His views of Africa tended
to conform to white stereotypes. He once told this story:

> A friend of mine who went to Liberia to study conditions
> once came upon a negro shut up within a hovel reading
> Cicero's orations. That was all right. The negro has as much
> right to read Cicero's orations in Africa as a white man does
> in America. But the trouble with the coloured man was that
> he had on no pants. I want a tailor shop first so that the
> negro can sit down and read Cicero's orations like a
> gentleman with his pants on.[30]

Washington was keenly interested in sending American Negroes to Africa, not as an answer to their problems in the United States, but to be of service to Africa. Various Tuskegeans went to Africa to settle, especially in Togo. Their experience at first was not noticeably better than that of other settlers. They were struck by fevers and other disasters. Two were drowned when their surf boat sank. A Tuskegee alumnus wrote:

> Way down beneath the briny waves,
> Two martyrs Simpson and Drake,
> Who gave up school and native land,
> For their race and country's sake. [31]

Working with a German commercial concern, Kolonial-Wirtschaftsliches Komite, Tuskegee graduates introduced cotton to various parts of Africa. Washington himself played a major part in the campaign against the repressive colonialism of the Belgians in the Congo. His influence, however, was mainly in the United States.

Washington's ideas, while conservative and reassuring to whites, at least argued the necessity for more widespread education for the blacks who would inevitably have to stay in America — by far the majority of the black population. Yet the potential mass appeal of the Back-to-Africa vision was not weakened. In the many abortive schemes that followed Turner's, there was always a healthy number of inquiries from the black lower classes. Many individual groups made their own way to Africa without sponsorship, with varying success. In 1903, a party of fifty-three blacks from Georgia arrived in Liberia. Within three or four months, twenty were dead, and the rest desperate to return to America. Many Negroes were also fleeced of thousands of dollars in crooked schemes that followed in the wake of Turner's.

But what Turner had proved was that black repatriation movements should and would be handled by black people: from now on the leadership of such movements would be entirely black. Turner's effectiveness was that, despite his four visits to Africa, he never lost his dream of the ideal Africa, and ultimately the black masses believed him rather than the bedraggled parties who returned with tales of horror from the swamps of Liberia. So the vision never died, but merely stayed in abeyance until new visionaries should come along.

In October 1913, the British Ambassador in Washington, Sir Cecil Arthur Spring Rice, received a puzzled letter from the U.S. State Department:

> It appears . . . that a negro in Oklahoma who represents himself to be an African chief from the Gold Coast is urging the negroes in that section of the country to go to the Colony, where political and industrial conditions are pictured to be much brighter than in the United States, and it also appears that many of the negroes . . . are disposing of their property and are about to start for Africa. For the guidance of these people and in order to save them from what may prove to be a disastrous venture, I would appreciate very much any suggestions that you may be able to make in the premises.[32]

Next came a letter from the Governor of Oklahoma to the British consul in St Louis. 'Sam seems to have cast a spell over many of the negroes and they look upon him as a modern Moses.'[33]

Finally, a citizen of Clarksville, a Dr James E. Guess, wrote directly to Sir Edward Grey at the British Colonial Office, asking if a certain Chief Alfred Charles Sam represented British Government policy.[34]

The British were as puzzled as the State Department, but despite the fact that certain other, European, confrontations were looming, they were worried. A Colonial Office Under-Secretary of State replied to Dr Guess: ' . . . for climatic and other reasons emigration of American negroes to West Africa could not be encouraged.'[35] Behind the smooth dismissal, however, there was some alarm at the prospect of a sizeable exodus from the United States to the Colony of the Gold Coast. From the Colony's Governor came word that 'every effort should be made to prevent the continuance of Sam's operation in the United States . . . for were he to succeed in inducing a number of American Negroes to attempt colonization in the Gold Coast his victims would be fore-doomed to disappointment.'[36]

But the British were too late. On August 21st, 1914, this 'Chief Sam' and a number of black Americans set sail from Galveston, bound for Africa aboard a British merchant ship, renamed *Liberia*.

Alfred Sam had appeared in Oklahoma in May 1913, surrounded by a certain African mystery but bounding in energy. The community he made for was Boley, a town in Okfuskee, Oklahoma, one of the all-Negro communities that had been developed in pre-Statehood days. Such towns had been set up as experiments, and far from being regarded as ghettoes, they were seen as an avenue to Negro self-fulfilment. They attracted first the labouring classes, and then the middle class from the Deep South and were briefly successful. The communities were fully elective and they gradually spread and grew. By the time of the holding of the State Constitutional Convention in 1906 it was found that, at least in Okfuskee County, blacks held the balance between the Republican and Democratic Parties. After Statehood was declared, the Negroes of Boley elected two black representatives as county commissioners, much to the horror of the whites. In panic, the whites on the County Election Board pronounced the Negro votes invalid, and this decision was upheld in the State Supreme Court. By this blatant gerrymandering and subsequent lynchings, the whites smashed the hopes of Negroes for a form of equality in the West. Other violent pressures which they put upon the blacks were the forcing of small black farmers off their land by intimidation and exclusion of black labour from certain white farms.

Sam was a native of Akim Busomi in the eastern Gold Coast. He was educated at the Wesleyan Primary School in Saltpond, on the coast itself, and after this minimal education became a merchant in palm oil and rubber, which he exported to Europe. He is still remembered in Saltpond as a bluff, popular man, although his claim to chiefdom was tenuous. He was certainly the head of a family and possibly a sub-chief, so to that extent his claim to be an 'Ashanti chief' was accurate, though meaningless. Since the Asantehene, King Prempeh, had been exiled after the last Ashanti War, at the turn of the century, the final arbiter in the matter was absent. (One of the reasons for the profound sympathy shown to Chief Sam, and later to Marcus Garvey, by the Ashantis of the Gold Coast was their conviction that here they had a means of bringing Prempeh back from exile in the Seychelles. The more militant believed that black Americans would come in battleships and drive the British out.) Sam conceived the idea of an all-black trading company, the Akim Trading Company, which would export exotic goods to black Americans; a subsidiary idea was that he should import black Americans to Africa. Like most of his kind, he disregarded such details as the total reluctance of the colonial authorities to allow black Americans into colonial territories. He went to the United States in 1911. Seeing no point in understating his intentions, he proposed to found 'a college of agriculture and industry in all the trades of manufacturing and agriculture', and the construction, owner-ship and operation of 'hotels, restaurants, bath houses, theatres, or other places of amusement'.[37]

He saw ideal immigrants in the disgruntled townspeople of Boley, and he began promising them abundant riches in the Gold Coast.He talked of bread growing on trees and of diamonds being found in gullies after hard rain. Briskly, he sold stock — which entitled the holder to the trip to Africa — in Okfuskee County, and in the face of accusations of sharp practices and fraud, he bought an old British merchantman, the *Curityba*. His only problem was that he had 5,000 stockholders, while the ship would only hold a hundred or two. Sam warned his pilgrims not to sell their property, but his warnings went unheeded. Large numbers sold up and moved to what they believed were temporary camps, 'Gold Coast Camps'. At first the camps were alive with carnival spirit and expectations of Africa. But as the winter of 1913 wore on, they became cold and muddy, and the emigrants grew impatient as they waited for their ship to arrive.

At length, some moved to Galveston, and just in time to forestall open rebellion, the renamed *Liberia* appeared. The next problem was that of numbers. Of the thousands now both in Galveston and in the tents back home, the *Liberia* was capable of embarking only a few score.* Sam was optimistic: 'Our people are not homeless', he insisted. 'They are not idlers or drones. Our plan is to establish a government in which our race will be supreme. When our colony is established and the people

---

* Most official claims — repeated in the one good book on the subject, *The Longest Way Home*, by Gilbert Geis and William Bittle — were that only sixty sailed on the *Liberia*. A group of old people in Saltpond, whom I interviewed in April 1973, were unanimous that two hundred black Americans actually landed.

of our race see that we are successful, this boat will be crowded on every trip she makes to Africa.'38

There is no way of knowing what success the little colony might have had if the British had not created so many absurd difficulties for the settlers. (Certainly, the Fantis on the coast maintain even now that the immigration could have been completely successful, and today black Americans still find an especially warm welcome in the Saltpond area.) But even before the passengers were allowed off the ship, the British authorities demanded a £25 bond from each of them. The colonists decided to pay up and ignore the boorishness and peevishness of the British. The Africans of Saltpond were fascinated by the new-comers. When I asked one old man what he thought of the Americans, he simply said: 'I never knew there were people of this colour in Europe.'39 To this day, he still cannot conceive of the pilgrims coming from America. Another African remembered them as more copper-coloured than himself; he thought them a little stern and not at all out-going, but prepared to be friendly. All the Africans I spoke to said that relations between the excited and bemused Afro-Americans and the intrigued Africans were never other than excellent.

One reason for the cordiality was, perhaps, the new techniques of distillation which the Americans brought with them. It is claimed that *akpeteshie,* the native spirit banned in the Colony until Independence, was in fact introduced by the Americans. (This is doubtful since distillation of spirit was certainly known in other parts of the Gold Coast long before.) The Africans had a long tradition of weaving *kente* cloth in long strips, but the Americans taught them new methods of weaving. They also gave gun-powder to the natives. In each case, the British saw the Americans not as benefactors, but as subversive elements. The British were anxious to preserve their monopoly in the provision of spirits. Thus, a series of prohibitions was placed upon the Americans.

Several of them were already disgruntled both with the project and with Sam himself. The engineer of the *Liberia*, William Hurt, from Bristow, Oklahoma, wrote:

> Well, I am sorry to say that this Negro, our so-called leader, Chief Alred C. Sam, has only lied and frauded the people out here . . . I found out he is a trader on the race.

He fooled our people; he said the cattle here were eight
feet high. I learned there isn't a cow in the place — this
was a fraud . . . This is one of the dirtiest things our race
has ever gotten into since the world began. We are here . . .
starving sometimes, no bread on board, no water; our
people are crying to come back home, and if the people
don't help us we are lost for ever . . . you all can see from
[this] that death is at our doors.[40]

This letter was published in the Tulsa *Star*.

Partly because of the pressure from the British authorities
and partly because of their own impatient wish to get to the
lands promised by Chief Sam, the group decided to move to the
interior. The destination was a spot sixty miles inland. A
certain Professor Johnson, who adopted an 'African' name,
Orishatukeh Faduma (in the manner of countless Afro-Americans
before and since) wrote of their arrival at a village about three
miles from Akim Swedru:

The reception given to Chief Sam and his party was the
most elaborate and orderly we have witnessed along our
route . . . *Nsefu* (native palm wine) was drunk fresh and
sweet. Beating of drums and dancing were a part of the
programme. A unique sight was a band of young musicians
with brass instruments playing at intervals 'Hold the Fort',
'Joyful will the meeting be', 'Rule Britannia' and the
National Anthem. But the most unique of all was the
rendering by the band of Fanti songs, quick, lively, and
indigenous. Every time one of them was played the
motley crowd as if by a common impulse was inspired to
dance. The effect was electric. The writer has heard
rendered the most classical music of England, Germany
and Italy. He has listened to symphonies which were
soul enraptured, but he cannot forget the peculiar
feelings which swept over his soul at the rendition of
this native Fanti music. If he did not dance with his feet,
he did in his soul . . .

The party stayed a month in Swedru, then moved on through
the thick forest. 'Gigantic trees from two hundred to three
hundred feet high, mahogany trees, some over two hundred

years old with thick overhanging branches and dense under-
growths, greeted our eyes. The fauna and flora of the country
is rich and abundant. For another century the precious woods
will be inexhaustible. No railroad runs through. All kinds of
animals, except lion and elephant, are found here.'

Finally they reached their destination.

> The village Chief, Ohin Kwami Dokyi, was the one who
> sold 64 square miles of land to Chief Sam, a fact which
> was denied by American papers and others in authority.
> Inasmuch as all of the party were anxious to know the
> truth about the land, Chief Dokyi who had a copy of the
> deed of sale was asked to produce it. By his permission it
> was handed to the writer in the presence of Chief Sam
> and read publicly. The land is bounded eight miles on
> each side, having the river Brim on the north . . . Joy was
> boundless after this verification . . . Time has proven
> beyond doubt the following facts:
> 1. That Alfred C. Sam is a recognized and well-known
> chief in the Akim District.
> 2. That he did buy 64 sq. miles of land in his own
> name.
> 3. That the said land is to be used as a settlement for
> U.S. Negroes who may wish to settle on it, subject to native
> laws and the laws of G.B. governing the Protectorate.

They named the land *Asequoi*, and Sam intoned Chapter 6
of the Second Book of Chronicles:

> Then said Solomon, the Lord hath said that he would
> dwell in the thick darkness.
> But I have built an house of habitation for thee, and
> a place for thy dwelling for ever . . .[41]

But the dwelling was not for ever. Those who stayed on the
land at Asequoi found that they were completely unsuited to
the climate and to the style of agriculture of the region. The
bush was so thick, said one settler, 'that you had to stoop down
and squint to see only a few feet'. She 'couldn't think of
building a house with gopher wood'.[42] The life was monotonous

and hard and, sure enough, the fevers sought out the settlers.
Further, there had certainly been chicanery on someone's part.
The 'deed' was unenforceable, and amounted only to a paper
permission from the chief allowing them to farm his land.
Slowly, all the settlers made their way back to the coast. Some
of them started court proceedings against Sam in Cape Coast.
He is said to have been summonsed ninety-nine times. In due
course, Sam took to his heels.

He was variously reported to have fled to Liberia or to have
been imprisoned by the British. There appears to be no trace of
what happened to him.* Some of the colonists struggled back
to America, others drifted along the coast, to Liberia or to
Nigeria. I heard a probably apocryphal story in Accra that one
of the group travelled further inland and managed to convince
the *jasi*, or king-makers, in one village of his direct descent from
a line of chiefs, whereupon they made him chief. What is known
is that hardly any stayed in the Gold Coast. One who did became
a trader in firewood in Cape Coast, and two others took to doing
odd jobs in Accra.

Sam may well have been a charlatan — his disappearance
would support the belief that he was — but unlike most
charlatans, he did achieve at least a part of what he promised.
Pressure from the British helped to sabotage the scheme. But
the idea of even Southern blacks immediately taking to West
African agriculture has been proved time and time again to be
misbegotten.

The episode had a strange sequel, one that illustrates that the
Back-to-Africa fervour of many blacks was — and is — no
maudlin defeatism, but could contain a special buoyancy and
humour. In August 1920, the Governor of the Gold Coast
heard from Mr Hurt, the engineer, now back in Bristow. The
correspondence that followed was inconclusive, but not
untypical.

---

* I tried for six months to trace Sam's family in Ghana. His
daughter, Miss Dorothy Sam, was said to have died in Saltpond
before the Second World War. His house still stands in Saltpond,
but it is now occupied by another family. The name Sam is not
an unusual Ashanti name, but none of the people named Sam
whom I asked in Ghana could claim any connections with the
late Chief. He did, it seems, vanish completely.

Dear Governer of the Gold Coast Colony [Mr Hurt's letter began]. This is one of the decenents of W.Africa asking you for a point of information as to the sale of land in the Heman lands. I want to know how that land be bought and get a clair Deed for same. I were in a noshon of Bying a tract of it if I can get a good deed on it. I were out there in the year 1915. I have seen part of the land and it sute me all right all I want to know what every trade I make with the owner . . . Now I would like to get your deceshion on it and what you deam best and what will it cost me to get a Fantee Translator so I can understand the language of that land. Say dear Govner I am trusting in you to let me here at once I would to get one of your Bylaws of the Constitution of the Gold Coast Colony this is your humble Servent. In Obeadence to you all . . . 43

There was some mystification in the Governor's office, and a flurry of inter-departmental memoranda. Did he mean Hemang in the central province? Or the Himan lands in the Tarquah district? It was decided that he must mean the latter, which were, however, already the subject of litigation. A dry, discouraging letter was sent to Mr Hurt by the secretary for Native Affairs, C.W. Welman. In December 1921, the unsinkable Mr Hurt wrote again:

I receive your mighty letter sometime ago, was glad to here from you about that land deal it just save me losing money on it. Say Mr Welman I would like to no is there eny land in that Fanti country can bee bought at eny price and get a Good Deed for it. If there is will you please give me there names, or where the land is at Sir I felt that you give me the true wird about it, I see it wont be good to bye that all now, not until they settle it them self right. I would like to get a place where I can put an oil mill where I can grind your Palm kirnals and cooco beans, If I can buy a place to set the mill on. This will bring life in your country . . . Mr Welman I am preparing every day to come back to Africa next year, and I hope to see you persnealy on bisness for you no I no there is over five million dollars wirth of kernals go

110

to waist each year there . . . Say Mr Welman if I can get fix I will bee over in short.[44]

In April 1922, the new Secretary for Native Affairs, J.P. Furley, wrote: 'I regret I am not in a position to give you detailed information as to where or from whom land may be acquired in Fanti . . .'[45]

That July, the delightful Mr Hurt, not to be put down by a stuffy British official, wrote:

> I am in hipes I will find a Track of land large enough for me to put a steam mill on, I am tending to come over in Janery 1923. I am bying up my mill machinery every day or to. I have dun inployed Elder Dempster Steam ship co. ltd. to hall my stuff over we will land where we can dock then get of on land. I will be in England for meny days before I sail for the West Coast of Africa so I will bee over home some day and put our world and country in mothon . . .
>
> I will come over home to open up our Farther lands, I hope you are well and doning well this leve me and family allwell so I will look to here from you at an early date, you let me no and I will cend all money to you for delliver to day is Sunday it is hot and dry here. Everything is growing corn and cotton grapes apple and peaches we have plenty. But our home neads us neads us back to it the [prophets?] say that every man shall wirship God under his own vine and fig tree.[46]

Here the correspondence ends. Mr Hurt never did return to Africa. He eventually died, early in 1957, in Bristow, an exceptionally good mechanic in oil-field installations.[47] His reasons for not actually returning are obscure. He may have been vanquished by British officialdom. Alternatively, he may have become embroiled in the movement — in full steam by the early 1920s — that was the most powerful and dynamic the black American community has ever seen.

Marcus Moziah Garvey was born on August 17th, 1887, in the small northern Jamaican town of St Ann's Bay. His parents were opposites: his father, a master mason, was stubborn, gloomy, formal and litigious; his mother was beautiful, gay and gentle and a profound influence on her son. Garvey himself claimed descent from the proudly ungovernable Maroons.

He early developed a race pride that derived from his belief in his undiluted black heritage, against a background of increasing racial disharmony in Jamaica. He had a strong dislike for mulattoes who had been upheld as a buffer bourgeoisie by the British. This dislike, which he shared with many other black West Indian leaders, he never lost. Although he had little formal education, he later liked to claim that he had, and even adopted a mortar board and academic gown, especially when his critics included intellectuals of undoubted scholarly talents, such as his arch-enemy, W.E.B. Du Bois.

At the age of fourteen he entered the printing trade as an apprentice. He moved to Kingston and advanced in his work. In 1907 he led a printers' strike on the island. The strike collapsed when the union branch treasurer absconded with the union funds. Garvey's alienation from organized labour almost certainly dates from this strike. It was to be an important factor in the movement he led. He not only wanted to form his own organization in his own ebullient image, but no doubt felt that, by holding a power base outside the unions, he could entirely dictate his movement's policy. It is doubtful if many unions would have lent their support when his doctrine appeared to veer sharply to the right, away from what might be held to be orthodox labour beliefs.

In the years following the 1907 strike, Garvey drifted round central America, working on banana plantations and attempting to start newspapers. In 1912 he went to London, where he became an associate of the part-Egyptian, part-Negro scholar Duse Mohammed Ali, publisher of the *African Times and Orient Review*. In London he read Booker T. Washington's *Up From Slavery*, 'and then my doom — if I may so call it — of being a race leader dawned upon me . . . I asked: "Where is the black man's Government? Where is his King and his kingdom? Where is his President, his country, and his ambassador, his army, his navy, his men of big affairs?" '[48] It is an irony that it was the author of the 'Atlanta Compromise' who should have first inspired the fiery, intransigent orator. Garvey came to hold a low opinion of existing black leaders. 'I would not exchange two five-cent cigars — even though not a smoker — for all the

Coloured or Negro political leaders, or rather mis-leaders, of our time. The fraternity is heartless, crafty and corrupt.'[49]

In 1914, he returned to Jamaica, and within five days had formed the Universal Negro Improvement and Conservation Association (U.N.I.A). Its aim, he said, was to 'establish a universal confraternity among the race; to promote the spirit of race pride and love; to reclaim the fallen of the race; to administer to and assist the needy; to assist in civilising the backward tribes of Africa; to establish Commissionaries or Agencies in the principal countries of the world for the protection of all Negroes, irrespective of nationality; to promote a conscientious Christian worship among the native tribes of Africa . . .'[50] He was consequently not proposing much that radically added to the aims of, say, Bishop Turner, except that he urged the creation of a 'central nation for the race'. What did set this squat, egotistical Jamaican apart from any of his predecessors, however, was his personal magnetism and its impact on the frustrated era in which he lived.

At first, his campaign centred on attempts to set up educational institutions for the betterment of Negroes in the West Indies. In 1915, he wrote to Booker T. Washington to enlist his support. The reply from Washington was polite and non-committal, but Garvey felt that it was warm enough to warrant his going to America. By the time he arrived, in March 1916, Washington was dead. It was Garvey himself who was about to snatch the limelight, as he moved his theatre of action from Jamaica to New York.

The foundations of grave discontent upon which Garvey built his movement to such remarkable heights were laid in the post-First World War years. The death of Washington removed coherent black leadership at a time when anti-black discrimination was running highest. Negroes, who had put large amounts of money and considerable numbers of men into the war, saw that in their absence, organizations such as the Ku Klux Klan had been reborn (in 1915). During the war, many Negroes had migrated to the North. Boll weevil was rife in the cotton areas of the South, and the lure of the industrial and affluent North was once more strong. The attraction of the relatively wealthy North had overwhelmed the lure of Africa in the years immediately before the war. But, yet again, disappointment was at the end of the road. There was vicious discrimination and then race riots. Once more a hopelessness over civil rights set in, a hopelessness that had so often fostered Back-to-Africa movements.

Garvey's estimates of his membership — as with his claims for the total numbers of Negroes in the world — were certainly exaggerated, but public displays of this membership were impressive. Garvey provided abused Negroes not only with what they wanted to hear, but with what they needed to hear — that they were equal to white men, and that the equality derived from their heritage. The heritage was Africa, and the heritage had to be reclaimed. 'We have come now to the turning point of the Negro where we have changed from the old cringing weaklings, and transformed into full-grown men, demanding our position as MEN.'[51] The race must organize, he said, not in footling little cells meeting clandestinely, or in sad little store-front churches. Negroes must march through the streets of New York, the movement must graduate from the little chapels, put on uniform and form ranks. Its strength was in its numbers, he said, and these numbers should be united. The movement, however, should not just provide unity and organization. It must provide *excitement*. 'Negroes, teach your children they are direct descendants of the greatest and proudest race who ever peopled the earth', he stormed.[52] And: 'How dare any one tell us that Africa cannot be redeemed when we have 400,000,000 men and women with warm blood coursing through their veins?'[53]

The highest point of glory and hope for the Garvey movement came in the August of 1920. The U.N.I.A. held a magnificent parade in New York. There was a massive parade, at which the full panoply of the movement was unfolded, with marchers of the African Legion in dark blue uniforms and Black Cross nurses in white. In Madison Square Garden, 25,000 black people gathered to sing, to three massed bands:

> Ethiopia, thou land of our fathers,
> Thou land where the gods loved to be,
> As storm cloud at night suddenly gathers
> Our armies come rushing to thee.[54]

In a hubbub of excitement Garvey appeared, dressed in academic cap and a gown of purple, green and gold. 'We shall now organise the 400,000,000 Negroes of the world into a vast organisation to plant the banner of freedom on the great continent of Africa', he told the excited crowd. The banner would be red, black and green, red for the blood of the race, black for its skin and green for the new hope of Africa. Garvey went on: 'We do not desire what has belonged to others, though others have always sought to deprive us of that which belonged to us . . . If Europe is for the Europeans, then Africa shall be for the black peoples of the world. We say it; we mean it . . . The other races have countries of their own and it is time for the four hundred million Negroes to claim Africa for themselves.'[55]

Garvey was designated Provisional President of the African Republic. Plans were laid for the establishment of a symbolic Black House in Washington. Orders such as the Knights of the Nile and Distinguished Service Order of Ethiopia were inaugurated. From henceforth, the word Negro would be spelled with a capital 'N'.* Everyone had his place in the movement. Even the poorest Negro could don his uniform, carry his red, black and green flag, and be acknowledged as a brother in the race by Garvey.

The previous June, Garvey had formed a shipping line, the Black Star Line, incorporated in the State of Delaware, noted for its accommodating laws in company matters. On board ships of the Black Star Line, said Garvey, black Americans would go home. In the feverish bustle of the movement's activities, the first declared intention of improving the education of Negroes was forgotten: that could wait until they got to Africa.

A flagship, the *Yarmouth*, had been bought for a grossly inflated 165,000 dollars, and its maiden voyage to the West Indies was to start from the line's 135th Street pier. A jolly, cheering crowd invaded Harlem to see it off. About 5,000 black people milled around the flagship, some paying a

---

* Fifty years earlier, Blyden had insisted that it was wrong 'to designate one of the great families of man' with a common 'n'. He said that the term Negro was a scientific notion and that it should therefore be spelled with a capital 'N'. Garvey did, however, persuade newspapers to give the word Negro an initial capital.

dollar to walk round the decks of this maritime promise. A spruce U.N.I.A. band turned out to serenade the casting off and setting out. What the crowd did not know, however, as the ship proudly steamed away was that it would travel precisely 112 blocks. The discovery that it was under-insured forced it to drop anchor opposite 23rd Street. It was obliged to remain anchored there for several days while the insurance was adjusted. Thus, a pattern of pathetic ineptitude in the running of a Back-to-Africa scheme was once more set.

The *Yarmouth* steered an unsteady course over the next two years, mostly pottering round the Caribbean. The flagship's boilers never made enough pressure to enable the vessel to travel at more than seven knots. On one occasion, its inefficient master ran it aground off the Bahamas. On another, while carrying a consignment of liquor to Cuba, it had to jettison most of its cargo when it began taking water. What was not thrown overboard was consumed by the crew. Finally, to make good a debt, the line was forced to sell the *Yarmouth*. She fetched 1,625 dollars, so more than 99 per cent of the company's expenditure on the vessel was thrown away.

The rest of the fleet fared hardly better. The company bought a fifty-year-old ferry boat, the *Shadyside*, for 35,000 dollars, to make promotion trips for the line along the Hudson. In the heady months of its beginning in 1920 it made frequent trips, but the revenue was never enough to cover the cost of the fuel. After five months it was taken out of service, and even at its berth quietly sank to the bottom of the Hudson.

Garvey's third ship, the *Kanawha*, was actually the plaything of the Standard Oil millionaire, Henry H. Rogers. The Black Star Line bought it for the ridiculously inflated sum of 60,000 dollars. On its maiden voyage the yacht's boilers gave out, and it limped back to New York on one boiler and some makeshift sails. Repaired in a highly amateur manner, the *Kanawha* lurched round the Caribbean, its boilers leaking and exploding, from one repair yard to another. After running up astronomical repair bills, the vessel was left to rust to death in harbour in Antilla. The promised *Phyllis Wheatley*, which was supposed to take the faithful back to Africa, never materialized. None of Garvey's followers was ever sent to Africa by Garvey to settle there. Although various of his emissaries went on periodic visits to Africa, Garvey himself never set foot on the continent.

In February 1922, Garvey was arrested and charged with using the mail for fraudulent purposes. He had made many enemies, black and white, and it is not difficult to understand why. Strongly motivated and self-aware Negroes were not the most welcome sight to a great many sections of influential opinion. Typically, Garvey conducted his own defence, and he gave the court an eloquent run for its money. But he was found guilty. There seems from the evidence scant proof of intention to defraud his stockholders, much less of conspiracy to use the mails to defraud. There was, of course, plenty of evidence of incompetence which had cost the company hundreds of thousands of dollars, and in fact bankrupted it within three years. Happily for his white contemporaries, ineptitude is no crime. It has been pointed out — with some truth — that the real crimes were those of shysters who fleeced the company, charging absurd prices for useless vessels. All the same, Garvey was fined 1,000 dollars and sentenced to five years in prison.

Out on bail, pending appeal, Garvey redoubled his efforts. He sent envoys to Liberia, and he was given assurances that the Liberian Government — sorely in need of funds — would welcome immigrants. But one envoy, Elie Garcia, who had been sent to Liberia even while the Madison Square Garden convention was closing, had a disturbing report for Garvey. The ruling oligarchy, said Garcia, was 'the most despicable element in Liberia'. Dishonesty, said Garcia, was prevalent. He went on:

> To any man who can write and read there is but one goal, a Government office, where he can graft . . . The Liberian politicians understand clearly that they are degenerated and weak morally, and they know that if any number of honest Negroes with brains, energy and experience come to Liberia and are permitted to take part in the ruling of nation, they will be absorbed and ousted in a very short while . . . Human chattel slavery still exists there. They buy men or women to serve them, and the least little insignificant Americo-Liberian has half a dozen boys at his service — for he, himself, will not even carry his own umbrella in the street, said article has to be carried by a boy.[57]

Garvey kept Garcia's report secret, but, perhaps fearing that this not uncommon verdict might become known to the mass of American blacks, Liberia withdrew its welcome. There was also an amount of pressure from the colonial powers, Britain and France. Britain, fearing for the stability of its colonies in West Africa, undoubtedly took Garvey more seriously than it claimed, for instance by banning his publication *Negro World* in the Gold Coast and Nigeria.

The fact that the homeland was positively spurning the movement did not give Garvey pause. The Liberian consul in Baltimore said: 'I am authorized to say that no person or persons leaving the United States under the auspices of the Garvey movement will be allowed to land in the Republic of Liberia.'[58] The Liberian government itself said they were 'irrevocably opposed both in principle and fact to the incendiary policy of the Universal Negro Improvement Association, headed by Marcus Garvey'.[59]

But Garvey had a powerful message to counter his repudiation by crooks: 'When Europe was inhabited by a race of cannibals, a race of savages, naked men, heathens and pagans, Africa was peopled with a race of cultured black men, who were masters in art, science and literature; men who were cultured and refined; men, who, it was said, were like the gods.'[60]

Garvey pronounced that God himself was black, and that the day of the black man created in his image would soon come, together with redemption. 'It is in the wind. It is coming', he said. 'One day, like a storm, it will be here. Let Africa be our guiding star, our star of destiny . . . Wake up Ethiopia! Wake up Africa! Let us work towards the one glorious end of a free, redeemed and mighty nation. Let Africa be a bright star among the constellation of nations.'[61]

Garvey's importance has perhaps been discounted by the left because of his ready espousal of ideas of the right. It is true that his populism and racism appear to make him a figure of the right. He was accepted by the Ku Klux Klan, since his message presupposed a renunciation of the possibility of Negro rights within the United States. Garvey did accept the existence of the Klan — indeed met with Klan representatives — because here, he felt, the white man was showing himself honestly as he was. As he himself was the voice of what many black men felt but never dared to say, so, too, were the Klansmen the only truly honest white men.

Garvey was not an attractive figure to white liberals. In 1937, he looked scornfully at Italy's invasion of Abyssinia. 'We were the first Fascists', he said. 'Mussolini copied Fascism from me but the Negro reactionaries sabotaged it.'[62]

Garvey lost his appeal against his sentence, and was taken to jail. In 1927 he was deported back to Jamaica, where he tried to resuscitate the Back-to-Africa movement. He achieved some success, though never on the scale or in the manner of his American activities. In 1935 he moved to Britain, where he died five years later. In 1964 his body was taken back to Jamaica to rest in the Marcus Garvey National Shrine, and each year his birthday is celebrated in Harlem.

His spirit lived on in Africa and in America. His influence in Africa itself, however, has always been underestimated. The French and British banned the U.N.I.A. organ, *Negro World,* in their colonies. (The penalty for being seen with the *Negro World* in French Dahomey was life imprisonment.) Nigerians slept on the beaches at Calabar to welcome the new Moses with bonfires. In the mid 1930s the Kikuyu of Kenya had formed a separatist church, and in about 1935 they brought in one of Garvey's bishops to train and ordain pupils. It was from these churches and schools that the Mau Mau grew.[63] In his autobiography, Kwame Nkrumah said that he had been influenced by early reading of Hegel, Marx, Engels, Lenin and Mazzini. 'But I think that of all the literature that I studied, the book that did more than any other to fire my enthusiasm was *Philosophy and Opinions* of Marcus Garvey, published in 1923 . . . It was unfortunate that I was never able to meet Garvey as he had been deported from the country before I arrived . . .'[64] Among the members of the African Legion were Elijah Mohammed and the father of Malcolm X. In an interview shortly before his assassination, Malcolm X said: 'All the freedom movements that are taking place right here in America today were initiated by the work and teachings of Marcus Garvey. The entire Black Muslim philosophy here in America is feeding upon the seeds that were planted by Marcus Garvey.'[65]

I have never met a former member of the Garvey movement who laid any blame whatsoever on Garvey for the failure of its practical aims. He helped his supporters to stand upright in an oppressive world. His followers remember the excitement and not the failure. This belligerent, rumbustious ranter — whom

Claude McKay described as being shaped like a puncheon — is recalled with fond pride. An old lady I met in Ghana, who had finally come to Africa at the age of 77 to do charitable works, told me she had been a founding member of the Garvey movement 'when there were thirty-five of us meeting in the basement of the Lincoln Theatre on 135th Street'.

She had run a dressmaking and design business with 15 sewing machines in New York. Always involved in hospital and charity work, she had stayed in America, hoping to go home some day to Africa. In the early 1920s, she had, she told me, just finished buying a house on 130th Street, and borrowed 1,500 dollars to buy shares in the Black Star Line. When the line failed, her house was repossessed, and she also lost her small seamstress's business. She struggled to regain her home and business and possessions, putting her dream of Africa into abeyance. Forty years went by before she came to Africa. She was, when I met her, running a day nursery for the children of market women near Accra and raising funds for local hospitals. She had adopted a little African girl. One evening she asked the girl to sing a song for me. The ten-year-old Ghanaian girl solemnly sang the Garveyite hymn 'Oh, Africa awaken'. I asked the lady if, in retrospect, she did not now feel rather badly about Garvey. 'Oh no', she said. 'He knew nothing about Africa, not like I now know it is, and really you know, it all had nothing to do with Africa. But he made the black people of the world, America, the West Indies, Africa, feel they were all one. I don't condemn him at all. He did his best.'

A strange sect, the Rastafarians, which still exists, grew up in Jamaica in the aftermath of Garvey. Where racial or tribal self-awareness is particularly strong, the colonial situation has given rise, almost as a by-product, to messianic or quasi-messianic religious movements among the colonized.* The

* This has been most striking in Central Africa in this century, in the Simba movement in the Congo, for instance. In *The Religions of the Oppressed*, a world-wide study, Vittorio Lanternari noted: 'It is the impact made upon the so-called "primitive" societies by the colonial powers that has brought about conditions favouring the rise of messianic movements.'[67] The religions promise, he says,

racial position in Jamaica had certainly not improved by the 1920s: the whites, mulattoes and blacks were, if anything, even more entrenched in their racial divisions and attitudes. In the 1920s, various prophets of black salvation appeared.

One, named Alexander Bedward, claimed that he would ascend to heaven on December 31st, 1920. After actually trying to fly to heaven, he was removed to a lunatic asylum, where he later died. The more significant prophet, however, was Marcus Garvey.

In the late 1920s he reportedly said in Kingston: 'Look to Africa, when a black king shall be crowned, for the day of deliverance is near.'[66] The *Daily Gleaner* of November 11th, 1930, carried on its front page coverage of the coronation of the Prince Ras Tafari as Emperor Haile Selassie of Ethiopia. This was seen as the fulfilment of Garvey's prophesy. *
It is not exactly clear who Garvey had in mind when he spoke. Later, he had nothing but contempt for the Lion of Judah: 'Haile Selassie is the ruler of a country where black men are chained and flogged . . . he proved the incompetence of the Negro for political authority . . . The Emperor's usefulness is at an end. He will go down in history as a great coward who ran away from his country', he said.[69] Garvey was, and is, not alone among black leaders in invoking anti-Semitism. 'The new Negro doesn't give two pence about the line of Solomon. Solomon was a Jew. The Negro is no Jew. The Negro has a racial origin running from Sheba to the present, of which he is proud. He is proud of Sheba but he is not proud of Solomon.'[70] Perhaps Garvey had himself in mind for the position of King of Africa.

'freedom from subjection and servitude to foreign powers as well as from adversity, and salvation from the possibility of having the traditional culture destroyed and the native society wiped out as a historical entity'.[68] The Rastafarians of Jamaica may be said to have been the only group to have founded such an indigenous religion in the colonized New World.

* A black American aviator, Colonel John C. Robinson, was one of the few Afro-American volunteers who managed to obtain a passport to go and fight in Abyssinia. He became known as the 'Brown Condor'.

He may well have considered that the title of King would be less vulnerable than that of Provisional President.

Basing their beliefs on a curious mixture of scriptures, a number of Rastafarian preachers began drawing support from the oppressed working-class areas of Kingston, especially from the dock areas of Dungle and Back O'Wall. The key text was Revelations 2: 'And I saw a strong angel proclaiming with a loud voice, Who is worthy to open the book, and to loose the seals thereof?' The Italian invasion was thought to have been foretold in Revelations 19: 'And I saw the beast, and the kings of the earth, and their armies, gathered to make war against him that sat on the horse, and against his army.' The next verse was said to forecast the defeat of Mussolini: 'And the beast was taken, and with him the false prophet that wrought miracles before him, with which he deceived them that had received the mark of the beast, and them that worshipped his image. These both were cast alive into a lake of fire burning with brimstone.'

Independent missions, such as the King of Kings Missionary Movement and the Ethiopian Coptic Faith, developed, and leaders, the most successful of whom was Leonard Percival Howell, emerged. Fanned probably by Fascist propaganda, white Jamaican newspapers fumed about a 'black peril' and an 'ominous secret league' and saw a connection between the Rastafarians and the secret league of *Nya-Binghi* — 'Death to Whites' — which originated in the Belgian Congo. At one time the Rastafarians were, in fact, known as the Niyabingi Order. Howell founded a colony of 1,600 Rastas. Apparently fulfilling scriptural instructions, they grew and plaited their hair, becoming known as the 'Dreadlocks'. Following an obscure Biblical exhortation, they took to smoking *ganja*. (The community called itself *Gangungu Maraj* and traded extensively in marijuana.) This began a long and bitter history of police attention which developed into a vicious circle: Rastafarians would be sentenced for possession of and trade in marijuana; in prison they were meeting actual criminals who in turn found Rastafarian society relatively easy to mingle with on their release, thus bringing further harassment from the police.

The Rastafarian movement was full of people who would 'dream' of their return to Africa, and turn up at Palisadoes

122

airport and on the piers to await transport. A convention held in Kingston in 1958 ended in a riot. Some brethren had sold their property believing that at the end of the convention they would all sail to Africa. There was another riot in 1959. Cards at a shilling each were sold to 15,000 people. Each one read:

> Pioneering Israel's scattered Children of African Origin back home to Africa, this year 1959, deadline date October 15th, this new Government is God's Righteous Kingdom of Everlasting Peace on Earth, 'Creation's Second Birth'. Holder of this certificate is requested to visit the Headquarters . . . August 1st . . . for Our Emancipation Jubilee commencing 9 a.m. sharp. Please preserve this Certificate for removal. No passport will be necessary for those returning home to Africa. Bring this Certificate with you on August 1st, for 'Identification'. We are sincerely, 'The Seventh Emmanuel's Brethren' gathering Israel's Scattered Children for removal . . .

Regrettably, no ships awaited, and the Jubilee ended in clashes between the police and the Rastafarians.[71]

A report in 1960 urged Government aid for repatriation. The report also said that *ganja* traffickers, revolutionaries and frauds had found a 'serviceable instrument' in the movement, and only the mutual competition of the three groups had prevented a major upheaval in Jamaica.[72]

Odd attempts have been made by Rastafarians to stand for political office in Jamaica, but few have approached success. Some members of the society have actually returned to Ethiopia and now scratch a living in southern areas. But as with all Back-to-Africa movements, the significance of the Rastafarians is rooted in the New World. The despotic Haile Selassie, though periodically threatened and finally ousted in his own country, has remained a godhead for thousands of believers in Jamaica, and, at second remove, in the grey streets of South London. In Jamaica, harmless Rastafarians are pursued by the police and despised by the middle classes. The dynamism of the movement, however, may in the future have untold political significance in the Caribbean.

CHAPTER 4

'And Lo! I was in Africa'

'For what though friends and kindred all
No more around me stand, —
Am I not near my father's hall,
FREE in my native land?'

(Poem in the *African Repository*, 1829[1])

Scene at Kotoka Airport, Accra, summer of 1972.

Young Afro-American tourist arriving: 'What's that fuckin'
white man doing in there?'
Senior Ghanaian Army officer: 'Sorry?'
Afro: 'I said what's that *fuckin'* whitey doin' in there man?'
Officer: 'What white man?'
Afro: '*That* fuckin' white man. An immigration man or some
fuckin' thing.'
Officer: 'There's no white people in our immigration department,
sir.'
Afro: 'Look, there's a fuckin' white man in there, and he's
immigration or customs or . . . listen, what the fuck are *white*
people *doing* in *Africa,* man?'
Officer: 'I'm afraid I don't understand. There haven't been any
white officers in our immigration or customs departments for
some years.'
Afro: 'But shit, man, can't you *see*? There's a *fuckin' white man*
. . .'
The argument maunders on in the fearsome humidity. Finally,
the Army officer wanders off, promising he'll look into it. Two
days later, he visits the hotel where the Afros are staying. 'I
should tell you,' he explains, 'that the man you are referring
to is a Pan-American representative. He actually came on your
plane with you and is supposed to be looking after your party.'

Black Americans and West Indians have many preconceptions of Africa, although they may deny this, and perhaps not even be conscious of having them.

New Worlders have many motivations for travelling to Africa, too. There are, of course, the misty-eyed tourists who are fundamentally like American tourists anywhere, playing a losing game against bewilderment. They travel to West Africa on the increasing numbers of charter flights,* and for some it may be their first time out of America. Their special relationship with their particular ideas of Africa makes them either hypercritical or hyper-appreciative. They are middle class and therefore have an affluence which is not typical of the mass of black Americans and is at any rate far greater than that of middle-class Africans. The young come either as poorer but more adventurous travellers, or as students to special courses run by, say, the University of Ghana at Legon.

The relations between the black Americans (young and old) who arrive *en masse* like this and the Africans they encounter is ambiguous and sometimes uneasy. One tutor at Legon said to me: 'They [the visiting students] can't apply academic rigours to a "subject" so emotionally charged. I expected them to be able to objectivize their history, but they were too sensitive. Besides,

---

* From a negligible number of black American tourists visiting Ghana up to 1970, the figures shot up to between six and seven thousand in the summer of 1972, and were still rising dramatically. By 1973, they represented ten per cent of all tourism to Ghana. They were a choice target for Western newsmen, all too keen to make an easy point: 'Young, as their ancestors were when they were pressed into slavery, the blacks return as they left, herded together in groups.' (Associated Press, St Louis *Post-Dispatch*, January 18th, 1973.)

127

they were more interested in talking than listening.' I also heard
a story, supposedly at first hand, from several educated
Ghanaians. It goes like this: 'I am sitting on the bus with an
Afro going to Kumasi, and I'm pointing out all the things along
the route. We stop at a refreshment place, which is just a
collection of huts with a pot of stew and some rice cooking on
a fire. The Afro says to me:[6] "Golly, if this is what Africa's like,
I'm sure glad my forefathers were taken away from it." ' There
were several other accounts, probably equally apocryphal, of
penniless Afros turning up at the airport expecting to be
supported by the Motherland. There was one such case which
I was able to substantiate. Otherwise the broad feeling is that
the black Americans are overbearing, inclined to kibbitz and
complain and push their basically urban problems on to
unwilling rural Africans. From the American side, the Africans
are wonderfully friendly at first, then never turn up when
you arrange to meet them.

The editor of a West African journal told me:

> The Afro-Americans who come fail to observe the
> conversational rituals, the little niceties that African
> people appreciate. I mean, you don't just go up and
> say, 'Hi man', to some gentle old African soul. There is,
> of course, no colour-consciousness in most of these
> places, but there is a kind of caste-consciousness. Now
> this is not an exclusive or prohibitive affair; it's based
> on many things that have nothing to do with race, tribe
> or colour. Age, for instance. And a young Afro who
> expects immediately to 'relate' as it were, to anybody
> rather older than himself is mistaken. You can always
> tell an Afro, by his hyperactivity and general bearing.
> The Ghanaians have a great tranquility and conservatism,
> they are not really flamboyant in their dress — the
> materials may be highly colourful, but the cut of their
> clothes and style with which they are worn are very
> conservative — and if I were to put one description
> to them it is that they are very much at home with
> themselves. This, of course, may mean that they are
> quite simply bloody inefficient and I may be putting it
> charitably. But they have a certain quality that I'm
> afraid Afro-Americans just don't.

One centre of tourist activity, and the place where
Africans see the more raw areas of the great black American
hurt, is Cape Coast castle in Ghana. Built in 1664 by the
British, it served as a depot for slaves. It is a totally dreadful
place: five of the thirteen dungeons that formerly held
three hundred slaves each are visitable by the public, and one
feels that the guide cuts his cloth according to the background
of the visitor. The place is charged with its hateful history. The
grille on the ground below the chapel through which the slaves
were allowed to hear the pious mutterings of the proceedings
above, the dank dripping roofs of the dungeons, the crumbling
handcuffs on the floor, are all relics of violence. Below the
battlements on the shore is a huge rock, the fetish shrine, *Nana
Tabir.* Part of this rock was brought into the dungeons in
1953 so that now, in accordance with the fetish custom of
pouring spirits at shrines, it is surrounded by old bottles of
Bramsco Schnapps and Lawyers' Gin. It looks, to the casual
eye, like a rubbish tip, but it is actually a revered spot.

The black American reacts with completely understandable
emotion. One black leader from Chicago, for example, took
his shirt off and tried to hammer down the pillars holding up
the roofs of the dungeons, and then attempted to bar entry
to white people.

The visitors' book reveals the gulf this very hurt places
between Africans and black Americans. Anglophone Africans,
from Ghana and Nigeria, note: 'Splendid . . . very interesting . . . most constructive . . . ' etc. and the francophone
Africans from Ivory Coast or Upper Volta remark: *'Pas mal
. . . assez bouleversant . . . tres joli . . . ' etc.* The margins have been
scored heavily, however, with remarks by Afro-Americans:
'The white man is *still* the devil . . . Yeah! . . . they shall reap
what they have sown, the white man . . . Of the Devil! Right
On! . . . This place really makes me feel hate for the white
people. They must be crazy to do anything like this. Today
they are still the same, they are trying to still rip us up. Every
Black American needs to see the castles . . . The whites must
die . . . The white is a PIG . . . Wake up black man. The beast
is still around! And he's very sick.' The authors, sometimes
signing themselves as professors or doctors, are from Detroit,
Los Angeles, Ann Arbor, and so on.

'How can we live up to what they think we are?' said a

young Ghanaian one evening after I had been the object of a
vehement harangue from a young Afro. (I should say that it
was the only such incident. All other black Americans and
West Indians I met in West Africa treated me with unfailing
courtesy, even when I knew their patience was severely
stretched.) 'He acts like a victim. The white man has succeeded
in him, in a way that Ghanaians would never show. The white
man may have hurt the Gold Coast, and there are many
Ghanaians who remember many things, but the black African
would never reveal how much he has been hurt, especially to
a European.'

This gulf is frequently reported in American newspapers.
A recent account ran:

> A Cambridge-educated Nigerian judge and a visiting
> American civil-rights leader met at a diplomatic reception
> in Lagos not long ago, and their conversation turned to
> the race problem in the United States. The black American
> told of brutal treatment he had received at the hands of
> Alabama policemen and, starting to unbutton his shirt,
> he offered to show the scars that they had left on his
> back. But the Nigerian stopped him, saying: 'I am simply
> not interested.' Later he explained, 'That young American
> assumed that he and I had some special common bond.
> But all we really have in common is that we both have
> black skins, and that's evidently more important to him
> than it is to me.'[2]

I have no doubt that felicitous experiences far outnumber
tetchy encounters, but as with most social phenomena, it is
what is believed to be so that becomes true and shapes
attitudes. I saw more American tourists happily munching
kenkey (corn-dough balls) and smoked fish in unbelievable
squalor and more eager, if uncomprehending faces, than
sour and ill-natured rows. Unhappily, the loud, the overbearing, the arrogant and stupid are much more visible and
audible than the contented. Meanwhile, the Ghanaian tourism
authority was pressing on with plans to attract more and more,
with little regard to the subtly profound consequences that
large-scale tourism can have on a developing country. (They
only have to look at the North African coast.) At the same

time, a curious interaction was taking place between Afro-Americans and Africans. The decidedly un-African 'natural' hair style of the Afros was quite the vogue in Ghana, as were 'shades' and slim moustaches. James Brown blasted from every street corner, the many young Ghanaians were affecting the hip bearing of the Afros.

But what of the settlers, many of whom felt a backlash of African opinion after the departure of the tourists at the end of the summer? What had motivated them? A substantial group were West Indian and black American wives of Africans. They had followed their husbands with a greater or lesser amount of stoicism.* For some of the remainder, it was angry or terrified reaction to segregation or violence. One young American girl missionary said:

> I felt I was a prey in Chicago. The atmosphere was unbelievably violent. I had black friends who were actually murdered. I found that I was saying to myself, well next time such and such happens I'll react violently myself. That was what was frightening. I'm a Christian and that hurt me. I felt that it was all getting to my spirit. I came to see Africa from afar as a land of purity where I could find some peace. Yes, I have found this peace.

For other settlers, it was contact with impressive African individuals and the idea of an independent Africa that spurred them. A black American professional man in Accra explained his own experience:

> I was at [Lincoln] university in epoch-making years in the late 1930s. Africans had been coming to this university for quite some time. I just didn't know that. But Kwame Nkrumah was there when I arrived. He and these other Africans shattered the concepts I had, but in a pleasant way. They made me enthusiastic and anxious to be friendly with them. Just watching them negated so many of the concepts and gave me hope that the things people said and the things written in books might not necessarily be so. The primitiveness of Africans, the backwardness of them — I

---

* See Chapter Six.

mean, these people were sitting in my classroom and making life hard for me. I mean they were flunking me out in English. And in chemistry and biology and physics they were doing as well as I was, or better. Nkrumah stayed like himself. So we thought of him as an older man. He never acted like a young boy, he was a very studious type. Some guys even called him Mr Nkrumah. Nobody tried to be that friendly with him, there was not much kidding and ribbing and joking with him as there was with other Africans. He was studying to be a presbyterian preacher. When he went off practising preaching they would send a choir or a quartet with him, and I was singing in one of these quartets. His lectures were mainly centred on the colonial system, how this British Empire functions, and so the notion of colonialism I picked up from him. I'd never even thought of it. Nobody in any classroom of mine made any big issue of colonialism except that America had been a colony. There were lots of pages on that one. But they hardly spent any pages at all on describing the fact that the Gold Coast was a colony, just like America. The analogies were not made. I got the notion there was a struggle going on, that this wasn't going to be permanently British Africa. I went to New York after university and started in my profession. I lived out on Long Island and I tried to do so many things and co-operate with the town I was living in, but they just wouldn't let me do it, so I got tired of that. I decided in the early 'fifties that at least I'd come and have a look at Africa. I found that the struggle here was much more meaningful than all the segregation struggles and the prejudice. Something could really happen here in a way it never would back home . . .

It is obvious that there are also numbers of black Americans who go to West Africa solely to make a large amount of money, more than they could make in the United States. Many realize that if there were any suggestion of their own incompetence in their failure to make money in America, then that suggestion will become a certain recipe for disaster in Africa. A small number of black businessmen do make fortunes in West Africa, but only those who have fairly advanced skill in areas lacking in developing countries or who have spent a ridiculous amount of their time on making their fortune. And, to be sure, numbers of young black Americans go to seek their 'identity'. Usually these energetic seekers after abstractions find that they already have a load of identity from which they are unable to shake free, and they grow sour, unforgiving of America, Africa and themselves in their inevitable failure. Groups of West Indians are in West Africa as a result of what they describe as an inveterate Caribbean urge to travel away, away from economic depression, from smallness. These become businessmen or professionals, and, since they never consciously strive to rid themselves of a perfectly serviceable identity, they adapt very well indeed to Africa.

Again, many settlers have highly individual motivations. A Jamaican nun said to me, 'My vocation was always tied up in a picture I had of myself sitting under a mango tree — always a mango tree, I don't know why — in Africa converting ignorant heathen natives. I'd always be surrounded by children at my feet and that would be my mission. The fact that the children here are total strangers to the truth and all forms of honesty only gives my vocation trial, and, in a certain way, a strength.' And a young black American teacher in Ghana said: 'I came here, number one, to get away from home, number two, to get a master's degree in chemistry, and number three, to make a lot of money.' And another, in Kumasi, said in a rather mysterious manner: 'I'm here because I'm not in the States. Man, that United States are too deep for me.'

But mostly the settlers have a saddened realization that 'there was a ceiling through which we couldn't break,' as a black American businessman in Ghana said:

It was a white system that limited us. I was never angry about white people, just the system which · created those moments when you know you may never play with the white kids again, and those moments when a *look* in the eye tells you everything. When Ghana became free it gave us a fantastic sense of pride, it gave us the same taste of pride that other Americans had. Before that, there was no bridge we could cross over to Africa. Sure, we had Garvey's Africa and all kinds of other Africas. But we were surrounded by Germans and Italians and Poles who all talked of the Old Country, and Jews were hearing about their homeland and so on. But when we looked at Africa, we found nothing there. The white man had depopulated it, so it was Garvey and all the rest of them that invented people for it. But *now*, why here was a homeland that was real, and they were real people in the United Nations and all. I was doing all right in the States, like in the middle income group, but here it could be even better. If I'd hated whites it would have been terrible for me here. You know what I felt? I just felt goddamn *weary*, just sad and weary with it all. I felt tired and I needed this vitality of Africa.

The first day, the first hour, even the very first few moments in Africa are a shattering assault on the senses for the New Worlder. It is perhaps only in those first moments that they really understand the power of the preconceptions they had had. Even after many years, most remember their first day, with its release, relief, sadness, fright, lingering terror and happiness. There are moments of calm, but also of incredible vulnerability as the senses are invaded by a three-dimensional, vivid, breathing, smelling reality. W.E.B.Du Bois, himself a strange convert to the Back-to-Africa movement, wrote in *Dusk of Dawn:*

> When shall I forget the night I first set foot on African soil? I am the sixth generation in descent from forefathers who left this land. The moon was at the full and the waters of the Atlantic lay like a lake. All the long slow afternoon as the sun robed herself in her western scarlet with veils of misty cloud, I had seen Africa afar. Cape Mount — that mighty headland with its twin curves, northern sentinel of the realm of Liberia — gathered itself out of the cloud at half past three and then darkened and grew clear. On beyond flowered the dark low undulating land quaint with palm and breaking sea. The world grew black. Africa faded away, the stars stood forth curiously twisted — Orion in the zenith — the Little Bear asleep and the Southern Cross rising behind the horizon. Then afar, ahead, lights shone, straight at the ship's fore. Twinkling lights appeared below, around,

and rising shadows. 'Monrovia,' said the Captain . . . and lo! I was in Africa.

Here [in Africa] darkness descends and rests on lovely skins until brown seems luscious and natural. There is sunlight in great gold globules and soft, heavy-scented heat that wraps you like a garment. And laziness, divine, eternal, languor is right and good and true. I remember the morning; it was Sunday, and the night before we heard the leopards crying down there. Today beneath the streaming sun we went down into the gold-green forest. It was silence — silence the more mysterious because life abundant and palpitating pulsed all about us and held us drowsy captives to the day . . . [3]

Du Bois lived most of his nearly one hundred years in America, and only shortly before his death did he decide to go and live in Ghana. He bacame a kind of sage during the early years of Ghanaian Independence, and is remembered by a plaque at Christiansborg Castle in Accra.

The first impressions are not always as reassuring as those of Du Bois. A young wife from Chicago told me:

I remember as a kid being sent to some relatives on a farm in Pennsylvania. It was my first holiday away from home, and really my first time in the countryside. I hardly knew the relatives I was going to stay with for two months, and they weren't there when I got there. There I was on this farm, looking like it was deserted, and there was a rooster crowing. It was so scary, me being so young and in a strange place, and whenever after I heard a rooster like that I got the same feeling. When I got here, we had to stay in a hotel, and my husband went out to fix something or other, and outside the window I could hear this rooster, like going around the street — in the middle of town, for God's sake! — and it all came back to me again.

Nervous vulnerability may make settlers prone to short-lived nebulous fears and to more mundane ones, too. A black American, joining her Sierra Leonean husband told me of her arrival by ship:

135

The captain went on and on about how I would hate it here, no electricity and no water and so on. He said I'd be back inside a month. We started approaching Freetown and I began packing in the dark. The captain yelled: 'Come up here and see for yourself. Didn't I tell you there was no electricity?' It didn't occur to me to look out of the porthole. I clambered up and looked out at Freetown and Christ Jesus! it was like 1,000 stars, the lights all over town, up the hill, round the bay, all over. And he said: 'There now', and he smiled and all those little fears just disappeared — and never came back, well, not quite like that. The first thing I remember hearing when I got ashore was Elvis Presley. The second thing I heard was Sarah Vaughan, and then Ella Fitzgerald, and I thought, oh well, this isn't going to be too bad. Except for the incredible heat. I couldn't believe it. My husband was based up-country and I remember when I got there I thought my God, look at those vultures! Every time I saw one I'd gather my children up, and my mother-in-law, who didn't speak English tried to tell me they were harmless. It was stupid really, I didn't really understand. Then there were the bush spiders, all muddy and hairy. I was taking a shower one night in the dark, or at least with a candle, and I felt something watching me, and there was this spider. I called to the watchman, who was a bit tipsy, and the spider dashed into the bedroom. He dropped on to the bed. I searched for two or three hours, then I shooed this crazy watchman out, I was sick of searching. I thought I'd go to bed, and I pulled back the covers . . . and there it was!

Inevitably, it is the heat and humidity that most people notice first. If you arrive even in the middle of the night, the moist heat meets you like a blow and envelops you in glowing, dripping discomfort. A black American girl who originally went to Nigeria with the Peace Corps, then returned with the United States Government, described it in this way:

Well first, I arrived with one hell of a hangover. It was a charter flight for the Peace Corps and they'd said they weren't serving booze so we took our own. We drank and

136

sang for the first half of the flight from New York to Lagos. For the first half we were drunk; for the second half we were sick. When we go to Lagos, it was 5.30 in the morning, and I walked to the back of the plane to get off, and we were just *hit* by the muggy heat. I thought Christ if it's this hot this early in the morning how'm I going to live here for two years? I nearly got back on the plane. Anyway, I did get off, but it was a very unpleasant arrival. I still get smells that I associate with those first few days. There is a smell that is associated with damp and mildew. It's like the sheets on a bed in a non-air-conditioned room. It's not exactly mouldering, or even unpleasant. I just associate it with darkness, damp. When I came back here a second time, I smelled it immediately. I could have been blindfold, I'd have recognized it anywhere. They took us to Onitsha market. I remember being in the bus, so uncomfortable in my clothes, wearing loafers which filled up with sweat. I'd arrived wearing high heels and hose. I soon ditched them. But I remember vividly my damp squishy shoes, riding along in the bus, being amazed by all the colours, a maze, the people, too much! When someone new comes to the place now it blows your mind walking with them, all those first things come back, the palm trees . . . wow, the palm trees, like that. Goats! Goats? People with stuff on their heads, and that scary feeling at the back of your mind and in your stomach.

Another wife, from the West Indies, joining her husband in Nigeria, gave me an account of a series of emotions that are perhaps more widely shared than is admitted:

I remember getting a most peculiar feeling in Dakar. You get it when you come from an island, I suppose, but I felt at Dakar that it was a vast expanse that went on and on and on. I looked at the modern airport, with the lizards running around, and the men in long gowns and then out at this stretch of land that went on for ever, and I remember feeling for the first time something I have often thought ever since. Take an airport or something that's familiar going on, and you think that this is the veneer of

137

Africa. Only the veneer is really much more a thick crust of what you know. You start to recognize it and you may be able to relate to this crust, but under that there's a dark and maybe loathsome abyss, you just don't know. I can hardly describe it, except that I get it from time to time, that same feeling, when I'm walking down a street in Lagos. You know, walking along comfortably as if you know the place really intimately, not really needing to look where you're going — and after all I've been here 11 years — when you'll catch some indescribably awful smell that makes you think of this abyss of evil. Why do I call it evil? It's only that it's something you will never learn to know, it's something *they* know, though. You're living on this crust that separates you from something sort of unspeakable. I've had this feeling when dancing with my husband. He'll be very intent on dancing, and I suddenly get this throw-back feeling of the airport and the vastness, and he's like a stranger, at *home* in some extraordinary depths I can never know. I don't know why I call it evil. It's just that it's something that makes me terribly lonely and scared and cut off from Africa and also from my own people. I never felt this with my husband in London or in the West Indies, but I do here.

Yet another wife, from Trinidad, also talked of the start of irrational fear, of an unaccountable welling of troubled feeling: 'First thing, we drove up from Accra to Kumasi. I'd never seen so many trees. If G . . . hadn't been with me I would have wept. I felt so desolated. I don't know why. I felt tears about to come the whole time, I could hardly stand it. It wasn't self-pity. I was very glad for both of us that we were starting out in Africa. But I kept feeling there was no-one else there, no people in all those trees.'

In his book *Black Power,* an account of his search for kindred spirit in pre-Independence Ghana, Richard Wright also caught this disturbing effect of the inrush of half-understood impressions:

> Ten minutes out of Takoradi was enough to make Africa flood upon me so quickly that my mind was a blur and could not grasp it all. Villages of thick-

walled mud huts heaved into view, tantalising my
eyes for a few seconds, and then fled past, only to be
replaced by others as mythical and unbelievable . . .
The soil was rich red like that of Georgia or
Mississippi, and, for brief moments, I could almost
delude myself into thinking I was back in the
American South . . . [but] . . . the kaleidoscope of
sea, jungle, nudity, mud huts and crowded market
places induced in me a conflict deeper than I was
aware of; a protest against what I saw seized me . . .
My protest was not against Africa or its people; it was
directed against the unsettled feeling engendered by
the strangeness of a completely different order of life.
I was gazing upon a world whose laws I did not know,
upon faces whose reactions were riddles to me . . .
faced with the absolute otherness and inaccessibility
of this new world, I was prey to a vague sense of
mild panic, an oppressive burden which I could not
shake off . . . [4]

Several immigrants spoke of the awesome bewilderment at
the outlandishness of it all and their failing will in their new
venture. Some spoke of a sadness at not immediately
recognizing Africans, after all, as brothers, and of the
intrusive environment as something much too daunting, if
absurdly and needlessly so. A young businessman spoke of
his experience of this:

First thing, I'd been met and we were going by night
to Kumasi [about a hundred and fifty miles from Accra]
and the truck broke down. The driver went off to find
somebody to fix it and I was left there at the side of
the road. Now I'm not very impressionable and I
thought I was pretty well prepared for Africa. But
there I was, at night, at the side of the road with this
great mahogany forest. Suddenly I heard drums, and
boy! was I frightened, it was ridiculous, nothing less
than all those Tarzan memories coming back. I stood
there absolutely terrified. The driver came back and
laughed himself sick. It turned out to be kids, nothing
but small small children, going to church.

An incident of equal pathos happened to Leslie Alexander Lacy (he describes it in his *Rise and Fall of a Proper Negro*) when he reached Dakar and African soil for the first time. Spotting the crowd on the harbour, he greets them:

'Brothers, I'm so glad to be home. This is the greatest moment of my life. It was worth spending every hour in America just to be able to live this moment. You have made me very happy. They tell black people in America that the Africans don't want them. I know now that they were lying to keep us apart. Black people in America belong on this continent, and I bring you greetings from all those who cannot be here. I am truly happy.'

'Give us a dollar', the man said enthusiastically.

'Dollars? But I don't understand.' I was confused.

'Yeah. You from America. You got plenty dollar. You be Big Man. America rich country. This be poor country. We need dollar. You give dollar.'

Suddenly it was as clear as the hot sky above.[5]

This innocence is not very widespread, but impressionable young Afros do turn up at international airports in Africa, struggling with expensive cameras and duty-free liquor, and do leap off planes and kiss the ground and fling their arms round the necks of startled policemen. They are certainly as easily clipped as white people by the notorious West African airport taxi drivers.

But there are also some who are, as one young Afro-American put it, 'surprised I was so unsurprised', and feel at home, if not in a satisfyingly mystic sense, then at least without the powerful feelings of sadness, apprehension and regret. The same young black, newly arrived, said,

It had the physical lay-out of a tropical country that I didn't find strange — it reminded me slightly of Hawaii, Accra being on the ocean and all — and I felt immediately comfortable. The things I noticed were small things, so small I can't remember. You noticed that the people, outside Accra, had their lives involved in food, and clothing and shelter, everything revolved around the provision of those three things. In Accra, a metropolis, you get other jobs and functions, sign writers and so on, but outside, everybody had his own function regarding food, clothing and shelter. The biggest impression of surprise was the Westernness of the place, the clothes many of the people were wearing. There was still a visible relationship with the ex-colonisers, the British, in the cars, street lights, even the 'Stop' signs.

For most blacks, however, it is perhaps a recognition of the familiar in outlandish surroundings that makes those familiar things, the Coke signs, the Mobil and Shell signs, skyscrapers and cars seem themselves outlandish amid the flame trees, the sound of fruit bats, the light of kerosene lamps flickering ominously. One man explained: 'I was unprepared for the modern airport, with a runway and all. I wanted it to be like Casablanca or somewhere, with a dust track and a guy with a machine gun. But the idea of a real modern airport really threw me, there in the middle of the bush. It was only when I did get out into the bush that I got over that feeling of strangeness.'

Many remarked on the surprise, mingled with pride, at seeing black people in responsible jobs, as soon as they disembarked.

Black cops, black customs men, black pilots, black guys refuelling the plane, black managers of airports, black, black, black, man, [said an American.] But you know, you get this funny feeling too. You've been so long indoctrinated that these jobs, well they're so skilful that no black guy can do them. You honestly feel Christ! what's a black guy doing around that plane? It's all gotten so far inside you that you too, just for a moment, wonder if they're really competent. How about that? You hear yourself thinking that, and by God you laugh, and I remember laughing, why of course they're competent, I'm home! It's *them* that runs it all, it's *us!* How can you explain that to anybody who has never felt the discrimination of the United States? You are just so

happy, and man, you just want to shout, hell,
black can do it . . . black guys *do* it!

This exultancy frequently has a visionary element. Edward
Wilmot Blyden wrote, in the last century, of seeing the
Pyramids for the first time:

This, thought I, was the work of my African
progenitors . . . Feelings came over me far different from
those I have ever felt when looking at the mighty works
of European genius. I felt that I had a peculiar heritage
in the Great Pyramid built . . . by the enterprising sons
of Ham, from which I descended. The blood seemed to
flow faster through my veins, I seemed to hear the
echo of those illustrious Africans. I seemed to feel the
impulse from those stirring characters who sent
civilization to Greece . . . I felt lifted out of the
commonplace grandeur of modern times; and could my
voice have reached every African in the world, I would
have earnestly addressed him . . . 'Retake your Fame'.[6]

A black American who subsequently became a businessman
in Ghana described his feelings when during the last war his
troop carrier sailed past Northern Africa:

We had been starved of information about Africa;
you heard of remote things, jungles and wild animals,
and you never saw anybody in the States who seemed
to be black the same way as Africans were. It was not so
much a matter of nowhere to go, but nowhere to have
come from. American blacks — and there were many on
the ship I was on — seemed to be more concerned with
their blackness than with their African-ness. But when
we went through the Straits of Gilbraltar we all looked
at Africa. I felt it was my homeland, as simple as that, a
vague feeling that suddenly became clear. All my
ancestors were *present* over there. It was really my home,
and we knew nothing about it, but all the centuries of
knowledge sort of flooded over me as I watched it
going past. All the guys went to the starboard rail, and
I knew they were feeling it too. In the night we passed

by Oran, far to the south, and as a storm built up, you could just see the outline of the continent in the distance, oh! we wanted to get off that ship and walk on the land. All the life and the things we hadn't experienced in the States we would be free to know over there. I just stood there, with this excitement, and I knew that I'd have to come back.

It is natural that different eras and different backgrounds produce different reactions. The young black American may become apoplectic with rage at the sight of a white person on *his* Africa. He has just arrived after a matter of hours in a plane from a highly advanced and tangled urban society. But in the 1920s and 1930s, a number of individuals from the West Indies travelled to West Africa, sometimes via London, sometimes not. An important group, for instance, was comprised of doctors who went to the Gold Coast a few years after the First World War. One said:

> It's hard to remember the first personal impressions now. The Garvey movement had been going on back home for some time, but I don't recall being unduly influenced by it. I practised up-country, and I remember most of my reactions, personal or otherwise, were overwhelmed by the sights that greeted me. Disease was appalling, and I might say that of all the revolutions in politics or economics, all are put very much in the shade by the gradual beating back of malaria. As for colonialism and white people, well, I worked for a while in a poor area of London before I went, and I knew it wasn't the English people who were doing all these things in the colonies. I recognized that the same people who were overbearing colonialists abroad were overbearing bosses in England, so I could never blame English or white people.

Others remember the chaotic arrivals of those days. (One white former colonial administrator who arrived in the 'forties described his experience of disembarkation: 'I thought they were putting on a show of *Sanders of the River* for me. They put me in this little boat off the ship and we came

143

into shore; I remember them singing something that went
a bit like "Ali-o-ho", well it couldn't have been, but I
thought the whole thing was straight out of Korda.') A
Jamaican trader who arrived in the Gold Coast in the 1920s
had a similar memory:

> I don't remember being all that elated, or feeling a
> great deal of brotherhood. But it was rather extraordinary
> being hoisted out of the ship in what they called a mammy-
> chair — a kind of crate affair — and into a surf boat. This
> boat would precariously bump and swoosh up and down
> as you headed for shore. So, out of that kind of horse-box
> with planks for seats, into this terrifying ride in the
> surf-boats; you were in quite a state by the time you
> landed. And after the sea, the heat hit you, along with all
> the gaiety of the port, and the colour and smells. It was
> all very weakening.

Different situations also produce different reactions in the
wives in those early hours. Many are already apprehensive
about the new life ahead in a strange and bizarre country.
They are also aware that not only are they meeting their
in-laws for the first time, but that their in-laws are seeing (or
even inspecting) them for the first time too, and that these
early impressions are likely to make all the difference between
acceptance and a completely intolerable hostility on the
family's home ground. Those who are agonizingly aware of
the importance of those first few moments with the
husband's family are often surprised at how easily they can
be got through. Others find that they 'get no Brownie points
for being black' as one put it, and that a tough struggle
ensues, the battlefield being marked out at that first meeting.

A black Brazilian wife arriving in West Africa said:
> It wasn't at all easy, although it was very exciting. We
> had dancing and they put their shoulder cloths on the
> ground for me to walk on, and there was more dancing
> and I was sweating so they dried me, and then we all ate
> yams. But I know I was resented, especially by the
> sisters. They were materialistic people and they felt that

if I hadn't married their brother, there would have been more money for them. Now I could understand the grandmother and people of her age not accepting this foreigner, even though I was black, because that's the way it is for old people, but I came to have a lot of trouble with those sisters, and I felt it straight away.

But sometimes small things could be reassuring to the new family. A West Indian wife in Accra told me:

We arrived in Takoradi, and relatives and friends came to meet me. We went to the house of a cousin there. I had no idea if he was a close cousin or anything, but we just turned up. I knew the wife was gesturing at the husband that he shouldn't have brought us without warning. How difficult, just coming with a stranger like that. I would have been furious. Apparently she only had some corned beef and some yams in the house. They said, 'Will you eat it?' And I said, 'Of course I'll eat it!' I ate it and said it was very nice — which actually it was — and this was very relaxing. The wife took me aside and said, 'If you have any complaints about your husband, you just come and complain to me.' It was simple and it was wonderful. I never had any problems whatsoever. I don't know if it was that or not, but it was all such smooth sailing from then on.

These first moments are for many a period of unprecedented intensity. Often people said they felt that they were suddenly forced to flex sensual muscles that had previously been dormant. It was, they said, a period so charged that they could never be the same again. Attitudes were firmly set, and a whole way of perceiving created, on their first day. 'It was like a trip,' said otherwise conservative people. The senses were engaged in a gear that had somehow been unsuspected.

The gentler reaches of this strange, sweaty, remarkably alive interval before adjustment begins were summed up by Edward Brathwaite, the Barbadian poet who spent eight years in Ghana:

Takoradi was hot.
Green struggled through red
as we landed.

Laterite lanes drifted off
into dust
into silence . . .

. . . *Akwaaba* they smiled
meaning welcome . . .

. . . Here is plantain
here palm oil:
red, staining the fingers;
good for the heat,
good for the sweat.

Do
you remember?

Could these soft huts
have held me?
Wattle daubed on wall,
straw-hatted roofs . . .

If you should see someone
coming this way
send help, send help, send help
for I am up to my eyes in fear.[7]

CHAPTER 5

A Home in Canaan

'Spies sent from different sections of this country by the
coloured people — and many a spy not commissioned —
have gone to that land, and have returned and reported.
Like the Hebrew spies, they have put forth diverse views.
Most believe Africa to be a fertile and rich country, and an
African nationality a desirable thing. But some affirm that
the land is not fit to dwell in, for " it is a land that eateth
up the inhabitants thereof" . . . Behold then, the Lord our
God has set the land before us, with its burning climate,
with its privations, with its moral, intellectual and
political needs, and by this providence he bids us go up
and possess it without fear or discouragement.' [1]

(Edward Wilmot Blyden, 1862)

'Their problem is to "acculturate" if one might use such
an expression; they must make a change. The first
generation never really makes the change. Many come
with a certain idea of Africa in the abstract. For those
who do, it is rather like going down a set of steps and
finding there is one more at the bottom they hadn't seen.
It gives them a nasty jar.'

(West African diplomat in London, 1972)

Daybreak is the best part of the day in Accra. It is cool, and the only sounds may be those of the puff adders swishing back to the maize patches after their warm night on the roadways, followed by the sudden awakening of millions of birds. The air is clear and fresh. Over the next hour or two, however, it begins curving under either the burden of the winter particles of Sahara dust carried on the *harmattan* which blows from the north, or the weight of the dense humidity. By nine or ten o'clock the coolness is finished. The city is enclosed in a bowl of dampness, the sky itself seems to seethe and moulder, and the day is fit only for the ubiquitous lizards. The orange-headed salamanders that continually do their push-ups on balconies, on sidewalks, on grass verges and in the road, seem to be the ideal form of life. Anything that is animal flesh or less etiolates in the crippling heat. The air does not have a flat Hellenic clarity. It is a diffusion of light, reflective and deceptive. But somehow human life persists, even if it does not invariably prevail. Soon the smells of the city are rising, and they hover, trapped about six feet from the ground, for the rest of the day. The predominant smell is a kind of mixture of smoked fish and diarrhoea.

Accra is a fearsomely overpopulated city, and Westerners who come from cities that are collapsing under their own size and complexity find that Accra too is collapsing, but from a lack of what might be called 'urban-ness'. Facilities are hopelessly inadequate for the daily infusions of people from the depressed rural areas, and so these people gather in the fetid compounds of shanty-towns such as Nima and Jamestown. Somebody told me that the middle-class sections of the city are a sort of paradigm of the Ghanaian spirit. Streets do not have names, and houses have completely unmemorable numbers, so that, to visit someone, you have to know them well enough in the first place to know exactly where their house is in the sprawling city; and to find that out demands a deviousness and initiative that would defeat most people who have the misfortune not to be Ghanaian.While I was there, one street changed its name three times; with Ghanaian finesse, however, it ended up as a two-part street with two names.

Around the city are scattered bumptious reminders of the glorious 'fifties, reminders such as Black Star Square, modelled on some ludicrous parade ground, and the vainglorious State House which succeeding governments have been too embarrassed to fill or staff adequately, possibly because the lifts do not work for the greater part of the time. Up in the hills of Aburi behind Accra stands a deserted Peduasi Lodge, built specially for Kwame Nkrumah. (One of the more infamous bars in Accra was once described to me as Pederasty Lodge.) Against this increasingly shabby evidence of *folie de grandeur,* yet another government attempts to grapple with the incredibly onerous economic problems of the country.

Against this backdrop, too, the dwindling band of expatriate Europeans — all too visible to visiting black Americans — meet to gripe, play polo, wrest a living, and drink at receptions. Diplomatic receptions are still a regular feature of white expatriate life in Accra. The Queen's birthday is celebrated with a garden party (despite the fact that the Queen has been inconsiderate enough to have a birthday at the beginning of the rainy season).

At one reception a Ghanaian military band, dressed up in Hussars' uniforms, oom-pah-ed 'Colonel Bogey' on the lawn. At another, one evening at a certain High Commission I noticed an odd gap in a group of people standing in a loose circle. On the ground, a guest was stretched at full length, breathing stertoriously in a gin haze. His companions had thoughtfully left a space for him should he recover from his overtiredness. Some expatriates are exceedingly hospitable, charming and thoroughly pleasant. Others are very odious indeed. If one does not move from Accra and mixes with certain European expatriates, one's overwhelming impression of Ghana is that it is stagnant, corrupt and lazy.

Yet there is a non-belligerent pride about Ghanaians; the

hectoring and shrewish bullying of some of their neighbours are absent. Absent too is the preciosity and pretention of many metropolitan Africans of francophone Africa. There is instead a gentle, pitying cynicism. 'They've talked themselves politically into silence', said a friend of mine. Perhaps they have lost the innocence of gullibility which many Europeans still have. Most Ghanaians I know are a walking celebration of themselves. And in a languid and sophisticated way, they have the quality of celebrating you, too.

It is to Ghana that the majority of black American and West Indian emigrants to Africa have gone in recent years. There is, of course, still a trickle of immigrants into Liberia and Sierra Leone, and there are black Americans in Togo, Ivory Coast, Senegal, the Congo Republic and Ethiopia. There is a small group in Conakry, Guinea (Stokely Carmichael was there for about four years) and a larger group — 'the angriest group south of the Saharah', said a local correspondent — in Tanzania. There are blacks serving in diplomatic missons, and also a fair number of black Peace Corps volunteers all over Africa. But since the late 'fifties the focus for those intending to settle permanently has been Ghana.

The presence of New Worlders in Ghana is by no means new. In the early nineteenth century a party of Swiss missionaries from the Basel Evangelical Missionary Society moved to Akropong, the capital town of Akwapim in the Aburi hills thirty-five miles from Accra. In the twelve years they were there, eight missionaries died and not one convert was made. Finally, according to Andreas Riis, the leader of the missionaries, the local chief, Nana Adow Dankwa I, said, 'When God created the world he made Book for the white man, and juju or fetish for the black man; but if you could show us some black men who could read the white man's Book, then we would surely follow you'.[2] Accordingly, the Society recruited eight West Indians from the Moravian mission in Jamaica.

They arrived in Akropong in June 1843. Their influence survives strongly. They held meetings under the great and ancient *Mpeniase* (the Mpeni tree that still stands), constructed stone buildings which survive in an Akropong street known as Hanover Street, and introduced the now common cutlass for agriculture. John Rochester, who introduced the cutlass,became known as *Kwesi Dade** — 'the man of Sunday with steel'. The Jamaicans are reputed to have introduced mango, avocado, cocoyam and coffee. Their first baptism was in 1847. By 1852, they had 117 baptized Christians in their flock. In 1848 they founded the Presbyterian Training College, which is today the second oldest institution for teacher training in Africa, second only to Fourah Bay College in Sierra Leone.

Their conversion record is impressive, but it was not achieved without considerable rivalry with local fetish shrines and customs. Four miles away across the valley is Larteh and one of Ghana's main fetish shrines, the shrine of *Akonedi,* and the whole area is steeped in fetish belief. Near the Akropong mission† is the *dente,* a fetish grove inhabited by the *bosompra* spirit. The Jamaicans entered this grove one day in 1855, and for just having seen the shrine they were 'fined' one cow, nine sheep, nine fowls, and nine eggs. There are many stories of missionaries trying to set up shop in strongly fetish areas and being chased away. Today, the two seats of religious belief sit, glowering at each other in amiable enmity across the valley, reminding one of a Don Camillo story. When the sound of drums drifts across the valley, it has been known for the pastor to hang on to his bell to drown it.

In the 1970s, the area has a curious significance for black Americans. Parties regularly turn up at Akropong to see round the college and to watch displays of native dancing and arts. At the mission itself I found a beautiful and determined young Afro-American girl from Chicago who was aiming to form a nucleus of equally determined immigrants, which

---

* The name *Kwesi* is given to boys born on a Sunday, but it has also come to mean 'White Man'. Calling Rochester Kwesi may have been in accordance with the custom of calling all foreigners white men.
† By a strange reversal, it was the Akropong mission that sent the first-ever African to do missionary work in America. The Rev. E.N. Abboa Offei conducted his mission in New York and Detroit between 1959 and 1961.

would attract yet more like-minded pilgrims. (She made the interesting point that young white Americans were just as alienated from materialism and violence in the United States as blacks were and that there was some evidence that the Salvation road to the East was slowly becoming a hitch-hiking road to Africa for young whites.)Meanwhile, across the valley, groups of Afro-Americans were taking up residence at Darteh. Some thirty-one were initiated into the shrine in 1972 by the high priestess, Nana Abena Oparebea. The group was led by a dance teacher from New York named Yaw Opare Dinizolo, who claimed to have traced his descent from the priestess's family. He further claimed to have come originally from near Aburi, and that his great-grandfather was a great priest, Atwidan, who had never died but ascended to heaven, casting his sword to the ground, where it was still stuck.[3]

Those who had seen the Americans drumming and dancing were struck by their skill. Some of the girls, said African on-lookers, had cut tribal marks on to their faces and bodies, and their dancing certainly looked authentic to them, although the singing was somewhat harder to decipher.

Authentic or no, the new fetish acolytes angered some sections of Ghanaian public opinion. The Ghanaian jazz drummer Guy Warren wrote a letter to the *Daily Graphic* in Accra, part of which said: 'Whilst we in Africa must welcome home our brothers and sisters from America WE MUST ALSO CAUTION THEM ABOUT OUR CULTURE, for whatever these brothers and sisters may say to the contrary THEY ARE AMERICANS, BORN AND BRED. THEY THINK AMERICAN, ACT AMERICAN AND SPEAK AMERICAN. And typical of Americans THEY ARE VERY BRASH.'[4]

When Nana Abena visited America in 1969, Dinizolo said: 'It was just like the miracle of Jesus' walk on the sea. All black America was shook up.' A temple was established, the *Bosom Dzemowodzi,* and soon it claimed to have 250 adherents worshipping the Larteh shrine in the United States.[5] It is by now almost a cliché to assert remarkable affinities between fetish ceremonial and, say, the services of Holy Roller Tabernacles, or certain Pentecostal churches. It is repeatedly said that the call and response structure and general participation of the worshippers in the main stream of the service shows the direct line of descent of such services

153

from African forms. The forms of the respective services are undoubtedly a bridge between the two continents and between the present and the past, but the content is divided by irreconcilable notions which may not be apparent to hasty observation. (Certain fetish objects may, however, be found in churches in the Caribbean and South America.) Hence, many black Americans told me that on arrival in Africa they had 'recognized' fetish from their Southern non-Conformist chapels, but that they had been very quickly disabused about deeper similarities. Dinizolo's claims must speak for themselves: they may be an attempt to provide Imagined Africa with some household gods, or they may be an example of Afro-American religious forms becoming the content of fetish worship.

African religious and other retentions were much stronger in the Caribbean than in even the southern United States. They were stronger still on the mainland of South America. This, in part, explains the total assimilation of black Brazilians into the communities on the coast of the Gulf of Guinea. The black Brazilians — repatriated to West Africa in the mid and late nineteenth century — have been little investigated, so complete was this assimilation. There are a number of houses in Lagos that are obviously of South American architecture, and along the coast various Portuguese names, such as Da Sousa and Ribero, persist. (One president of Togo, Sylvanus Olympio, later assassinated, was of Brazilian descent.) Otherwise the waters of Africa closed again over the returnees.[6]

For years, the Portuguese conducted their slave trade from the Congo and Angola, then they moved into the Gulf of Guinea, and started taking Ewe and Ga from Dahomey, Togo and Ghana, Ashanti from Ghana, and Hausa from Nigeria. These were baptized, classified as *peças de Indias* (pieces from the Indies), and shipped to Brazilian mines. When they were repatriated to the Gold Coast, the coastal Africans gave them some land near what is now Accra. This area of land, Adebraka, is now a very choice piece of real estate, accounting for a huge section of inner suburb, something of an equivalent of Kensington and Chelsea. Hardly any written material on the repatriation survives in

Ghana, but the queen mother of the Brazilian *Tabons* told me this:

About a hundred came back here in two or three boats. They were highly literate and skilled in all sorts of ways, for instance in the digging of wells — they found one here when they dug up the road recently — so they were welcomed by the people on the coast. In particular, they were taken in by the Ankrah tribe of the Ga nation and given their own stool [symbol of tribe] and they gave them this land. They called them the *Tabons,* which is without doubt a corruption of the pidgin French they spoke, *très bien,* or *très bon.* They were settled like that on the coast. Now the Ankrahs were not stupid. They were threatened frequently from the sea, people raiding from further down the coast, so they wanted the Brazilians to fight for them, to stand between them and the sea. Well, they did this and fought many times. They were excellent teachers and interpreters, so they were of good service to the Ga people in many other ways, so the barriers started breaking down. In time there was inter-marriage and so the divisions were broken down more. Also there were many things in fetish that had survived in Brazil. We had *Shongo*, our protector, and snake fetish would actually be kept in the Christian church. How did they become assimilated? They were educated and they were useful, they became traders in beads and salt and fish and palm oil all over the country and they gradually stopped being a separate community. Now it is very difficult to keep a group together, they are so dispersed among other Africans. There are a number of people of Brazilian descent who, through marriage and so on, are entitled to sit on the Ga Paramount stool. [The Ga throne is, in fact, succeeded to by family rota, but in theory several Brazilians would be entitled.] As for Afro-Americans . . . why did they not come back when *they* were free? We were very lucky to have come back when we did. But why didn't they?

So, unlike the Creoles of Sierra Leone and the Americo-

Liberians, small groups of New Worlders did find it possible to assimilate into tribal Africa. The descendents of the Jamaican missionaries are proud today of their ancestors, but they are indistinguishable from other Christian Africans. The Brazilians find it extremely difficult now to assert any kind of South American allegiance or identity. The assimilation of these groups of a few score of people in the nineteenth century is a very different matter from the adjustment of black Americans to Ghanaian society in this century, of course. But in a limited sense, the experience is instructive. It shows, firstly, that the descendents of Africans taken into slavery were, and are, not inherently incapable of adjusting back to Africa, just that the further south the place from which they were repatriated, the easier the repatriation was. Secondly, those with something positive and valuable — that Africans saw as positive and valuable — to offer may, like the Creoles, offer it at a haughty distance, or, like the Brazilians, offer it from intimate proximity and be therefore submerged virtually without trace into Africa.

These two points are the cardinal ones in successful immigration, and they are precisely the ones that have been distorted by the cultural and political developments of the last hundred years. In Africa itself, tribal society was in much greater flux in the nineteenth century than it is now. When the Jamaicans arrived in Akropong for the first time, they found that the buildings originally constructed by the Swiss had been practically destroyed in one of the civil wars that had raged and continued to rage in the area. The Brazilians played an even more direct role in the inter-tribal friction of the time. The British colonial system only really became established in areas away from the coast with the fall of Kumasi in 1896 and the end of the Ashanti wars. Thus, the extraordinary solidification of African society in the last century has produced a far more daunting, more national, entity to which to adjust.

But more dramatic cultural developments have taken place in the New World that would seem to militate against the successful adjustment of black Americans to Africa. In face of insult and discrimination, American Negroes grew, as we have seen, to take a pained pride in their race and culture, a culture that inevitably developed independently, away from its African roots. The growth of mass media to disseminate this culture served to standardize it but also to make it available to nearly everyone. The media itself created tastes and directions. This inter-action of medium and message has produced a more or less complete, separate culture, with a full range of artistic expression and political connotations. This has led some to suppose that the black American is now a member of a different race from the African. This only demonstrates the power of such a mass culture. But the only African culture with access to this media — which ranges through written forms and literature to the modern entertainment industry — was the culture expressed in a language alien to Africa, English or French, and which was therefore already removed from its well-spring before it even left the continent. (African music has only lately had access to mass media.) African culture was only available to blacks in the New World through African politicians or artists who spoke a European language. Perhaps this unavoidably distorted cultural awareness of Africa was more misleading than total ignorance.

The last hundred years have seen the true mass rise of the articulate self-aware American Negro, and, as important, the massive upsurge of the means of access which most black Americans have to self awareness, through mass education and literacy, for example. This upsurge is a much more recent phenomenon in Africa.

A further factor is the emergence of the urban American Negro. Migrations to the north at various times through the last century produced a class of black industrial workers, often settled in huge urban masses such as Chicago's South Side. The physical conditions of these areas are now among the very worst in the United States, but the attitudes and culture they engendered were, nevertheless, urban. Again, the very squalor has itself produced a series of particular attitudes, even in people who have long since quit such areas. But the main point is that the adjustment any black American must make in Africa may be as much the adjustment from the essentially urban to the essentially rural. Not all black Americans live in ghettoes, of course, but few can be said to be untouched by their existence, which permeates so much of black American culture.

The Back-to-Africa movements were working-class movements in America. In the last century there came the highly significant switch in the direction of the movements from the white middle class to the black working class. Non-academic Africa-awareness is of the proletariat. But it is not usually black Americans of the 'mud sill' who emigrate to Africa. It is more often the middle-class Negroes. They will have, naturally, a number of attitudes that may be shaped by the conditions their poorer brothers endure, but their own life-styles are bourgeois.

This is not the contradiction it seems. In order to acquire the skills he must have to adjust successfully to Africa, the black American must almost certainly, in the nature of things, have moved into the middle class. His — not insuperable — difficulty is therefore going to be that of any urban middle-class person adjusting to a rural working-class society.

On top of all this is a simple arithmetical fact. The American Negro, whatever his station, lives as part of a minority in a white society. The United States is a nation of minorities, but the black minority, while one of the largest, is highly visible, exploited and perennially disappointed. This gives the Negro a different racial attitude from the African. This attitude is at the heart of nearly all misunderstandings that crop up between black Americans and Africans. There are many tensions and frictions in West African societies. With few exceptions, they are rarely racial tensions. Naturally, I came across a number of quasi-racist attitudes among African as well as among European individuals. Some Africans I met were anti-Semitic, anti-Levantine, anti-Indian or anti-white, but these had been affected by individual incidents or situations. But far from governing any kind of overall situation, racial attitudes were minimal or, more often, non-existent. Africans I came to know were free from colour reaction. A Jamaican settled in Ghana put it to me in this way:

When an Afro-American is talking about colour and race he is using terms that are *totally* alien to Africa. (Here we're not talking about Southern or Portuguese regimes.) He is still searching for roles which can't be conceptualized. The Ghanaian knows he belongs body and soul to Ghana. When an Afro says, 'I am a black man', what does he mean? What can the African take that to mean? A Nigerian is a black man, but a Ghanaian doesn't conceptualize him as a black man, the term is to him meaningless. It is like saying a ball is round; how can a ball be aware of its roundness and not its ballness?

On a casual level, Africans told me, this imposes a burden of irrelevant experience on Africa and Africans. It is natural, they said, that black Americans should want to interpret their experience of Africa in terms of their own background and previous experience, but they did not always observe the fine distinction between interpreting Africa to themselves in this way, and *prescribing* for Africa from their own vantage-point. The black American view of Africa may be an understandable and valid one, but it is not the only perspective. Educated and politically-aware Africans whom I met, often said that the supremely irritating thing about some black Americans was their desire to be the latest in a long and varied line of people of all races and nationalities who have Known What Is Best For Africa. This, it was noted, was particularly true of American blacks who have migrated to Africa since Independence came to so many countries.*

Most black Americans I met had come to Africa in search of opportunity and not of identity. Those who did seek an identity were angry and bitter. 'These Afro-Americans blame the white man for the white propaganda about them, when they should blame themselves for having believed most of it. Perhaps, you know, that is what they do. It's very difficult to live with people who blame themselves like that and who did believe more than they admit of what the white

---

* The *anni mirabili* of Independence in Africa were from 1956 to 1960. In those years, twenty-one countries became independent. In 1956: Morocco, Sudan, Tunisia. In 1957: Ghana. In 1958: Guinea. And in 1960: Cameroun, Central African Republic, Chad, Congo (Brazzaville), Zaire, Dahomey, Gabon, Ivory Coast, Malagasy Republic, Mali, Mauritania, Niger, Nigeria, Senegal, Togo and Upper Volta.

man said about them. Trouble is, they only know they believed so much of it when they get here.' These were the words of an elderly Ghanaian professor, who himself had plenty of evidence all around him of well-adjusted black Americans on his staff but preferred instead to look at the ill-adjusted among his students. Another Ghanaian said: 'Afro-Americans criticize us for being British. They say we are still the lapdogs of the British and they say our minds have been colonized. But we never believed the sneers of some of the white men. We always thought they were mad. How could they have so little pride in themselves, such people, if they could think such things of us?' So, to the extent that the Afro-Americans believe that educated Ghanaians are black British, and educated Ghanaians believe Afro-Americans to be ultimately unknowing victims of white people, there is a great divide in racial attitudes between them. And this division the white races have made between African descendents and both their forefathers and their present-day brothers in Africa.

This is a subject that does not readily admit of generalization. It is, moreover, the many exceptions to the generalization who do adjust well to Africa. They are the people who understand the true perniciousness of certain white racial attitudes. But the point at which generalization does hold up was illuminated by a number of West Indians who said they had adjusted to Africa much more easily than could an Afro-American because, ironically, of the British culture that they and Africa had experienced. They had also both equally understood the limits to which they would allow the white man to influence them. Subsequently, and in a similar fashion, they had both disentangled themselves from white rule. They were able, both West Indians and Africans told me, to relate to White in a much more mature way than could a black American. This, too, is a sore point of misunderstanding between all three groups, Africans, West Indians and black Americans. The black American attitude was summed up by Richard Wright:

> The gold can be replaced; the timber can grow again,
> but there is no power on earth that can rebuild the

mental habits and restore that former vision that once gave significance to the lives of these people [Africans]. Nothing can give back to them that pride in themselves, that capacity to make decisions, that organic view of existence that made them want to live on this earth and derive from that living a sweet if sad meaning. Today the ruins of their former culture, no matter how cruel and barbarous it may seem to us are reflected in timidity, hesitancy and bewilderment. Eroded personalities loom here for those who have psychological eyes to see.[7]

Poor Richard Wright. He disliked his experience of modern Africa and found few affinities between himself and the Africans he met. Wright talked of a 'sense of trespassing' and of Africans being 'split deep within themselves'. It should be remembered that the theme of 'alienness' was very important to Wright. The dedications of at least three of his books stress this personal preoccupation. Typical was his dedication in *White Man Listen*, to those 'who seek desperately for a home for their hearts'.

The Fanon view of the colonized person, the 'coiled, plundered creature', the man whose very mind has been colonized by the oppressor, might well be applied today by the independent Africans to certain Afro-Americans, and in particular to many of those who now visit Africa. For Wright's description of the symptoms of timidity and hesitancy, Africans might well substitute the qualities of brashness and dogmatic self-assertion.

For most New World settlers in West Africa, with or without damaging racial assumptions, much of their success or failure in adjusting depends on how thy acclimatize to expatriate life as such.

It is a highly individual way of living, a very private one. It makes tremendous demands on the personality, and only those with fair reserves of intimacy with themselves can manage it happily. A large number are with a husband or wife and often with a family, so for these, the more extreme toll of expatriate living is greatly reduced. For those who return to Africa alone, it depends to some extent on how African they believed themselves to be before they arrived.

It seemed to me that the more consciously a person felt himself to have been an African who had lost his way for a few years and had now returned intact to the homeland the more likely he was to become disillusioned and to fail. It is most unlikely that any will completely assimilate. Very nearly complete adjustment gives the illusion of assimilation, and in practice amounts to much the same thing. Some parents view with equanimity the fact that only their children or grandchildren would ever be truly African; others felt resentment and frustration at this. As ever, much depended on the expectation.

In Sierra Leone I met two delightful elderly sisters whose missionary father had brought them as babies from the West Indies to West Africa more than eighty years before. Surely they must feel completely identified with Africa now, especially as they had never been back to the West Indies? 'Definitely not!' they said in unison. 'Oh no, most definitely not. We are from the Caribbean and we never forget that. We still have that, oh, that uncertainty about how people are going to react.' This was no doubt attributable to a missionary upbringing in formative years, which would produce the sense of being at a remove from Africa. A businessman from Trinidad who had been in West Africa for more than fifty years said: 'I have never completely lost the sense of being an expatriate. This is not something that is constantly on my mind or so. Actually I never expected to stay. But, well, Africa holds, and now I can't imagine leaving unless I was forced to. But me African? No.'

I met a number of young Afro-Americans — the pained expression on the face of one of them being possibly due to the circumcision he had recently had performed by an Ashanti native doctor — who, even while they were vociferously repudiating their American identity, seemed precisely by doing so to be expressing it most eloquently. Many had followed the mode and adopted 'African' names which were gobbledegook in any African language; many others manfully struggled with Swahili, despite the fact that it is an East African language, hardly spoken at all in West Africa. We are African, said these young men from Detroit and Atlanta, places one felt certain they would be returning to at a smart pace.

Most black Americans and West Indians soon realize, by force of circumstance or by choice, that if they are going to establish any identity at all, then it must be black *American* or West Indian, if it is to be at least acknowledged by Africans.

A West Indian who is married to a beautiful African woman and has held an important political post in one West African country told me:

> In the West Indies it would only take an English-speaking expatriate a month to adjust, whether he spoke Oxford English or broken English. Here, it would be unfair to expect people to speak your language all the time. I have been with friends who were talking English. Then they tell a joke in the vernacular. They say, 'We must translate this.' Then they say, 'Well, you can't tell this joke in English.' It isn't society that is repelling me or preventing me from moving in a normal way. Language is crucial to this. But, with a European language you can adjust in six months. They may know you are not French or whatever, but you make yourself understood. Here, there are so many vernaculars. Which one are you going to learn? And then how can I learn it? An adult coming to a country where he is going to earn a living, where is he going to find the time?
>
> This society also has a certain hidden thing that is against the integration by an outsider. The funeral customs and so on, you don't understand what certain things mean and you ask for an explanation. That involves the whole ethos of a people and besides, your having to ask underlines your outsiderness. It would take a person a lifetime of struggling and enduring before they were completely integrated, without people saying, even implicitly, that we don't want you. Even then there would be one or two little things that would be impossible to overcome. Identity with a village, for instance. When really asked, a person would never say they came from Lagos or Accra or Abidjan. They always say some little village which may be just outside town, or is in the town but is still regarded as a village. Then

if you said you were such and such a man from some place, they would say what family? They would *know* if you were real or not.

Then it depends on a man's aspirations. The majority of people who leave their homeland and go to another country — unless as a philanthropist or a missionary or a bum — they go to where they can better their lives. They think there is some way of utilising their abilities better than in their own country, and they can better move up their ambitional hierarchy. Sooner or later they will realize that although they want to like people and have them like them, it is part and parcel of their own self-advancement. Sooner or later, someone will ask why so and so is in this job. Here, people don't talk as dispassionately, impersonally, objectively, as they do in the U.K. If you have done something contrary, not to the law, but to social custom, they will sometimes tell you, but more often they won't. A former boss of mine, an older man, asked me several times to consider a certain proposition. I repeatedly said no, it didn't interest me. But I flatly refused, you see. When I did that, I found the rest of the people present began talking in the vernacular. I was later told that I should never have said No. I should have procrastinated to an older man. I learnt a tremendous lesson from that. Ever since then I have said, 'I'll think about it', and from that they know you mean No.

These may seem small things, but it is only in the small ways that you are reinforced as what you are to them. You may try to be African, you may even think you are, but there are many many things that crop up during just one day that assure that you are not and never will be. However much you are with them, there are certain ways you still feel an outsider. I am saying this with no rancour. I do get on well with them. They never would do you the gross discourtesy of even suggesting that you should stay in your place outside, and they will do many things for you. It's just something you have to have the wit to understand if you are going to have the remotest chance of being happy here.

A black American put the same idea in this way:

There is such a lack of objective accounts of African
history. Africans are *aware* of their history through oral
traditions and they are aware of their identity, but
their account of history is not an objective one that
can be imparted to an outsider, any more than their
identity, and how they see that, can be. I would say
that they have a true knowledge of their history and
themselves, but not an objective understanding. So
it's little wonder that we come and don't know
factual things. We're like foxes that have gone away from
the lair and mixed with human beings. You go back to
the lair, and the others suspect you because they
think you are now part human. You are still a fox but
you have knowledge of human beings so that makes
you different to them, so it's got to make you
different to yourself too. In that sense I'm no
African, any more than you are. I'm a wierd kind of
Frankenstein.

And another black American said: 'When you really
really realize you are not African, it's the loneliest
moment of your life, and if you can withstand that,
you can make it here. It goes on being lonely, and it's
how you adjust yourself to that loneliness that
matters, not how you adjust to Africa.'
This is not a question of retaining a group identity with the
country you left or your erstwhile countrymen. There is not,
in fact, a great amount of conscious group activity among the
permanent expatriate blacks in West Africa. There is a
certain tea-time mixing among at least one group
of expatriate wives, but attempts to set up associations
usually peter out, and such other mingling as there is is
desultory and isolated. One West Indian businessman said,
rather melodramatically: 'We don't want to become an
identifiable group, a visible minority, because we know what
happens to such minorities in Africa.' This is his own, not
particularly justifiable view, but the last time a visible black
expatriate community of New Worlders developed in Ghana,

in the early 1960s, is not remembered too kindly.

The ideas of New World black intellectuals and politicians have tremendous importance in the political development of modern Africa. Blyden, Du Bois, Garvey, C.L.R. James, George Padmore, Frantz Fanon, all made a very great impact on Africa in their different ways. The British Empire owed much of its dynamic to a triangle of trade: slaves from Africa to the West Indies, molasses from the West Indies to Britain, manufactured goods from Britain to Africa. In this century a new triangle, that of ideas, took shape between the West Indies, North America and Africa. West Indians were active in political movements in America and in Africa, and an increasing number of Africans were gaining a political education in America.

The very first Pan-African conference was organized in London in 1900, and was sponsored by a Trinidadian barrister, H. Sylvester Williams. A series of conferences followed, dominated by West Indians and Afro-Americans: Paris, 1919, London, Paris and Brussels, 1921, London, 1923, and New York, 1927. Only with the sixth, in Manchester in 1945, could there be said to have been significant African participation. The previous five had been led by the remarkable Dr Du Bois, and although the sixth had been organized by George Padmore, a Trinidadian, it was most clearly an African conference, dazzled by figures like Nkrumah and Kenyatta. It signalled the end of African patience: 'We are not ashamed to have been an age-long patient people', said part of the concluding declaration. 'We continue to sacrifice and strive. But we are unwilling to starve any longer while doing the world's drudgery in order to support by our poverty and ignorance the false aristocracy and a discarded imperialism.'[8]

It was only in 1958 that the Pan-African Congress, which had been formed in the Caribbean, came home to Africa, to newly independent Accra. Cross-fertilization of political ideas between the New World and Africa went on all through this century. African leaders, such as Azikiwe, Nkrumah, Banda and Eduardo Mondlane, were all educated in America.

In the period immediately following Ghanaian Independence, many Afro-Americans flocked to Ghana. 'They came like bees to a honeypot; straight from the ghetto

166

to the royal court', says one (white) by-stander. This is an unfair assessment from a partial source (the greater criticism is precisely that they were *not* from the ghettoes, but were bourgeois intellectuals) and denies the important role black Americans have played in the evolving philosophies of post-independence Africa. But it was true that a distinct community of black Americans gathered in and around Accra. Ghanaian Civil Servants remember with some resentment the ready ear that Nkrumah lent to his black American advisers, speech writers and ideologues. They became part of the ruling elite. In time, Nkrumah found he could command an unswerving loyalty from them which he could not do from as many senior Ghanaian figures. As we have seen, this is almost certainly because they shared his vision of an idealized, united Africa, which chimed with the Imagined Africa of the United States.

But they were not entirely a band of unscrupulous opportunists. Another section of the community was a highly talented group of black American artists and a significant number of academics and other professionals. Around these people, however, grew a further band of hangers-on and, probably, black American intelligence agents. As a kind of disillusion with Nkrumah crept into Ghana, the reactions of the black Americans polarized. They either remained completely loyal to the Osagyefo, or returned to the United States to denounce him. In either case, black Americans' reponses, invariably delivered in vigorous American terms, won them unpopularity, and as a group they came to be regarded with considerable suspicion.

Some of this suspicion was certainly justified. It is inconceivable that the Central Intelligence Agency did not have black agents placed in Ghana at that time. And, of course, other criticism from Afro-Americans had the familiar ring of the years through which disillusioned returnees have libelled the continent from afar. The opprobrium that was meted out to black Americans by Ghanaians unfortunately stuck to most of them in a particularly unfair way; many of them had, in fact, returned to Africa with perfectly acceptable ambitions and ideas, and had disapproved of the clique at Flagstaff House as much as had Ghanaians. Some of the backlash remains. A senior Ghanaian educationist

167

asked me in Accra: 'Do you think Afro-Americans can subvert independent Africa?' I said I didn't know a proper answer to that, with scores of unasked questions hovering behind it, but at least at face value the answer was No. He did not look convinced, but he said: 'You know, for the last three hundred years we haven't thought about them too much, if at all, and I don't suppose they've thought about us in any real sense.'

The black American, then, faces not only a number of particular problems in Africa but also general problems, shared with all expatriates anywhere and by people in more situations of a different kind than one at first suspects. (I was constantly struck by the similarities of the 'problems' of black Americans in Africa to those of newly-weds. The problems inherent in many white and many black,situations were simply made explicit and immediate by the merciless location, as if Africa were some violent kind of barium meal that showed up particular aspects of general living.)

Most other kinds of expatriate experience are, say those who know them, about the discovery of resources that would otherwise have stayed hidden, a curiously practical kind of self-knowledge, but also a fertilization of emotional qualities. For a black New Worlder, the surroundings have a direct bearing on this. It can be a joyous, if baffling, experience, as a black American doctor explained to me:

> When I first got here to Ghana in the early 'fifties I had all those emotional things, an exhilaration, a sort of pleasant anxiety. After a month or so of going around it became sort of like when you leave home as a kid and go to camp and there's the forest and then the moon comes out at night, here you are you're out in the forest by yourself, you and one or two other boys and you've got that Fine Feeling. You are starting out again in so many ways. So when I went into a village I began to look at the people. I had to get used to just *looking* at them, people moving in their own environment. How comfortable they felt moving in it; I was the one that felt uncomfortable. I found that this feller could be in

a village today and he'd put on his tie and go to the office tomorrow. Things like that, I mean he didn't have any hang-up about living in this village with all the rest, and working in the city. It was so good to see that already Africans were running the country. People were anxious for Independence yet I did not notice that there was any revengeful hate in these people. I never heard anybody discuss throwing any European into the sea or throwing bombs at anybody. I never saw anybody strike anyone. We would argue, but arguments never seemed to even be on the verge of coming to blows.

In the States I was used to that situation where survival was not just a matter of working and eating, but life itself could be threatened. You were always sharp, and always tense, like an antelope, because if you made the wrong leap it could be dangerous. You could find yourself in jail with no hope of any justice at the bar. The police department was no protector to black Americans. That was fifty per cent of your life. How can you grow like that, I mean you don't even know who you are half the time. Well that meant a great relaxation here at first. As for racial affinity, I think the feeling is growing. The longer I live here the more I realize what we have in common; we just don't know how to express it. But I'm patient. In the beginning I just assumed we had these affinities, then I went through a long stage of believing that there were so many irreconcilable differences, and now again I feel there are affinities. To a great extent the problem is the language. I should have concentrated on that when I first got here, but now people will always be able to tell I'm not a Ghanaian until the day I die. But I'd say I have five friends here. That's not bad you know. I lived for thirty-five years in the States and had five friends. But you have to understand that you've been brought up with all this racialism, and this has held back a part of you, not let you live, and now you can. At the same time you have a whole way of thinking aside from that, I guess a rational way of thinking things out, and they don't have that here. At least it's a different way, no, an alternative

way, sort of parallel. They might end up at the same
conclusion or they may not, but it's a whole mode that
you've got to accept as being just as right as yours, and
you've got to question your whole way of thinking.
This isn't as easy as that. You have got to really
understand their reactions, even if you don't understand
what this makes them do. What sort of things? I'd be in
good shape if I could answer that. It's responses to
different stimuli.

Take this: I want to put a little dam across a river on
my farm. Now this would be a wall twenty feet high,
with a million gallons of water. Isn't gonna cost them a
penny. Well, I run into trouble. A man would come and
tell me I can't put this thing here. If I put this dam here.
I'll cause lots of trouble. He'll go away. Next one would
come and say all the same things. There was so much
dissatisfaction. You could see the people weren't happy.
You'd expect them to be happy that somebody's going
to bring water that's never going to run dry. So much
water you can drink it and throw it away, even fish in
it. Plenty water. While all this was going on, I put a hose
in a little stream of water, to keep the people from
standing in the water, because there's Guinea worm all
round the place. I bought this hose, a long hose, two
hundred, three hundred feet long, and a pump. I put
this hose there, made a concrete pillar and mounted
the pump. They saw the water coming out the other
end, and I called these kids together and I said, 'See,
you don't have to stand in the water again.' I called the
head man of the village and said, 'Do you understand?'.
Oh, he understood it. I came back the next day and
somebody had cut the hose into about a hundred little
pieces. Anyway, I finally had it out with the chief,
just recently. I said, 'I don't come around your stool
too much because there's too many things I don't
understand.' I told him about the water. He said,
'Look, you know our people, er . . . ' I said, 'No, I don't
want one of those answers. Why do these people object
to the dam? You know, why don't you tell it to me?'
Finally he told me. He explained that there's this fetish

belief that the river god won't like that and you got to
do a certain ceremony before you can put that dam
there. I said, 'Really?' He said, 'Yes.' Now I don't want
to laugh at them, but that sounds kinda funny. So now,
I got to get this fetish priest and tell him to do this and
if he's agreeable we'll have to do this ceremony. One
sheep, two bottles of schnapps. But . . . Now a European
doesn't have to think twice about a thing like that. But
I have to say, well, I relate to these people in a different
way. I don't have to say *I* believe it but I have to know
if I have the instinct to accept it. Sure, it sounds funny,
but they believe that God is everything, not a man with
a beard. He's a composite of forces that make everything.
He's in that river, he's in all the animals, in all the people,
trees, everything. People are conscious of their
environment because they're inside their environment.
They're no better or worse, they just happen to be
human beings. They don't go around shooting animals
just to see them die. But I just want them to tell me, so's
I'll understand. I think I have come to understanding.
Not of this country in every way, because, you see, I
don't always know the questions to ask, never mind the
answers. But an understanding more of myself. A balance.

    I go and visit my mother in South Carolina, and after
a week or two, you feel the hostility in town, and I get
tired, my muscles start getting tired. I get fed up. I don't
want to test this hostility and get that unpleasant feeling
of finding it is true, that these people, the white people,
feel hostility to me. My mother took me to see a white
friend of hers, and she walked round back of the house.
My mother thought I wouldn't notice. I just sat there
and let her get on with it. She'd think I was making a
big fuss about nothing. But I sat there and listened to
her condescending friend and when she'd finished I
thanked her very much, and she asked me if I'd ever
come to live in this again, and I said no, and she wanted
to know why. I said that would take me a long time,
and I don't think she'd really stand that . . . so . . . I see
my mother get tense and she thinks I'm going to start on
it, but I'm not going to make her unhappy. I come back
here and relax.

A black American girl from New York said:

You're away from the racism, and that's the plus side.
But when you get here all your supports are removed too.
Not just family and friends or anything, but all the
other things, community, television, familiar food, a
familiar street with lots of things you understand going
on in it, all these things support you. Then you get to
realize that these things kind of divide you from
yourself, you put them on like clothes that disguise
you from what you are, and you don't have time to
wonder. Here, the whites support each other, they have
contact with all the familiar things from back home.
But when I came here I wanted to forget about back
home, cut myself off from the bad things, and just, well,
forget it ever happened. When I first got here I found
there weren't all those distractions, and you'd sit in a
room and it was like an empty room, not even you in it.
You'd notice yourself doing things in a way you didn't
before. White people come here, say, at my age. They're
twenty-six and they can go right ahead being twenty-six,
they're just in another country. But when you come
like I came here then you go back to being a little girl,
starting again; and then later you find that you are a
much older twenty-six than you were before.

Some Afro-Americans go to Africa hoping to see black
people 'kicking a few white asses', as one put it. But for
most it is a short-lived hope that recedes into being a time-
wasting irrelevance. In Ghana the black American business
community is now a small one, mostly concentrated in light
engineering concerns on the huge Kaneshie Industrial Estate
in Accra. Businessmen agree that to conduct a business in
Africa demands more time than it would in the United
States, just as many expatriate wives talk of the increased
amount of time they spend on and with their homes and
families once they are cut off from a highly developed
system of child-distraction. While the wives talked of having
to find new resources to amuse their children in an educative
way, the businessmen talked not only of vastly increasing the
amount of time they spent on their business but of a new and

172

different kind of initiative needed, and of correspondingly more flavoursome rewards. One explained:

> You've got to adjust to the fact that people ain't going to show up at the time you expect them, even on the *day* you expect them. They're going to do the opposite of what you instruct them to do — I guess this is a hangover from the colonial days when they didn't listen to what the white masters said and really went their own sweet way — and just getting things done, Lord, what an effort! The phones don't work, I mean you don't simply ring up and order an expansion valve or something, and most of the other services aren't really up to efficient management. It all goes at a puzzling kind of pace. I spend twice as much time on the business as I did in the States. But what the hell? Here I feel it's *mine.*

The tone is often this combination of commercial impatience — a universal emotion — and a desperate desire to be counted in. The frustration of the incomprehending and incompatible colonial is often reflected in these new managers, but the expression of this frustration is uneasy, since the New World black is more edgily and emotionally involved than the colonial. Their early days sometimes brought them into conflict with the former colonists. A black American manufacturing electrical goods said to me:

> I came here strictly for business motives, although I had always a strong feeling for Africa. Despite everything — shortages, inefficiency, not being able to get hold of things when you want them, having a hard time if you need something like concrete — I have never lost that feeling of having come back to my original home. What I did not anticipate was the tough struggle it would be to get established. I sort of assumed that we would be more welcome than the British. This was not so. When I got here, just after Independence, I found I had to fight the British to get any foothold on the market. There were British advisers who were effectively making industrial and commercial

decisions. There seemed to be an unspoken agreement
between the Americans, British and French that this
was British territory. Only comparatively recently
have the French started moving in. I hadn't expected
this at all. I expected that if you went into an office
and asked a Ghanaian a question you'd get an answer.
But instead, he'd say come back tomorrow, and
meanwhile he'd have asked the British adviser.

In the context of being owner of industrial capital, the black
American boss has a slightly contradictory attitude towards
his nominal managerial overlordship. He is especially
sensitive of any appearance of exploitation inherent in any
boss situation, black or white. Being highly motivated
towards success, he is often uncomfortable in a situation
which places him in direct succession to white former
colonials. His problem is: does he express frustrations that
echo those of the colonials who frequently introduced a
racist edge into their carping, or does he accept practices that
he knows, as a Westerner, to be industrially inefficient? The
success motivation is much deeper and more personally
involving than for the white boss. A contractor from
California told me:

> I wanted to spend my life as much a man as anybody
> else. I hadn't been doing badly in the States — maybe
> about a hundred and eighty dollars a week — and
> California was never particularly heavy race-wise. I
> never felt I was discriminated against in any direct way.
> But I wanted something of my own that I could not
> have had in the States. Do I feel a man here? Yes,
> without any doubt at all. In the States, when I
> travelled, every white man called you Boy, whether
> you were eight or eighty, they never seemed to call
> you by name. Here, you are Mister. I doubt if I could
> have done all this in America. No doubt I could have
> made a go of a business, but would I have been
> comfortable? Or happy? All that hustle and bustle. I
> picked up a magazine the other day, and there was a
> chap I knew better than my own brother. He was in
> Watts. The Government had given him loans and all, and

he had in a few years built up a billion dollar business. There are a lot of black Americans who have done very well since those riots. But I have no desire to go back to the United States. If they take this from me, I'll just fold up my little things and get out. That would be too bad, although I must admit I would understand them wanting to close people like me down, being a foreigner, better than I can understand being intimidated out of a black business in a white area in America. This is no place for the uptight Afro, this is no place to solve their problems. They should go straight back. What is exciting, maybe easier, but a hell of a challenge, is that you had the feeling the country was starting from scratch, and not just you and your business. This meant that all the fundamental analysis you have to do to start a business was being applied to the whole country and this makes your decision-making easier, if not necessarily less time-consuming.

Another black American said:

When I was a kid I had a dream about building a great dam across the Niger. I've no idea why, I don't think I even knew where the Niger was. I also had a crystal set, and a buddy and I later had this world map, and we'd pretend to talk to each other. I always had this feeling about Africa, I wanted to be there, even from being a kid. I remember at school, a teacher actually said: 'There's not much point teaching them anything, they're going to be nothing but janitors.' What would she say if she knew I was now technical director of a large company in Africa?

This status is richly satisfying for the black brought up with stultified expectations of life. It brings him a respect and an involvement that might have been denied the white, and a social level that might be denied the black in America. The black American owner of a prosperous electronics factory in Accra put it in this way:

You know that when you come here you aren't coming to the Promised Land, you are in a situation of more strenuous job survival than in the United States, but you have the chance to meet the challenge. I didn't feel the lifting of any burden when I came here, as it happened, but I feel I'm advancing at last in a thousand and one different ways. You slowly begin to learn what is expected of you. You build up a social group as you would anywhere. You fit into a small wedge of social life. Not roaming through the whole of society. The people you were close to, say, at school, you were just close to because you were with them every day, but here you have something more, you are close *despite* the things that might set you apart. One thing I didn't realize was this business of coming to see you early in the morning, four or five in the morning. This is a measure of very high regard, to ask your advice at four in the morning. This guy came round soon after I got here. Well, in the States if anyone knocks on your door at that time, he's crazy or he's a mugger or something, but I had the sense to sit there and listen.

The shade of Samuel Smiles looks kindly on those black Americans with application and with expertise in engineering or construction work, for instance. But the threat of dispossession is as strong for the black expatriate as for the white.

In 1970, the Ghanaian Government passed a Business Promotions Act which ruled that foreign-owned businesses with a turnover of less than 500,000 cedis (£170,000) a year should be turned over to Ghanaians. The measure was primarily aimed at Nigerian petty traders, and very nearly a million Nigerians were expelled, but the ruling did not affect the massive European trading firms. Some smaller Afro-Americans and West Indians who had not put their businesses into their Ghanaians wives' names were caught in the middle, and there was considerable resentment that the white-owned monopolies should remain intact.

Most of the New Worlders were big enough to escape the measure, but among those affected was the Majors family. Edith Majors, now a grandmother, arrived in Ghana in 1966, a week before the country's first military *coup*. She gradually built up a small catering business, supplying an aluminium company at the new port of Tema. She was relieved of her business in 1970, so she moved to neighbouring Togo, where she now runs a small hotel in the capital, Lome. Her experience has probably tempered her expectations about Africa, now more wisely based on business, rather than on emotion. She is critical of her stay in a formerly British colony, and some of her comments are fairly typical of many black American expatriates:

I tried to behave like a human being to my servants, but it didn't work. They just thought you were a fool. There was so much cheating and thieving, and that ain't pleasant for a black person in a black country. Their attitude was just like ours in the States. If white folks don't have money there, it's their own fault, because they have all the chances, therefore they are fair game. The Ghanaian servants thought that, well, we had the money to pay our passage here, so they never looked on it as cheating. They were simply profiting from somebody else's ingorance or inexperience. There seemed to be a greater bridge between them and the Europeans than between them and us, and that hurt, because you felt that they were looking at people of another nationality through colonial eyes. It seemed to be the only way they could look at people, the only way they could be comfortable. You'd feel so much about them, but they just thought you were crazy. I was once in the market and I saw this pregnant girl. A week later she was back at her stall scooping things in her hand into the baby's mouth. I said to the girl's mother, 'That's not right, you know,' and the mother said, pointing to the girl, 'See her? That's how she was fed. So?' See, they wouldn't let you be concerned.

So Edith and her family (which seemed to expand and contract before one's eyes, but which actually numbers thirteen) run the hotel, Edith's Inn, as a haven for Peace Corps and V.S.O. volunteers, youthful travellers, black and white, and other mavericks who have a taste for smothered chicken, doughnuts, cupcakes and peanut butter and jelly sandwiches on the shimmering coast of the Gulf of Guinea. Edith takes in the volunteers with smashed knees and collar bones, or with typhoid fever (there is also a dreaded hepatitis room) and talk in the hotel takes in animism and the bargains to be had in the markets in Niamey and Douala and Ouagadougou; Edith's elderly father, in flowing cotton, picks his way through the pell-mell of crash helmets with a *demi* of *pression* in his hand, smilingly practising his minimal French.

Edith's son Butch had arrived in Togo two months before I visited it and he was a not untypical example of the growing raft of young, decidedly *un*mystical Afro-Americans now travelling to Africa. His ambitions were: to make a wooden clock, with wooden working parts, a hang glider, the first in West Africa, and one million dollars. He will assuredly make all three. As he said to me:

Being mechanical you start ahead of the game in Africa. I was a good mechanic in the States, but well, you know . . . I always thought of myself as a lazy person, always having jobs that entailed afternoon or evening work, but here, man, I get up at six o'clock in the morning. All that racism stuff, that's behind me, that's for the bums. All that averted eyes, uh uh! Funny, I get on with white Americans just great here. I guess the worst kind of bigot just doesn't come to Africa. Here, you have a respected position in society as a technician. In Africa I've moved into a whole new social scene.

Before I could ask the obvious question, he went on: 'I mean I mix with ambassadors now . . . here, you move up in a way you couldn't in the States.' I said that a number of white volunteers I had met in the hotel had expressed misgivings about coming to Africa, finding that they were translated into a professional class in which they felt uncomfortable, and that they attracted an exaggerated respect which they considered they did not deserve and which set them apart from students and colleagues. In answer Butch said: 'I don't know. I don't know too many Togolese. I haven't moved outside this compound much since I

got here. I've been too busy discovering all the things
I never knew I could do till I got here . . . '

Expatriate black businessmen may ultimately gain personal,
emotional rewards that are very different from those awaiting
the white businessman. At the same time, they live
reasonably well, within a circle which may include a certain
number of African industrialists and customers. In many ways
they live like any other expatriate businessman: in Africa,
but not of Africa. They are shielded from the poignancy of
this by their relative affluence. To some extent this is also
true of black New Worlders who take up long-term
professional jobs in Africa. The academics are insulated
in much the same arbitrary way as any foreign academic
would be. The lawyers move towards a legal or
functionary circle. There is perhaps even less class mobility
among the professionals than among the thrusting
industrialists.

People with high academic qualifications do not seem to
have escaped the lure of Imagined Africa. But quite often
professionals arrive and find they have not got instant
communication with the land of their forefathers, but a
servant problem. 'What I can't stand is the petty thieving,
the petty petty thieving', cried the West Indian wife of a
Ghanaian professional man. 'One lot of servants have just left
taking a whole lot of the children's clothes, the coloured
ones they can't wear at boarding school. They don't steal
anything worth taking. Why can't they do a Great Train
Robbery? Why do they take old clothes and leave the new
ones?'

Rather more profound reservations also abound. A West
Indian who has held a professorial post in West Africa for
more than ten years talked to me about a number of them:

When I arrived, impressions followed very rapidly.
The airport hotel was a very primitive affair. The beds
were smelly, you didn't want to sit anywhere. Usually
airport hotels are the best in town, so we thought
if *that's* the best in town . . . There was no one to
meet us — our children were very small then — and
when we got here, we found a pile of our telegrams.

'Oh, these things take time', they said. Ugh, that
hotel! It was all shuttered and dark and gloomy, and
heat, heat, heat, I couldn't stop sleeping. I thought,
well, I've got to adjust, it is all so important to me. So
I thought I'd learn the language. The language here is
terribly difficult. It's all to do with intonation. But I
started. Then I stopped. I realized the awful blunders
I could make. I understand it now, but I don't think
I could ever speak it without giving offence. There was
an English professor of local languages, and I figured
he was a great, great expert, having lived here for
twenty years, but then I discovered they were
laughing behind his back. So it's the language that
always reminds you that you are in a foreign land, and
that's very disappointing. Take the word *okro*, well,
it can mean okra, of course, but given different
intonations it can mean rat, and spirit, and God knows
what else. Just think of the *faux pas* you could make
in more delicate abstract areas. I have seen the effects
of the mistakes people have made. I mean there are
people who still don't speak to me because I waved
to them with my left hand. Learning the language
would be like the first great step on the Moon. Maybe
living on the Moon would be more comfortable.

The children have lived nearly all their lives in this
country, but they now feel neither West Indian nor
African. They have become rather withdrawn. I'm
very worried about this. In the first place, they are
physically isolated. Secondly, I imagine it must be
very difficult to grow up in a community you are
not emotionally a part of, and which you feel your
parents aren't part of either. I do like Africans a very
great deal, and I don't feel rejected by them in the
least. Not in an everyday conscious way. They don't
try to push you out all the time. But some part of
you is certainly starved. Some part of your ego is not
used at all. You recognize this when you go back
home. Something clicks. In the plane, with West
Indian stewards, other West Indians, suddenly something happens to you that hasn't happened to you for
a long time. Here you have a kind of tenseness, always

being careful you're not going to offend somebody.
When you get home you feel so much this release of
tension. We have been going home once every four years,
and each time we go back we are more like strangers,
especially to young people. If this went on, we'd not
feel at home anywhere, so we may well move on, or go
back. Of course, the compensation is that we meet
a bigger variety of people than at home. I can't decide
whether the last ten years have been a plus or a
minus in my life. I would tend to say a plus because
I'm an optimist. My wife would take a balancing view.
She hasn't cared for it so much. Sometimes I wonder
what I have done to my family bringing them here.

For younger Afro-Americans the sharp withdrawal of illusion
can be indistinguishable from the pain of growth. A former
Peace Corps volunteer, a black girl from Memphis,
Tennessee, talked of this:

I went to college at eighteen, and meeting Nigerians was
the turning point. Their country seemed to have so much
more going for them than mine appeared to for me at that
time. They kind of adopted me, and I started going with
one of them. They did a real fine propaganda job on me.
There was no racial discrimination in Nigeria, they said,
black people had dignity there. This guy and I got engaged.
There was all the romance, then, of marrying somebody
who was so different from anybody I had ever known.
I had all these positive attitudes about Africa, but still I
didn't know anything about it as a place. I very definitely
felt that this was my real home. We had a beautiful plan:
I was going to marry him, my honey would come back
to Nigeria after my first year there, and I was going to be
the best Peace Corps volunteer the world has ever known.
Well, first thing, the Peace Corps didn't co-operate.
They sent me to eastern Nigeria. I was disillusioned. I
had naturally assumed it would be the west. Then, when
I got there I started getting some very negative attitudes
about Nigeria and our letters got colder and colder. I saw
so many negative things that somehow people hadn't
got around to telling me about. I was absolutely appalled

by the slums. They'd told me about the new buildings
in the Marina area. And then the open sewers in the
streets of Lagos. Also I didn't have the right kind of
clothes. I arrived for training with twenty cents in my
purse. I had gone to Chicago to see my honey, so I had
nothing. I was buying cigarettes with my pocket money.
I was uncomfortable and overwhelmed. After all I had
expected!

Affinities? I didn't expect to feel like a foreigner. In
Onitsha I was going round saying *kedu* [hallo] in Ibo.
At first people were interested in me because of my black
skin. They commented that I spoke Ibo perfectly and I knew
very well that I could hardly speak it at all. Many of
them said I would have no trouble learning it because I
was black, but I knew it wasn't true. I felt foreign
despite the fact that — or because of the fact that —
people were telling me I wasn't, and it seemed so
condescending. The school I was to teach at was very
new; there were a lot of teachers who didn't have the
proper qualifications, people just out of secondary
school. I can remember being in the house with a couple
of young girl teachers. They were my age, and I didn't
know how to talk to them. They were asking me about
dating, and I knew it was so different in Nigeria, but I
didn't know how. I just couldn't talk to them as I could
to girls back home. I was more comfortable with the
American principal and the two white American
volunteers, who were unfortunately leaving. The English
was spoken in a different way — you were aware that
for them it was a foreign language — and that there were
things they wouldn't be able to express, and not
necessarily just because of the language. You had the
feeling that the potential of what people say to you is
limited by their intellect or grasp of ideas or intimacy
with you, not by their grasp of language itself. I had
loved to hear my boy-friend talking as I'd never heard
English spoken before. But everybody in Nigeria was
talking like that, and it began to get irritating. I was
explaining about dating, where a boy would come to
your house and meet your parents, and he would take you
out for the evening somewhere, then he would bring you

home again, and go away. They kept calling boys 'my friend' — I had to get out of calling people 'my friends' — and their method was that everybody among their contemporaries knew whose 'friend' you were, but not the parents. It was sort of understood, but surreptitious. Even with older girls. This upset me rather because I had this idea that Africans weren't hung up on sex in the way Americans were. It upset me that things weren't free and easy.

I wasn't sure how to react in certain situations. Once, there were three or four young guys from the government secondary school who turned up at my place. I invited them into my living room, and they drank beer and talked and things, but as time went by I wasn't at all sure that this was the done thing, whether they should be there or not. I had a sneaking suspicion that they were checking me out. I didn't know what to do. I would quite often find myself in situations like that, and you just have to carry them through. I would quite often have a room full of people staying the night when they came into town, and I'm sure the people on the staff had some very strange ideas. But nobody came right out and said anything. Now, nothing that I would call untoward happened, but I would never know what was on other people's minds. All in all, you could say the year was a disaster. All my beautiful plans and ideas came apart. This guy and I broke it off, I was a lousy teacher, and I can't honestly say I liked the country, and that was certainly because I was expecting too much affinity. Now I'm less easily convinced of things. When you come to Africa you can live here and be very happy, but not if you are some kind of phoney African, not if you are a romantic, and not unless you apply yourself to it consciously and without illusions. Being black I would say I get more initial courtesy than white people — possibly — but it's no great help in making intimate friends, and I don't suppose that I have more intimate friends in Africa now that I've returned, than any white person here has.

Some who return to find a cure for alienation in physical exile find that all they have is exile. They find that it is not merely colour that has led to their alienation, but a much wider socio-historical pressure. Removing the colour cause of the problem does not remove the results of the wider pressure, at least not overnight. A young black from New York said:

> You find that you as a black person have been hated, discriminated against and all the rest. But it's what you represent as a black man that scares the shit out of the white people and makes them hate you and makes them drive you out by his actions. Coming here makes you realize what the white man has done to you. Just getting into an all-black society doesn't alter that. He hasn't insulted your colour alone, but your whole manhood. Africa's not going to give you that back. You've got to find it for yourself. For me, I could only find it in Africa. But it didn't come from Africa.

Others talk of the shock of Africa being the discovery, not of a new uninhibited self, but of precisely the contrary. They find they have not unleashed an unfettered, expressive personality but have become more enclosed in a reflectiveness that is fostered by the newly yawning amounts of undistracted time. They are sometimes appalled, in retrospect, at their naivety, and this experience is also salutary, although it probably means that they will not tarry for long in Africa. A young black from New York at the University of Ghana discussed this point:

> My idea of coming here was to work with people who had been untouched by the 'evil influences' of the Western world. That's hogwash, of course. But in the West you have lost perspective in the tinsel. What you do, physically or intellectually, is covered in a routine that seems normal, but is in fact irrelevant. Tinsel. One is trained not to rummage around in the tinsel to get at the core of things. Well there certainly isn't any tinsel here, yet the core is elusive too. You are dealing with a rustic society, and I mean that in the purest, most positive way. The core of things, as one might describe it, is also disguised, but in Africa by much more

dynamic things, like by survival itself. I realize now I
am most definitely a Westerner, an urban person, and
this is why I won't extend my contract. When I say I
want something at twelve o'clock, I mean at twelve
o'clock. I can't put up with not getting things done.
I think I have become much more hypersensitive here.
Prejudice never came home to me much in the States.
But I find the confrontation between black and white
much more clear-cut in Africa. Obviously there aren't
as many whites here, but the whole business is less subtle
here than in America. I find the European people are
really common, they've got no class at all. The British
are always saying they love black up one wall and down
the other. I say it's because they're sleeping with black.
   I find it's a whole different business, making friends
here also. I find I have not made friends I can confide
in. You find that goes on for a while, then you find
yourself not seeking the kind of friendship in which one
would confide. It teaches you a whole lot about self-
reliance. There is nobody to lean on. You're like a child
that runs around trusting until his face gets slapped a
few times. You therefore have to face situations alone,
find their solutions alone, and learn to live with those
solutions alone. It's more than being rebuffed, because
you consciously work situations so you know you won't
be rebuffed. I just happened to grow. This is perhaps why
I don't like Ghana because growing is a painful business.
But I am more self-aware, in the literal sense of being
aware of myself, seeing yourself as a psychic bulk, not
necessarily seeing in detail or understanding. You are
also aware of shades of meaning of words like alienation,
identity, self-awareness, outsider. These are not sudden
steps from a negative state. You don't just step into an
identity like you step into a room. I realize that I'm a
little alienated, and a whole lot more self-aware. I tried
to relate to Africa and I still dig so much of it. But it is
a question of me rather than it. I find that I haven't
been completely giving of myself here, and that a new
and private self has developed. You slowly develop into
a different mould of person as a black person in Africa.
When a brick is taken away from your psychic structure,

another one is put in its place, so you end up rebuilding most of it.

For older Afro-Americans and West Indians this reconstruction of reactions is not always painful. Many — notably West Indians, who had often spent some time in another country before they had moved to Africa — find it a positive and exciting experience. Of course, this change is never made in some, and they live reasonably happily in replicas of American homes all over Africa, apart but secure. But for most, some degree of inner reshuffle is necessary. There is talk of relief as poisons seep away, and one man talked of gaining a new knowledge, but also a new innocence. 'Not for one day in fifteen years has it stopped being an adventure,' he said. But one attitude that tenaciously clings is an impatience that comes perilously close to ignorant complaint. A black U.S. Government official gave me a lecture on the 'Balkanization' of West Africa, the need for national unity and further regional grouping. 'What is the viability of Togo or Dahomey?' he said. 'A vast amount of resources are wasted both in keeping groups apart and trying to keep them together.' He said this with seeming disregard for the amounts annually wasted by his own Federal Government in trying to keep the United States together, and the squalid political deals made in America to appease regional interests. Another said: 'They're just not Can Do people', a phrase with chilling connotations today in the United States. At the same time, many found themselves in a dilemma: which of the two potentially corrosive forces of complaisance and impatience do you succumb to? Do you become as inert as Ghanaian society can often seem to be, and at least achieve an undented peace of mind? Or do you continually hector and harry and complain and thereby try to get things moving, consequently earning for yourself unpopularity and a sizeable ulcer? The conundrum is as old as black immigration itself. One hundred years ago, Blyden wrote an account of the travails of the black immigrant Hilary Teague as a newspaper editor in Liberia. Part of it runs:

> To perpetrate an editorial he seats himself — not in the cushioned boudoir of the literate idler . . . but in a little

sooty apartment of six by eight. Beneath his dingy foolscap a portion of deal . . . on an empty barrel. At his side an inkstand . . . – the small end of a cow's horn – on his left a quiver of quills rifled from the upper surface of a porcupine.

The boy comes for copy . . . he thus begins. 'The press, the omnipotent press, is the most powerful engine which it has ever been the lot of mortals to possess. It is the scourge of tyrants . . . the Palladium of civil liberty . . .'

'There is no cassado for breakfast, sir.'

'Well go and get some and don't bother me.'

'I have no money, sir . . . '

'Can't you borrow some?'

'No sir: I've tried . . . '

'Well, go and collect some money . . . '

'Mr – says he has no money . . . Mr – says he don't like the paper now . . . Mr – says your paper is scurrilous. Mr – says there is too much politics and too little religion . . . '

'That will do . . . call again in an hour for copy . . . '

'The ram has gnawed the roller, sir.'

'Well, cast another.'

'We have no molasses, sir.'

'Well, shut up the office and go to dinner.'[9]

A West Indian stoic in modern Ghana said: 'I have realized that time is not that important to me any more. It is what you really do that counts. You come to understand that if they did get things done, if they could do all these things, then they wouldn't need expatriates, you'd have no use to them, and there'd be no point in your being here in the first place.'

But a young mother from Trinidad had a different view:

How are you supposed to bring up your children? They see you getting irritated with some of the people, and you don't want to pass those attitudes on. Especially when their father is African too. I must say my husband gets impatient too. But sometimes your irritations are exaggerated and you can't stop

yourself. You wonder whether you should try and
teach them [the children] patient understanding, in
which case they might end up as completely
ineffective people, or whether you should make them
impatient people who want to get things done. That sort
of person is the only kind who could get this society
moving. But then they grow up frustrated and they
would be unbearable to live with. What sort of expectations
and reactions should you give them?

Most black expatriates are aware that their actions and
attitudes are open to misunderstanding, that impatience, for
instance, can be mistaken for brashness and hostility. Their
sensitivity has to be greater than that of the white expatriate.
The judgments of a European are — so New Worlders claim —
slavishly heeded, but are, in fact, as often impassively
ignored. Unpalatable as it is to black expatriates,
Europeans do have a status in independent anglophone West
Africa; it is the status of former master, former mentor. It
is the complex and equivocal result of a long experience, the
qualities of which are debatable and insidious. They are
rooted in the massive crimes committed by Europeans in
Africa, in the overlordship itself, with its degradations and
benefits, in the pride at having shaken off this overlordship,
in the effects of some of the more advantageous aspects of it.
    The opinions of Europeans are accordingly treated with
a degree of either respect or contempt in the light of this
historical and familiar status. It is a position in no way
resembling the lofty status many Europeans in Africa seem
to think it is, and white opinions are treated with more
objectivity than they suspect. But the status remains a
kind of basis for interaction between white Europeans and
black Africans. It is, for better or worse, a social fact in
Ghana, a constant that has developed as much through
education as through unpleasantness in contacts with
Europeans.
    But for Africa, New World blacks are, for the most part,
still a social novelty, and in a country such as Ghana there
is no such widespread basis of familiarity on which to base an
assessment of black American opinion. Afro-Americans will
most certainly not be allowed to impose opinions

uncommonly similar to those of former masters who are no longer in a position to express them themselves. The process of setting up this basis for inter-action, especially between Ghanaians and black Americans, is under way at this moment, and as with even the less objectionable aspects of colonialism, it is a process that is not free of friction. Meanwhile, many prefer to be careful, as we have seen, even at the expense of a critical part of the expressive self.

Bridge-building between Afro-Americans and Africans is not always greeted with unlimited approval. American blacks are often disappointed that most Africans do not appear to have more than a summary interest in the slave trade or history of black America. One attempt at such bridge-building led to a stiffly executed minuet of conflicting interests and mutual misunderstanding among a group of black Americans, one European embassy and the Ghanaian Government.

Some seventy miles west of Accra is the village of Abandze-Cormantine, tucked into a bay beside Saltpond, where Chief Sam's men had stepped ashore in 1915. On a headland above the village stands Fort Amsterdam, originally built by the British in 1631 as a trading fort. In the ensuing rivalry of the slave trade, the fort changed hands between the British and Dutch many times. It was finally taken over by the Ashanti at the end of the last century, and since then it has fallen into some dilapidation. It stands at the western end of a spectacular arch of beach, lizards running around its rusty old cannon, overlooking the dun-coloured roofs of the fishing village below. Goats snuffle and nibble around the bottom of the steps leading up to it. The air carries the tang of the herring and mackerel that are smoked in clay stoves beneath it. The Fort might have grown slowly more encrusted with years, occasionally visited by students of the slave trade and by those tempted from one of the Accra—Takoradi roads that run alongside. In 1966, Dr C.L. Temminck Groll, Holland's leading Africanist, visited the forts of the Ghana coast, and his resulting study aroused interest in Holland in the castles. A collection was taken up among Dutch companies with interests in Ghana, and it was decided that two forts should be renovated or cleaned up. Onè was at Butri, beside Takoradi, and the other was Fort

Amsterdam. Some six thousand dollars were collected and work began on the site at Butri.

In 1971, an Afro-American organization was formed, the African Descendants Association Foundation (A.D.A.F.), and at a libation held in memory of Louis Armstrong at Fort Amsterdam, it was announced that a centre was to be founded at the Fort, where, said Dr Robert Lee, its executive director, 'we will learn to work together for the upliftment of Africa.' Dr Lee went on: 'It is a moving thing for brothers, long separated, to come together again to talk, sing, dance, and to clasp hands and rejoin the broken links that bound them together.'[10]

A local newspaper reported: 'A group of distinguished sons of Africa have bound themselves together and imposed upon themselves an historical and sacred task.' For Amsterdam, said the newspaper, had been 'acquired' by the group; renovation work would be carried out by them.[11] An agreement was entered into whereby A.D.A.F. would lease the fort, at a nominal rental, from the Government on condition they spent two thousand dollars a year in renovation and allowed free access to the public. A.D.A.F. instituted a fund — if you subscribed a hundred dollars or more, your name would be inscribed on the Soul Scroll at the Fort — and erected a notice: 'The walls have cracked and the roofs have fallen down from the moans and tears of the unfortunate men, women and children, and from the assault of greedy, lustful, inhuman men, and lastly from the weapons of the gods.'

While insisting that they found the inscription in no way offensive, the Dutch felt obliged to point out that an amount of Dutch money had been subscribed to renovate the Fort.[12] Perhaps sensing an inelegant squabble, the Ghanaian Government declared that there had been a military *coup* and a change of government since the agreement had been drafted, and therefore it had not been ratified. The Afro-Americans were, however, allowed to continue renovation work. An edgy, if *sotto voce,* three-cornered dispute followed, with the Ghanaian Government still insisting that nothing had been 'acquired' by anybody,[13] the Afro Americans determined to create a memorial and focus for visiting American blacks, and the Dutch embassy spending a

190

great deal of time extricating itself from the argument.

The incident was principally notable for the bafflement each party showed over the arguments of the others, arguments that seemed to be presented with reasonable logic. Dr Lee said: 'Just recently a very very highly educated African said: "What do you want to fool with this slave thing for? It's something better forgotten." I said: "Well I wasn't the one that created all this." I don't see why they should get all upset with me. The Fort's sitting there, look at what it is. There's no secret. They say that if you leave it alone, the whole thing will die out. I say no. I mean, the Israelis still remember.'

The bafflement and intransigence make this a much more typical incident between Africans and Afro-Americans than any open hostility would be. The matter simmered for a considerable amount of time, with much mutual indecisiveness. It was inertia that finally produced a non-settlement, with all parties still unclear about their situation. But at least ruffled feathers had been smoothed by the passage of time.

Such small incidents show, perhaps, that one kind of African inertia can solve some problems, but also that in a prickly confrontation Afro-Americans can appear to Africans to be acting in a peremptory or imperious manner, when in fact, within their own context, they are merely trying to create something they believe to be reaching out to Africans. These tiny diplomatic irritations arise too easily between Afro-Americans and Africans, as many report, with seemingly no fault on either side. A Ghanaian civil servant commented: 'They want to create a memorial for Afro-America! What is that to us? They want to take from us for themselves, not to give to us.' One assumes that once the bridges have been more successfully built and consolidated, contact on this level will be less highly fraught.*

---

*A good many Afro-Americans are infuriated — and Africans are just as infuriated at Afro-Americans for pointing it out — at the widespread fashion of wearing straight-hair wigs. An article appeared during the spring of 1973 in the cyclostyled magazine of Volta Hall, the women's residential hall at Legon. 'Wig-wearing and hair-straightening is contradictory

For the most part, Afro-American and West Indian settlers try to avoid, as far as is possible, such small confrontations, and many believe that communication will be achieved in quite another, indirect, way.

In the early 1960s, it was fashionable to describe, in Pliny's phrase, *(Ex Africa semper aliquid novi)* as Something New Out Of Africa the newly established dialogue between black Americans and independent Africans in Africa.[14] It was assumed that in some way the dialogue was in itself significant. A decade later this dialogue has made great inroads in the general apathy and ignorance Africans show towards the problems of black America. There is still an imperfect understanding, but at any rate an amount of good will and patience. This patience is crucial to what may yet turn out to be the Something New of the 'seventies and 'eighties, something a great deal more than dialogue, possibly a synthesis. Black Americans are much more likely to retain their American identity in the communications-ridden twentieth century than did the Brazilians in the nineteenth. It is improbable that organized repatriation will ever   ever succeed on any large scale. Back-to-Africa movements will undoubtedly continue to form in the United States, and they will undoubtedly be of great political importance to black America. But actual mass repatriation, no. It will continue to be individuals who attempt to re-form their patterns of life in Africa itself. Black Americans in independent West Africa will not form communities as such, but will have a very important individual impact. They will not assimilate in their own lifetimes. The tradition of immigration is still — outside of Sierra Leone and Liberia — a very recent one. But there are signs that Afro-Americans who emigrated in the 1950s — entirely different from the earlier West Indians — may produce a synthesis of an African Afro-American, with African traditions formed in *African* societies. A second generation of such immigrants is only now, in the first half

---

to the revolution that is taking place within your country and for Black people all over the world', said the American writer. This mutual irritation rises to a crescendo during the summer, with the visits of young and somewhat tactless Afro-American students.

of the 1970s, emerging. This generation of the children of immigrants has been educated in African schools, and will probably marry Africans, and that could mean a dilution of American influence, but equally an adaptation of American ways to an African setting.

Meanwhile, the parents will remain American. The most intriguing way for this synthesis to show itself is certainly through the marriages of black American and West Indian women to Africans. These marriages are among the most interesting and challenging of cross-cultural phenomena in recent times.

CHAPTER 6

My Son the African

'I once wondered how it would feel to arrive back in
Anomabu (home of Aggrey and Robert Gardiner) and be
referred to simply as Kodwo's wife, rather than as "the
American" wife of! For I am black, have been twelve years
married, dress in the traditional Ghanaian "cloth", speak
a bit of the Fante language, as a type have features
indistinguishable from my in-laws, have lived and worked
for eight years in West and East Africa. Politically, I am
firmly aligned with those working towards a genuine
economic and political liberation of Black Africa.
Nevertheless, for the likes of me in Africa, "Black" does
not yet fully mean "belonging".'

(From an article in *Africa* magazine, March 1973[1])

'I guess it's *fufu* for lunch, hamburgers for dinner.'

(Black American wife in Ghana)

A black American widow of enormous vivacity and courage gave me an account of an experience which, while not necessarily common, at least sums up many of the fears that must tread spectrally at the back of the minds of many black expatriate wives. She had been married to her West African husband, a lawyer, for some years, and shortly after the independence of his country they had decided to return excited and full of delicious apprehension:

I knew before I came what was going on here. We got newspapers over a period of six or seven years, a huge batch of them every month, so you could follow what was happening with the pictures and everything, you could see how many schools were being built, and you could read the ads and see what commodities were around. The fabric of the life was before us. I was thoroughly broken in by the time I came so I was more fortunate than others. But before I came I insisted that I was to be allowed to do exactly what I wanted within my four walls. When I went out in the early days — and this is still true — if the hostess said to go here, stay there, I stayed there, and tried not to offend by putting a foot wrong. But in my own house, I would do what the hell I liked.

Getting here was so nice. They brought me into the queen mother's house, and they were all dressed in white — does that mean happiness or welcome? — anyway my husband had taught me some of the local language, every Wednesday for eight years, so I understood a lot of what was going on. On the boat coming over I had sat in the sun an awful lot, so I was very dark. 'He's brought one of his own back,' they said, and I had real kinky hair, and that went down

197

just like gold. That first bit was the best bit of all. The
next thing you discover is how strong, real good and
strong, the family system really is. But it's only too
strong if the man doesn't let them know where he
stands with them. If he's a softy, people will take
advantage. Mr G. had his two worlds, and you can't do
this. You must, if you are married to someone not of
the tribe family, run against the family sometimes. He
didn't. He was a softy, and he let the family move into
our house. Now it was the educated ones in the family
who started pulling the clichés. The older ones, as a
matter of fact, were very nice, and it was always all
right with them. But now, for instance, I am left-handed,
and I hold things in my left hand. Everybody says this
is all wrong. This is the one they use to clean their *tuckus*
(bottoms), right? Now if you've been to university and
have been overseas, and you still feel this, then it's just
ridiculous. You know? You've made a meal and they
say they're not going to eat it because you used your
left hand. Christ! When they first moved in, after three
months of us being there, they said they wanted a piece
of what my husband had, as was their right, they said.
He should have told them to bugger off out of it, he
should have stood up to them, but he didn't. He was
a lovely, lovely man, but he was soft that time. Then,
they moved in. They were my watch-dogs. Every time
I wanted to go out, to go to the store or the dress-maker,
there was somebody in the car. Then one day I went to
a dress-maker I had found, and this boy wanted to come
in the room with me. I said, 'What the devil do you
think this is?'

Altogether there were two sisters, a cousin, and two
brothers in the house. And mummy. We wanted mummy
to be there. She was ailing and had to have a special
diet, I was happy to have her. She was really charming.
But this other bunch just moved right on in with us.
Somebody would just come here with all his clothing.
One guy showed up like that and said, 'I've come to
move into my uncle's house.' I looked at him on the
door-step and said; 'Don't say Good Morning, even.
Anyway, you can get the hell out.' 'But I was at the

port when you arrived', he said, so I said: 'Well, there were millions of people there. Why aren't you working?' — you know, American know-how . . . no answer. This guy just stood there with all his bundles. I wouldn't let him in. *That* caused a great fuss, but that time I was determined. The ones that did get in, though . . . they weren't clean, and that drove me up the wall. They lived upstairs and we lived downstairs. I considered myself responsible for the house, and I like plenty of soap. But they never washed their dishes for three or four days — in *this* heat? — and their toilet stank, you could smell it right out in the yard. And they were stealing from me. We put electricity in the locks, you know to give them shocks, so when they got the key in the lock they got a little shock. I almost went out of my mind. This might be their country, I said, but they're not going to kill me. I'm a coward. They were just rude and assumed they had a right to my husband's life and money. They were educated, though. That's what I can't understand.

After all this junk went on for nine months, I said: 'You'll have to go.' There was a tremendous showdown that I had to force myself, by myself. I never felt my husband was at my side in that, but finally they moved out, and they never spoke to me again for eight years, until he died. I should have let Kofi stay in the States. But . . . it was a new country, everything else was static. I said we should get in on the ground floor and make it work. Well, Kofi wanted to . . .and he didn't want to. I felt we should. So it was mostly my prompting. He could have waited for four or five years. I felt that all we were learning was for this country, and we should help to create it. Kofi *was* Africa. Even Nigerian friends in the States called him the Africa Man. He was conservative. He would bring out his cloth at the drop of a hat, though. Sometimes it wasn't funny. We went to this Presbyterian church in the States and he'd sing away in his own vernacular, with everybody else, of course, singing English. He really didn't care.

It was only a matter of time, I guess, but of course this juju thing came up. I don't know, somehow

Mr G. got involved in the juju man, and certain things
were brought to the juju man. Now I'll fight any man,
woman, dogs and cats, but I can't fight the goddamn
juju man. Bills were not being paid for eighteen months
because money was going to the juju man, God alone
knows why. I think I lost my lovely husband back to
Africa. In there, among his underwear and shorts were
amulets and bottles, and in the sideboard there were
herbs in bottles of vinegar. An educated man! I've
never understood it, whether he took problems to the
juju man, or what. Of course, nobody's ever told me.
One day I got really mad at it and threw the bottles
and the whole thing — and a lot of my precious crystal
— against a wall. That's one thing, I get really angry and
throw things around. Here they will poison you little by
little. I had every idea of being one of them. I was going
to bury my bones here. I can't afford to go back to the
States. I've got one or two business interests here and I
quite like it here. When did I realize it wasn't going to
work? 1961. I always made a point of us eating together
in the evening, around six. I'd wait for him to come
home so that we'd all be together. Old Faithful, that's
what I was. After two or three years, he stopped coming
home, but still I waited for him. The kids were starving
to death but I'd made such a point of it. But then he
took to coming home at two o'clock, and going out
again at four o'clock, and taking clothing with him, so
that was that. Hell, he hadn't paid the electricity bill —
that goddamn juju man — and there was no electricity
to play records I've carried around with me for twenty
years, and there was only a candle to read by. We
separated, and continued seeing each other. I said I
didn't want to destroy completely this fantastic
relationship we'd had. It really had been fantastic. So
we became firm friends. Well, the family didn't like that.
Then, well, then one day his brother came round, with
his clerk, and he told me Kofi had died in the hospital.
I looked at them. I'd seen him four days before! I asked
the clerk, 'Why didn't you tell me he was sick? You
know I know what to do for him.' He'd been ill
before, and I'd carried him out of the hospital. I

knew what to do for him. He had diabetes. The clerk just looked at the ground, and I knew the family had told him not to tell me. Kofi had always taken the family's side, sometimes against me, and that upset me, and now . . . When he died, friends warned, 'Don't touch that body. If you do you'll have to pay for everything, the funeral, new outfits for the whole family.' So there was this battle of wills, with poor Kofi lying in the hospital for five days, until they finally cracked and took him. But they still tried to make me pay £300 for the funeral. Then at the funeral, I found I was being edged out and edged out of the church until I was practically in the street. Then this guy comes and says he's going to take the stuff out of the house. He says he's the head of the family. I said: 'The hell you are. You ain't head of my family. I ain't never seen you at all.' I said *I* had bought all this stuff after we had separated, and with my money. So that was it.

You know, there was a very strange incident not long ago. I'd taken this taxi to go to do some shopping, and the driver said: 'I know you, you're Mrs G.' I said yes, then he said: 'I knew your husband. His family killed him.' I said: 'Now wait a minute, what's all this crap?' And he said: 'It's true,' and that's all he would say. My poor, poor dear Kofi. Africa was too much for him. It took him back . . .

Probably the most significant single group of all among the New World black expatriates in West Africa are the women who have married Africans. They are a comparatively large, if inchoate, group. There were scores in the six countries I visited and as more and more Africans travel to Britain and America to study, their numbers will certainly increase.

Their backgrounds are extremely varied, as indeed are their reactions. It is such wives who have to face the quality of life in Africa at more physical and spiritual points than any other kind of expatriate, including European wives, black and white businessmen and professionals, students and travellers.

The white European wife is a familiar figure in Africa. Her situation is largely delineated before she arrives. What is

expected of her is a muted notion, but precise and limited.
Many European wives I met had forged exciting relationships
with their new families, but they all realized that such
relationships, at least for the present, could not start from
anything but black—white, African—European, bases. The
family structure is of itself such that the outsider is excluded
from subtler areas of the family circle, and somehow as a
white outsider this seemed 'natural'. The black wife, however,
may be expecting her colour to act as a passport to these
inner circles. However mature she may be, she may find it a
shock to discover that she too is an outsider. Her expectation
of very nearly total acceptance on the basis of the kinship of
colour may well earn her the greater rejection, even hostility.

She may soon discover that she is in an anomalous position:
she herself may feel that she is an African descendant returning
home in a very real sense, yet she may be regarded as an
essentially American prize, and find that being black and
American contains a novelty and curiosity value that does not
last.

In many ways, such marriages are a paradigm of the Return
to Africa in general. Those with greater resources of emotional
adaptability, physical adjustment, and understanding of the
gradual changes this all brings about in them, find greater
contentment and stimulation. This kind of cross-cultural
relationship with its shifts of incomprehension but need for
mutual knowledge, its extraordinary moments of union that
may be vitiated by rejection is the only symbol for the return
of blacks to Africa. Those who embark on both cross-cultural
marriage and a return to Africa discover the true impossibility
of complete union (and complete affinity), but may recognize
the fascinating meaning of the distinctness of the two forces.
In rare cases, as we have seen, these two forces can collide
cataclysmically. But for the most part they co-exist, and can,
in children and grandchildren, become assimilation. Almost
invariably, the girls had met their future husbands as students,
on campus in the United States or in some university town
in Britain. Some West Indians who met their husbands in, say
London in the late 1950s, recalled that encounters with
African men were not always happy. A girl from Trinidad
told me:

They were very proud and nationalistic and dogmatic. They tried to make us feel unworthy, as if we were being neglectful of our past, and uncomfortable, as if they were about to attack us all the time. I was once even called a mongrel by somebody. This was very difficult and unfair, because my sympathies were always with Africa, or at least with the Third World and independence movements. When it came to this kind of argument — and it was very general between West Indians and Africans at that time — I'd try to say that Eric Williams had told us in Trinidad that if it could happen in India, independence could happen in Trinidad, if Sukarno can do it, we can do it, and if Kwame Nkrumah can do it, so can we. We didn't feel we had to apologize for not being African, but I felt that many of the African students behaved in a very unpleasant way, as if they were the ones who would show us how to do it. My reaction was that I kept away from company where there was likely to be a conflict of that sort.

At the same time, many West Indian and black American girls found that it was precisely this sense of pride and stature, an aura of national identity and destiny, that attracted them to this particularly politicized generation of West African students. 'They had a *bearing*', said one American wife. 'The Afro-American guys went around shooting off their mouths and going round the campus in circles. These guys were sort of quieter and more determined and you knew they'd do all the things they said they would. They weren't just bluster.' And another West Indian wife said: 'There was, it's true, a sense of mystery about them, and it's also true that they played that up terribly. Some of us had never met Africans before — how could we have? — and it was just the most exciting thing you could imagine. They never seemed to be wasting their time, like most of the English students did. They had strength.'

The components of the attraction were varied in other ways. Some dark girls from particularly shade-conscious Caribbean islands or middle-class Afro-American circles found a ready acceptance in African student circles, where colour in itself was unimportant. One girl said: 'One of the most dreadful things about the West Indies, well some parts, was this colour thing. Boys who had a fairish skin were never allowed to bring home anybody whose skin was darker than theirs. Some of these people seemed to be trying to make the West Indies lighter and lighter. And here were Africans who were not even proud of their dark colour. They had sort of got past that, as if it wasn't even worth mentioning, just a fact of life.' Another talked of the 'innocence' of Africa, an innocence of the discrimination she herself had experienced. Through the Africans she met as students she saw a way of regaining such an innocence. (This was a short-lived hope, as it happened, since her future husband himself experienced discrimination in America, and became embittered by it. Her seeming acceptance of prejudice became a *casus belli* between them, with his accusing her of loss of pride.)

Marrying into this group of overseas students has had several important results. In the first place, the view they received of Africa was distorted in crucial ways. In one extreme case: 'A friend of mine,' said a West Indian wife in Ghana, 'had Africa really built up for her. Her husband told her she would live in style, that he was a sort of prince, when in fact his father was just the mayor of a village. She thought she would come and live like a Princess Margaret, and ended up cooking on a coal pot. Needless to say, that marriage broke up.' This experience is not so typical, but some wives remarked that their husbands had described Africa as an exciting place of political ferment, where whole societies were being forged. In fact, they found that, while this was most certainly true in many ways, the Africa they were actually faced with was one of traditional values, a rural hierarchy that would be unlikely to change. African students tended to be more concerned with describing what Africa might become, rather than with the practical state of the society the wife would find.

However, such students were abroad to study subjects for which there were few advanced facilities in West Africa, fields such as medicine and law. Thus, on returning to Africa, their wives found them rapidly rising in their professions, in medicine, business, law and politics. The women then experienced a social life moving in circumscribed circles which they themselves would be unaccustomed to, a sophisticated contrast to life in their husbands' home villages.

But they may also find that being married to a 'been-to', one who has been to a white country to acquire what the Liberians call 'book-knowledge', is to be married to someone who himself has problems of re-adjustment. Such people are often regarded by their families and friends as Afro-Europeans, and they become burdened with a huge range of financial and emotional obligations and a decidedly equivocal attitude towards the perhaps rural culture they sprang from. A number of wives discovered that their husbands had greater problems attuning to Africa than even they had. Several wives told me that it was, in fact, they who had been keener to return than their husbands. The husband, once home, had experienced a violent oscillation between his own and his wife's culture, standing as they did at opposite ends of his spectrum of loyalties. What happened next depended on the husband's tribal or geographical background, and, naturally, the quality of his relationship with his wife. On occasion this oscillation was impatiently abandoned, and the wife was left alone to carry the complete burden of accommodation to her husband's culture. More often, however, where this conflict occurred, the husband would settle into moody alienation from his background. Either way, the wife realizes that she is very much stuck with her decision to return to Africa in a way that others may not be. A West Indian wife told me that she felt herself to be fully 11,000 miles from home, since there are no direct scheduled flights between West Africa and the Caribbean.

In short, the special difficulties of such cross-cultural marriages are: a redefinition of the relationship with the husband on his home territory; a uniquely complex relationship with the husband's family, which may later give rise to disputes over the upbringing of children; and the living conditions themselves.

The black American wife of a surgeon said: 'My husband is senior surgeon at his hospital and is earning what for this country is a great deal of money. But what he is earning is actually what I earned when I first left college in the States, and like elsewhere in the world, the cost of living is not far behind that of the States.' An expatriate wife married to an African professional does live in affluent circumstances that are much higher than those of the average African. The gulf between rich and poor is, of course, immense, and such families are without doubt considered rich. Yet the salaries coming into those families would be equivalent to those paid for very poorly rewarded work in New York or Chicago, or even Europe.

But the physical circumstances of the professional bourgeoisie into which many of these girls have married are, by African standards, and indeed by those of many other places, stylish and comfortable. There may be a large bungalow or house on one of the campuses or in one of the fashionable suburbs of a major West African city. Many of them live among the embassies in the airport residential area of Accra, or the modern Ringway estate, or the formerly white suburb of Tesano. They live in the hills above Freetown in clusters of gracious houses now vacated by the white colonials, and along the broad avenues that lead out of Monrovia. They have houses among the few trees in the cities, and tend shaven lawns that perennially threaten to become either dust-bowls or swamps. The birds of the cities gather in these compounds, brilliant blue, or scarlet and black, or yellow and green disturbances rushing through the vermilion flame trees and the frangipani. Often, there is a Jaguar or Mercedes Benz in the garage, and a driver to go with it. Their husbands are frequently the direct successors of the colonial administration, as judges, senior civil servants, government advisers, financial advisers to large companies, barristers, senior medical or administrative staff at metropolitan hospitals, heads of university departments. Many, but by no means all, live suburban lives that are at the same time acquisitively middle class and also African, two features that do not always easily mix.

To do their shopping the wives may try a chain store, and when they inevitably find that there is a shortage of what they are looking for, they must weave their way through the pyramids of tinned milk, toilet rolls, toothbrushes, mirrors and peppers in the markets and bargain for every item, which not surprisingly, proves to be a source of frequent irritation. As well as the driver, there will probably be a cook and a steward, and the husband and wife sometimes find that their relationship with them is far from straightforward. (One black American couple were amazed to learn that their steward had quit because of the shame he felt among colleagues at working for black foreigners.) Even if there is an unceasing barrage of unconscious assault from African culture and attitudes from husband and family, many black expatriate wives find that they are cut off in their suburbs.

The West Indian wife of a lawyer told me:

It was a bit of a rush decision to come here after Independence, so I never really had time to think of it. I had never asked very much, I realized later, so I had no feeling of coming home. I was married to him, and *he* was coming home. When I first came here, in those *very* early days, my friends were very much cut out for me because of our background. They were people from the establishment, very English almost, and I didn't really look at the country. Even now, after all these years, I can't say I know too much about the country. I was cocooned, it's true. You can find out certain things, mainly through watching. But people don't trust you if you have to ask, so you have a choice: either you remain ignorant and an outsider, or you ask and incur their mistrust, and feel even more that you are an outsider. They always seem to think you are trying to find out more than you are asking. I suppose I have learned small things, just from sensing disapproval when I do certain things, such as crossing my knees in company with my elders. If my husband was a West Indian we could, if we wanted, shut it all outside. You can't stay cut off physically, though. You can't shut yourself off from it all by yourself, because you love your husband. Yet he is a reminder and everything in the house is a reminder that you are an outsider. I came into a typically conservative society. It's like living in suburban London. I was made to feel a daughter among B.'s friends, they almost made me feel guilty that my mother had given birth to me so late.

An American wife said:

It seems such a small step to decide to go to your
husband's home. You feel as though if you are going
to have made sacrifices then it was in marrying him
in the first place. That's if there are going to be any
hassles with your family or your friends or whatever. I
never had any of these hassles, and it seemed to me to
be a pretty ordinary affair to go and live in his country.
It's only when you get here that you realize what you
have done. You've followed him. I mean, *followed* him.
You've basically denied yourself the decisions. I guess
women have been doing that for ever, but it's not
funny when you see you are doing the ordinary thing
and hitching your wagon to his star like that, I mean
up-rooting and all. Now I don't suppose it would
matter all that much, well it would be easier, if it had
been the other way round, like us going to the States,
but this way round, you have a whole lot of problems.
    Number one, you are expected to stay following him,
like making him a good home and all that. My girl
friends back home would think I was crazy. Everybody
was so envious and excited, 'Gee, going to Africa, oh
my . . . ' but here I am, it's not exciting, I'm Mrs
America 1973 — hey, how about that . . . a black Mrs
America . . . ? Number two, what are you going to do?
Get a job? Doing what, for Chirst's sake? I'm not
particularly qualified, so I'm not going to be a teacher.
Business? How the hell am I going to set up a business?
It's tough enough for the men. The only thing I'm
qualified to do is like going to be a market mammy,
and even they would skin me alive. You see, there's
this sort of vicious circle. The first thing and the main
thing you have to relate to is the house and home, on
account there ain't nothing outside of it to do. Then,
of course, you've got servants who do all the work,
so after a while there's nothing to do in the house
either, and you're making things to do. There's no easy
way out of the house like there is in the States, not in
terms of work and not in terms of leisure. Am I going
to play tennis all day long? Sit on the beach? Go to

the pool with the other bored housewives? Watch
television? You've got to be kidding!

What does my husband say about it? Well, there's
not much for him to say about it. He's got a real good
job and it's his country and he's excited, and he doesn't
want to come home and hear a federal case about how
bored his little woman is back home, like some soap
opera. He'd get good and pissed off it I went on at him
about it.

A large number of the West Indian and black American wives
are in fact qualified in nursing or in school or university
teaching or have strong interests in voluntary work. Some
help husbands in businesses, and a number have set up
shops and businesses of their own. But the problem of
the unqualified wife can be a grave one. The problems of
any isolated suburban wife anywhere in the world are
somehow exacerbated for the black expatriate wife in Africa.
There is, for instance, the feeling of non-participation in a
national life in which her husband may be involved, a sense
of failing a whole country. The weight her problems put
on a marriage may show up strains and cracks that might
not be apparent in another kind of marriage. A West
Indian wife put it in these terms: 'When we got here to his
country, I felt very strongly — much more strongly than I
suspected I would — that it was his country, and he took
on a whole shape of strangeness to me. It didn't in the
least seem to be my country, which I might have time to
feel if I weren't married to him. That was difficult
enough to adjust to. But if I complained about being
bored and left out he would feel I wasn't as happy as he
was, that I wasn't happy being married, and that he'd failed
and I'd failed in some way, and that would open up this
gulf of strangeness again.'

Even qualified, working or otherwise occupied, relatively
unbored wives are not exempt from a special form of
lonliness that is related to this gulf. One woman said to me:

I think it's a matter of a lack of a Time Before.
Naturally you get this in any marriage, and all husbands
and wives have only dim ideas about each other's child-

hood or early adulthood. When you are both in a foreign
country, as we were in England, we were just like any
other couple. But when we came here I realized how
totally divorced I was, not only from his Time Before, as
it were, but from my own. I thought of him not so
much as a stranger but as something much more positive.
Here were new things about him I had to learn to get to
know and that would be marvellously interesting and
important to get to know. He was with his childhood
friends and among places he had early memories of.
Memories he takes for granted. He would be with
friends and he would be laughing.

I mean, I wasn't resentful that he had childhood
friends or anything like that. It just made me aware that
there were many things about his background and
culture, the sort of things other wives would not have
to learn. But then you get to know that it's not as
simple as that, and that, frankly, it's impossible. I get
on very well with his family and they sort of accept
me as much as they possibly could, and I accept my
role in the family, and there are no problems that way,
you understand, because they do try to help me. I
understand what has made my husband what he is, yet
I don't understand. I can only understand from a
distance, even though I'm present. I'm a specator, and I
can only have the understanding of a spectator. I can
look at certain things, pouring the spirit on the ground
and ceremonies and music, and can see they're
important to my husband's background, and he takes
them as seriously as anybody, and I think these
ceremonies are nice. But they're not *me,* are they?
There's no bridge between me and all of that, except
my husband, and I see that he is on that side of the
chasm.

This does not make me unhappy, because I find
it all so wonderful and interesting. But there are some
things I can never fully comprehend about him, and
they're things that I'm with all the time. This would
not arise if we were not in his country. And all the
time I'm cut off from the places and friends and
relations and things that made me what I am. He

could understand my background much better than I could his. My husband speaks perfect English and spent many years in Britain, so he is familiar with many things that are not of his background. But when he speaks his own language among his friends — I'd never heard it before — he seems to have a different personality. We have so much fun, so many jokes, and he's a very funny person. But there seemed to be so much looseness, so much real ease, he seemed to relax one last little bit with his friends. I wouldn't describe my feelings exactly as loneliness. It's sort of tantalizing, though.

This, together with the flaws in the seeming comfort, calls for a special form of resilience. An American wife discussed this:

When I came we had a big, hollow, unhomey, uncomfortable house, with university-issue chairs, very hard, and there were all the smells of the area which I knew I was going to have to put up with, also drumming and dancing in the night, and problems with shopping, not be able to plan a menu, along with a water shortage and no electricity. This was in the capital! I think I got used to that very quickly, you get used to that being a constant in your life. I worked very hard to see that this didn't get me down. The trouble with many of the people who come here is that they are middle class — I am too — and they find it very hard not to be put off by this. Until I got a job these small discomforts were the most significant aspects of my life. The heat and the smells. The streets are the people's living rooms. The people are at home in the street. This is the reverse of what you are used to in the States. There the middle class is in tree-lined streets, it is house-orientated. Here, in the street you are literally in people's homes. Only the darkness gives these homes walls. But the way you use these streets takes some getting used to. You can't somehow be aimless in them. There's no window-shopping if you get bored, just to entertain yourself. Not that there's much in the windows anyway.

You definitely have to put more effort, more initiative, into getting out of the house as an expatriate wife. I was anticipating that neighbours would come and welcome me, whereas you are supposed as a newcomer to go and introduce yourself. Americans seem to be much freer on first contacts. You have to know these women better than you have to know your own to ask intimate things. I have to work hard to maintain relationships. If I see an American woman, I'll see her once or twice, then not see her for six months. It's all right, the relationship will still be the same. But if that happens with an African friend, they may be offended, and ask what happened to you. Once you get through the heat — I've never really got used to it — and through the rituals of relationships and the discomfort, there seem to be many more niggling things, which you have to build yourself up against, because they do become exaggerated when you're in a foreign country and especially being a foreign black in an African country. Our housegirl was arguing with the driver about who should use the kitchen first. I tried to step in, after all it's my house, and she said: 'Oh, you don't understand, because you are European.' That sort of thing, multiplied by twenty, means you have to lose certain sensitivities and gain new ones, sort of re-adjust your whole structure of sensitivity.

One extremely difficult area for expatriate wives can be the traditional attitudes towards the status of women in some African societies, and the way in which those attitudes survive in husbands who have long been exposed to a different, Western set of attitudes. Some women found that their assumption that their partners shared their Judeo-Christian ideas of monogamous rectitude and their Western views of sexual equality had to be reshaped to accommodate certain African facts of life. Some do not manage it. I heard about equal parts of reproof and approval for the almost casual African indifference towards illegitimacy. On the

212

other hand, many felt relieved of stifling Western coyness and guilt about it; on the other, it must be said that a great deal of the reproof was for the re-enforcing into subservient roles that this entailed for women. The equality that there is between men and women in African societies is aligned along quite different axes, and is not so much equality as a careful balance of power predisposed to tip in men's favour. But practices — such as polygamy — that have evolved over many centuries of rural subsistence-living in small societies whose existence has often depended on these very practices can be profoundly shocking to an American college girl. All this, too, calls for unusual qualities in the expatriate wife.

An Afro-American wife talked to me:

What I have really found it difficult to adjust to is the extra-marital activity. My husband has had three children — I have none — with two other women. The first was after we were married for seven years, and you know, it wasn't such a shock. He told me when the girl was six weeks pregnant. I was, in fact, surprised that I felt no great trauma. I was kept informed, we talked about it a lot — we've always been able to talk — and I felt I was a part of it. The baby came to us, and the girl went to America. I took the baby when it was nine months. When it was fourteen months I took it to New York to see its mother. My folks thought I was crazy, they really couldn't accept it. The second child came five years later. I had thought the first was *it*. That second one upset me a lot. Somebody told me about it and I laughed and said there was some mistake. But I found out it was true, but only two weeks before the woman gave birth. I had a very bad time then, with sleeping pills and whisky and the whole deal. It was awful, truly, because my husband hadn't told me, and because I was unprepared. But somehow I got over it, and the third, by the same woman, was not so bad. Yes, it was the second one that hurt. After the third I asked my husband, almost joking: 'How many more are you going to have?' He said very seriously: 'As many as God gives me.' And at that

I have to accept it. We are both Christians, and we married in a Christian church, but he is basically polygamous, and that's that.

I refer to the woman as his second wife, and he gets very annoyed. He places his wife in a very lofty position that the other woman can have no claim on. She doesn't come to the house, but when I see her in the street, we talk. And I always get the children to go and visit. When she gets older and no longer my husband's sweetheart, then I guess she'll come here. I now feel I'm totally adjusted to this (a) because there's no point being anything else, and (b) because I love my husband and don't want to leave him. I never allow it to give me a moment's resentment. It's the environment. And also, well, kids will love you if you're nice to them, and feed them, and maybe give them a stick of chewing gum once in a while. They're not concerned with who their mother is, just who shows them love and kindness. My husband is most passionate and loving and thoughtful towards me. He kept me busy with trips around Africa. Perhaps the most upsetting thing is not my husband having an extra-marital affair but people knowing. People can be very cruel. They talk about this woman in front of me. I cut it short. I just say: 'There's no palaver, O.K?' I don't think I've developed any special emotional equipment or resilience to deal with this. I think it's the help my husband has given me. He is a very personable and thoughtful man. My mother-in-law was *so* proud, of the first one. She told everyone. I felt like saying: 'Listen lady, it's not quite kosher. There's no call to be shouting it all over town.'

Despite her denials, this woman's attitude does show a special resilience, and perhaps the calm of retrospect. Many others would not find it in them to be as sanguine. Another American wife discussed the same situation from a different viewpoint.

Oh, you know it goes on, although as far as I know

my husband doesn't have some lady tucked away. Though, you know, they don't tuck them away. The guys I know who have other women are very open about it. My husband will tell me that So-and-So was with his girl at the club. But if it came to a formal party or a reception or something, it would be his wife that he'd take. I really don't see why wives put up with it. They've got it worked out better here, of course. The other woman will in no way threaten a marriage or the wife. A husband will spend a lot of money on his girl, but the wife will never go short. She has a special position that no other woman can touch. And, to be honest, a lot of African wives I know quite accept that their husband needs a screw some place else. But not me, baby. I know plenty of American girls who found out their husband was having an affair, and that was it. Off. Same goes for me, no question about it.

A West Indian wife, with three children (of her own) could not agree that it would be as easy as that:

Marriages just fall apart, and yet they linger. You can't just walk out. When you are together in a foreign country — as we were for some years in Britain — you spend a lot of time together with your family and your husband. You cling to each other in a way. But as soon as he comes back, well, it's like a disease, and you can't wipe it out. All men flirt, and many men will not allow that to interfere with their marriage, especially if there are children. They will have a fling and it will not break up their married life. But others . . . it's as if they can't help themselves. When you come here, you will be happy for a year or eighteen months, and that's the end of your happiness. Then you don't see much of your husband, he becomes brusque. This reflects on you, and you start shouting at the children. The girls here will throw themselves at him. Before he was away they weren't excited by him or attracted by him. As soon as he's a been-to they are all over him, and I think they do it viciously, actually trying to break up the marriage and home. They have caused a lot of havoc in this town. We struggle to help our husbands, and they have struggled not at all. They are not willing to share hardship with him, they just want what you have helped to make him into. Home spoilers, that's all they are. It makes me feel very embittered about Africa.

The phenomenon of the been-to is as old as, and possibly older than, that of the New World black immigrant in Africa. In the eighteenth century some Nigerians, mostly mulattoes, were sent to England for their education, and favoured sons of chiefs were often selected by missionaries for such an English education so that their zeal might be turned to usefulness in converting their pagan brothers. The problems of the been-to were once described to me by a West African historian as the 'Black Prince syndrome'.

The Black Prince was John Frederic, son of King Naimbana, and was Sierra Leone's first been-to. The prince, an extremely unpleasant-sounding boy, was sent to England with the Falconbridges for intensive ecclesiastical studies.

> His person [wrote Mrs Falconbridge] is rather below the ordinary, inclining to grossness; his skin nearly jet black, eyes keenly intelligent, nose flat, teeth unconnected, and filed sharp after the custom of his country, his legs a little bandied, and his deportment easy, manly, and confident withal. In his disposition he is surly, but has a cunning enough to smother it where he thinks his interest is concerned; he is pettish and implacable, but I think grateful and attached to those he considers his friends; nature has been bountiful in giving him sound intellects, very capable of improvement, and he also possesses a great thirst for knowledge.[2]

In England he underwent rigorous training in the study of the Bible and Hebrew, and his piety attracted the unstinting approval of the country clergymen in whose care he had been left. A tract, entitled *The African Prince*, depicted the boy on the cover spurning an improper book. He set off on his return to Africa in June 1793, dreaming of preaching the

216

Gospel there. He was shocked — as he recorded in his note-book — by the swearing of the sailors. Alas, the been-to never became a returnee, for on approaching Freetown he fell into a delirium and died of fever. It was rumoured among the Temne that he had been filled with the white man's secrets and had been killed lest he reveal them, but nevertheless, many other chiefs sent their children to England for their education. There is no doubt that had he survived, this priggish young man would have been a total misfit among his people. His book knowledge set him apart. He would have been sustained only by the rousing heroism of the Biblical characters he had learned about in England.

The problems of the modern been-to can be manifold, and infinitely more cumbersome than those the Black Prince might have faced. The been-to has, in fact, become a recognizable character in modern West African fiction. In Chinua Achebe's *No Longer At Ease,* the hero, Obi, is a country boy from eastern Nigeria, the bright boy of his village, and as for so many of his kind, the villagers invest in his English education. Leaving his home area at the age of eighteen, it is the first time he has even seen Lagos, quite apart from foreign parts. During his four years in England he develops a fond and idealized picture of his country, which he is determined his education shall serve and improve. Returning, he finds his illusions shattered. The village is stunned that he has not returned with a white wife, nor with a car nor other evidence of material privilege. Their expectations of him have also developed in his absence. They need a material outwardness that Obi's very education has taught him to spurn. But his principles will not stand up to the challenge of the true conditions he finds. He finally succumbs, ill-equipped and helpless, to the corruption of Lagos. Achebe describes this as a release of guilt, a kind of death beyond which 'there are no ideals and no humbug, only reality', and this reality is the corruption of petty officials and the need for Obi to form himself into the mould his people have expected and chosen for him.[3]

The Ghanaian Ayi Kwei Armah writes of the central character, Baako, in *Fragments:* 'The been-to has chosen, been awarded, a certain kind of death . . . He is the ghost in person returned to live among men, a powerful ghost understood to the extent that he behaves like a powerful ghost.' Armah talks of the been-to being expected to bring back a 'cargo' of wisdom, and this he does, but the wisdom is painful, full of guilt at the realization that Britain or America were not the paradises they were thought to be. He cannot reveal 'overseas' for what it is in face of such massive prejudgment. He is also guilty because the knowledge he has gained at a foreign university is in no way superior. He must see himself through his own eyes, educated and sophisticated and equipped to struggle in an imperfect Western world, but also through the envying eyes of his family's and villagers' culture.[4]

The been-to is alienated from and yet inseparable from his background on his return. All recognize this alienation as a force to be tackled. Some become desperately unhappy, and subsequently find they can only live as Africans in a foreign country. Their perception of their own culture becomes too strong and unbearable in proximity. (This trend, coupled with the material attractions of the United States and Britain, has concerned a number of African governments. In the early 1970s, the Ghanaian Government launched Operation Home Sweet Home, in which a group of Government representatives went to Britain to try to persuade qualified Ghanaians to return home and fulfil the terms of their scholarships by contributing to their own society. The operation achieved only modest success.) The 'alienation' may, of course, take the form of heightened objectivity and result in valuable service for their country. For many returnees it is a problem that can be overcome. But conversely it may loom large, and detach the returnee in a most painful way.

A return with a foreign wife quite often aggravates the alienation, and many wives I spoke to complained that their husbands seemed to have a sense of hopelessness, even an inverted sense of inferiority to their own 'authentic' people or, alternatively, an almost paranoid determination to succeed. It may produce impatience. A wife may see her husband becoming enmeshed in a complex web of reactions. There is a strengthened awareness of his own intellect, awareness too of Africa, coupled with a resentment at seeing things through foreign eyes, and a simultaneous effort both to repudiate and maintain this perception. There is resentment, most of all, at having a representative of 'European' culture — his wife— close by as witness to his confusion. It would be easy to exaggerate this alienation, which is very often felt only minimally, but most been-tos are unquestionably in a state of some turmoil on their return. Add to this the subtle consequences of 'European' culture being represented by a *black* wife, and the situation is potentially explosive.

In one West African capital I met a distraught West Indian wife who was actually about to leave the following week with her husband. She explained this decision:

> We have only been here twelve months and even now I don't know if he is leaving too. It's been an absolute nightmare. It's just impossible to describe. I felt my husband was disintegrating. He hadn't been home for six years. He talked and talked about it, but we'd just put it off. Then I knew he really wanted to come back so I agreed. We were really terribly happy in the first few days. It was a lot of fun to go and visit his grandparents in their village. There were libations, food and dancing, everybody with so many questions, but making us feel comfortable. Then he started work, and we soon had this sort of routine. I found it strange, but the family were really helpful. But my husband started getting depressed. I couldn't see any reason for it. We weren't earning anything like what we were getting in London, but it seemed to go almost as far. In London he seemed so sure about what he wanted. He didn't want to stay in London, well he wasn't sure about that, but he was sure that he would come back some day. When he did get back he didn't seem sure about that any more, and he was unsure about everything. His family were marvellous, but they carried on treating him as an honoured guest, I suppose that was the trouble. It never wore off. There'd also be remarks at work, I think, like, 'You're not in England now' sort of thing. He seemed to be on the outside all the time and wanting to be in, and not sure that he liked what it was really like on the inside. He

couldn't make up his mind.

Was he happy to be back? I'd ask. And he'd say: 'Of course', and he knew he was lying. We'd hardly had a cross word in England, but we started fighting. I'd tried to pretend that I was happy and had nothing to complain about, because he seemed to have so much on his mind already. But he insisted I must be unhappy, until it became unbearable. I used to get the horrible feeling that he was laughing at me when he was drinking with his friends. He was trying to put me in a position of being outside so that he could feel inside. We would have terrible, vicious shouting arguments. Then he started leaving for days on end, but being very contrite when he got back. We both knew it couldn't go on, and that this wouldn't lead to us settling down. It could only get worse. He honestly appeared to me as a changed man. I think he hated it because it didn't match up to what he'd told me it was and wouldn't ever admit it to me. We have now agreed that I'm leaving, and as far as I know he's leaving too. Such a terrible pity.

Such disintegration is, to be sure, an extreme symptom of a much more vague malaise. While some wives rail at being expected to become not only housewives and home-bound ancillaries but also supports to culture-shocked husbands, others calmly accept the situation, and try somehow to minimize it. A Guyanan wife in Ghana summed it up:

My husband was away for six and a half years. He was very young when he went away, and he developed all his adult faculties away from home. That wouldn't be so bad — I suppose that happens to most young educated men — except that there was such a difference between what this made him and what his friends all were. It is now very difficult to accept the point of view of some of his own people. He keeps saying: 'Oh, in America they do this or they do that', he really should be more patient. He would be talking about low-cost housing, 'See, in America, they have the right way of approaching this . . . ' One day his cousin was telling him about the problems with termites, and he said: 'That's because

they don't know how to prepare the wood, now in
America . . . ' It is very hard for an African to listen to
another African saying this. I spent a lot of time
preparing to come here, for the adjustments I
expected I would have to make. It's not easy. I mean
just small things, like not being able just to get on a
bus and go somewhere. People are always so surprised
to see you on your own. All that. But he, on the other
hand, didn't know what to expect, he didn't expect any
problem of adjustment, so he has problems. He is the one
who resents people coming in on us when we're at home
alone, he is the one who resents interference from the
family, and he's the one who complains about
conditions and the lack of services. He must stabilize
himself. But I have to help him settle here. He would be
annoyed at the country if he thought I was having
difficulties. I have to support him.

The Trinidadian wife of a doctor said:

My husband had the feeling I was unsettled. I never
said so and I was terribly careful not to give that
impression, because I knew that adjustment might take
some time. But he seemed to think that. I think it was
he and not I that was unsettled. He got a job in
Trinidad after we had been here a couple of years,
maybe to test me or to test himself, I'll never know
which. He said he would be released from his
government job. We were definitely going to leave,
alough I tried not to look too pleased — and how
glad I am now that I didn't look pleased. I went to
Trinidad and he was going to join me. Then he wrote
and said he had asked the government how much he
owed them from his government scholarship, and they
had said no, no, too many people have been leaving the
country, you can't be released. I have it in the back of
my mind, well I just don't know how hard he tried to be
released, and it's unfair, because he tries very hard to
make me happy. I know he can't afford to send me home
more often. I wouldn't put that kind of pressure on him.
We have a nice house, and a lovely garden that I love,

and security. After that one time, we never again
discussed leaving, and he has settled very well indeed.

Other surprises lie in wait for the black expatriate wife.
These can cause problems with more far-reaching and
profound consequences even than the alienation of a been-
to husband. An Afro-American wife talked of 'coming into
a community with ready-made windows on the world'.
Greatest of all the elements of this community, and indeed
those who are in control of the windows, their opening and
closing, are the family.

The tribal West African family is a vast, mutually
supportive unit, including sometimes quite remote kin, and
involving an intricate pattern of obligations.* These spread
out in tributaries from people further up the family
hierarchy towards those lower down. The African
family is not only a welfare organization; it is an advisory
and disciplinary body, whose judgments are seldom
questioned. Few practical or emotional problems are deemed
to be outside the arbitration of the family. Most problems,
from intimate, sexual matters to broad social affairs, such
as education or provision for a member in need, are dealt
with in the first instance by the family. Only reluctantly is
a professional outsider consulted. A recalcitrant child may
be visited by an uncle and soundly rebuked. (One or two
Ghanaian friends of mine remembered as children being
awoken very early in the morning and being harangued for
up to two hours by an elderly person whom they hardly
knew.)The entire family may in some way contribute towards
the cost of the education of a gifted member, potentially the
cause of most contention. It is an all but watertight system
that has its roots, of course, in the pure need for survival,

---

* The anthropology of these intricate patterns in, particularly,
the Ashanti area of Ghana, is contained in R.S. Rattray's
classic, *Ashanti* (Oxford, 1923) pp. 23-44. Rattray says, 'In
Ashanti, no [African] woman stands alone, for behind the
woman stand a united family, bound by the tie of blood,
which has here a power and a meaning we can barely grasp.'
(p.79)

but that has developed into one of elaborate interdependence, sometimes stifling but frequently indispensable.

One flaw in the system, however, is that it has a tendency to encourage a sense of exclusivity in a family, a sense of diminished responsibility for people not of the family. It is this sense of exclusivity and the rigid family structure itself that makes the intrusion of an outsider a difficult and delicate matter. On the other hand, the family is in every sense a varied community with which the foreign wife must come to terms. She will be allotted a place in this community — nowhere near the heart of it, however — and she will be faced at all times by this ever-present but non-absorbent social unit. It is for this reason that the wife in in contact with African society at far more points and at many more levels than any other expatriate in Africa.

This family structure is something for which it is difficult to prepare fully. A black American wife in Ghana told me: 'The family system is subtle and pervasive. It is so much part of the thinking of your husband that however much he has told you about his country he simply can't convey what the family set-up really means. It wouldn't occur to him to explain it. He may think he is no longer influenced by it, being educated in the West and all, or he may think it is not unusual enough to need explaining.'

As with Achebe's hero Obi, the man who has been sent to Britain or America for his education is often regarded as a very real investment, financially and inspirationally. And in a completely normal course of events, this investment must produce results, in hard financial terms, but also in softer-edged areas of influence. A Guyanan wife talked about this situation:

Uncle Kojo has provided some of the fees or the fare, Auntie Rose provided the tuck box, old cousin Kweku provided some clothes. Most of the family are illiterate or semi-literate, and when the man gets back he is regarded as rich and privileged. If the husband hasn't explained this, the wife will simply not understand where the hell all the money's going. And he may get embarrassed about it. I've seen so may marriages crack up with the strain and mistrust this can cause. It can be draining on a man whose real income the family actually don't know. Also he can be put in a very difficult position professionally, say, because he is then expected to get old Uncle Kojo a job. Then, he is regarded as wise and he can spend an enormous amount of time dispensing this wisdom. They look to him for advice on all sorts of things, and he ends up spending more and more time on the family, and many wives feel neglected. It's hard if she's not expecting it.

The obligations on the newly returned husband may range from his having, in turn, to provide for the education of a boy lower down the hierarchy to becoming fully responsible for his upbringing. A black American wife I spoke to was startled one day to find a boy on her doorstep. 'This kid just looked at me and said: "My mother said for me to come here and you'd look after me." I got the impression that this was some kind of problem child, and they could see that I'd brought up my own kids properly, with the right amount of discipline. It was very awkward indeed. I didn't want to offend the family, but I knew this kid would be one big problem. And you have to be firm or they'll walk all over you. I said "No" as kindly as I could. Actually this kid was a real distant relative so there was no unpleasantness with the immediate family. But it was touchy for a while there because he was thought of as Family, you know?' Being black, other wives added, meant a greater hesitation over decisions such as this, since such complimentary tokens might not have been offered to a white wife.

Naturally, many of the problems a black New World wife faces with a West African family are in their nature similar to those facing any wife anywhere, with the familiar mesh of resentments and suspicion. Perhaps only the intensity is greater. A wife from Guyana put it in this way:

You are in a sensitive position, because your being black doesn't smooth any paths, and this at first is very difficult to understand. I was conscious of their sort of wishing he had married an African girl. But not only that. In line with the custom, there would be somebody in particular that they wished he had married, and I'd

never know who it was. There's this unspoken thing
that you're in some way depriving an African girl of
this privileged position you've now got. I understand
that and I'm sure it's true to a lesser extent back home too,
so you learn to live with it. You can never be integrated
completely into the family. You sometimes wonder if
they're not just a bit disappointed that you are black.
Being white might give you higher kudos in their
eyes. But if you expected to be integrated you'd be
very unhappy. Once they were talking about
something, and somebody said: 'Don't let Anna hear' —
they actually said that — and they started talking in
their own language. It's like Rotary, you can never
expect to be part of the inner circle. It's natural, and
you mustn't let it upset you. I am an African on paper
only. It's like this: you are a visitor, I'll like you and
talk to you, but I won't show you my bedroom.
Maybe after some time has passed, I will show you my
bedroom, but there will always be a certain drawer in the
bedroom, and I will never ever let you know what's in it.

The obligations of hospitality and accommodation may be
completely unremarkable to the husband, but are sometimes
onerous to an outsider. A black New Yorker in Ghana
described her experience of this:

My husband's sister came to introduce me to things when
I first got here. There were so many things you had to
know. I mean when I got up from the table I wouldn't
have dreamed of then making provision for the rest of the
household, or remembering whether you give the driver
breakfast or lunch, or who gets what when. She was very
useful in that way. We had many visits from curious
relatives, people dropping in out of the blue.
    I started off getting on well with the sister, then started
finding it a nuisance. When would she go? After all,
there's a limit to the practical things you had to know,
and I soon got the hang of it. We were in a rural area,
and the A.D.R.A. buses, the pre-State transport buses
that were run by the Lebanese, passed through our
village. So people used to break their journey, or

occasionally get stranded there, so of course they came to stay. But then people started coming specifically to us. We lived in what they called a double battleship, a two-sectioned bungalow on stilts. We lived in one half and we could put them up in the other. Oh, some of them wanted to be helpful, but it could be irksome. One day I blew up. There were a number of people staying, including an aunt. I wanted to have a meal prepared, and it was the first time I had ordered a meal from our cook. I ordered roast meat and rice. My husband and I, we went out while it was being done. When we got back we found that that was not at all what had been cooked. One girl there said, oh, old aunt whatsername had had a chicken killed and had made a light soup and *fufu*. I was damned annoyed and we had a tremendous row. I felt I had no control over my own house. As it turns out, I rather like soup and *fufu* now, and the aunt turned out to be one of my favourite relatives. But nobody saw anybody else's point and there was a ruckus. I soon learned that you let them sleep on mats and not beds, so I stopped worrying about that too. You know, they just unroll the mats, so it's easy as anything. But occasionally people show up and say: 'I'm going to spend my holidays here.' They imagine we have a lot of money, which we don't. You say: 'Not on your damned life.'

Another black American wife in Ghana said:

In other countries you can make decisions as a couple or as a small family. Here the greater family is always in the background. The obligations towards the family play a very big part in your planning of your life. The larger family has an equal share on your husband's priorities. In Western society we are used to this growing problem of the elderly and ailing relative, lonely and sick and a royal pain in the ass, and everybody's terribly guilty about her. Here, it's true, that situation would never arise. But also, it's everybody you have to keep an eye on, and they're not ailing at all. There's the nephew's family and some uncle some place. The money is shared according to need, not according to who has earned it. My husband's time is divided between the immediate family and the extended family. This is not something I can — or should — fight. It's one of the 'givens' of this kind of marriage.

The possibly divisive force of the family on loyalties and resources can be more feared than real. It may be an outright struggle for influence over the husband, but will more often simply place the wife in a defensive position. 'I suppose any wife feels a bit of a usurper of affections or loyalties,' said an Afro-American wife, 'but when you are surrounded by the people you "usurped" from, you sometimes feel they might get their own back in ways you can't fight.' Another said, 'It's a curious situation. You're worried that the family may alienate your husband from you, but you also realize that he's very much a protector of you against them.' Even the faintest suspicion that a common heritage might be shared by the black New Worlder and the black African family disappears on intimate contact.

The most sensitive area of all can be that of children. Helpful gestures from the family appear uncommonly similar to intrusion. And relatively simple customs, such as 'out-dooring' — the presentation of the baby to the gods and the pouring of spirit as a libation to the ancestors — can be unnecessarily confusing. A Trinidadian wife talked about this:

> My husband had said all along, several times, that he didn't hold with all that. I hardly knew what it was. Then his brother called on the phone, and they spoke for a while in their language. I said: 'Who was that?' and he said: 'Oh, that was Bill; he's coming over.' This man turned up at 4.30 in the morning with presents and all the paraphernalia for out-dooring. I locked myself in the bedroom with the baby and wouldn't come out. I let him leave the presents, but I refused to let them do something I didn't understand and that my husband had specifically said he didn't

believe in. We didn't speak for three weeks. That may seem stupid but it was the principle of the thing. That it was the brother who was to decide what happened to our baby. My father-in-law wrote to me very upset, but I stuck to my guns.

A few wives told me that they had refused to attend when their babies were out-doored, were shocked by the 'paganness' of it, and up to the present day do not know what happened, whereas many others found it a rather charming and moving ceremony, and simply bemoaned the waste of good whisky on the dusty yard.

A Jamaican wife in Sierra Leone told me: 'When my first baby was born, the placenta was buried by a tree, and they said that as the tree would flourish so would the child. I liked that because I could see it was significant to them, and I found it very moving. There are, I suppose, some rather threatening things around, but so much of it is harmless, and I find it rather sweet.'

Some of the cruellest problems are raised by the differences between the matrilineal and patrilineal tribes in West Africa. These are the customary determinants of not only the practical line of inheritance of a child but also its tribal identity. The Ashanti of Ghana, for instance, are, like the Jews, matrilineal, and the child of a black American mother will be viewed in tribal custom as a black American. The Ewe and Ga tribes of Ghana, and indeed most tribes in West Africa, are patrilineal. The child of a black American mother and an Ewe father will be an Ewe. This is not always an obtrusive problem, but it can cause subtle distress. The Afro-American wife of an Ewe described her own feelings:

I never cared about it, because I wasn't even aware of it until my husband's sister told me about it. She made such a fuss about it, and was so bitchy about it, trying to make me feel that I had had their child. Now according to them, that's true, and if they want to make trouble for me, they can simply point that out and I haven't a leg to stand on. It's stupid, but this

sister's point did go home, and I found myself
looking at my child and sort of envying him that he was
truly an African. At the same time, I felt this terrible
feeling of loneliness, as if both my husband and my
child were really part of all this and I could never be.
I have to fight against that feeling, because I know it
could be overpowering. I can't forgive that sister,
you know.

Perhaps the problem was more apparent than real, although its
being apparent did not stop it being a potential souce of
anguish. Those wives who accepted their own outsider status in
a matter-of-fact way also tended to accept the tribal status of
their children. But they do sometimes see that the two
cultures of the parents collide in their children. As one wife
said:

> I think the children may later be a problem. We have
> three, and so far they are too young to understand too
> much about this tribal thing. When people ask them
> where they're from, they sometimes say 'from America'
> and sometimes 'from Ghana', although strictly speaking
> they are Ewe. I try to bring them up in a mixed
> environment. It's not as easy as making a conscious
> effort. I guess it's *fufu* for lunch, hamburgers for dinner,
> but there's only a certain amount you can do in this way.
> I try to expose them to their father's village as often as
> possible so that they won't disdain their background. My
> father was from a slave family in Virginia, and he used to
> take us there every summer. I'd meet my grandparents,
> so I never felt ashamed, because I knew them and loved
> them. I take my daughter to the village so that she will
> not only meet the relatives, but she will bathe in a
> bucket, and use an out-house. You explain that that's
> the way people live here, and there's nothing wrong in
> that. In fact, she thinks it's fun. She asked me some
> time ago what tribe she was from. I said Ewe. I said it
> automatically, but I surprised myself at how promptly I
> said it. It gave me a funny sort of feeling. But I
> certainly don't regret that she's not American, and,
> technically anyway, not of the same culture as myself,

because our house is not organized that way. It helps a very great deal that my husband is so familiar with my culture background. But she's finding it a little difficult to understand. Little things come up. Like she'll pick up some food with her hands, and I'll say: 'Use a fork', and she'll say: 'Well, the people in the village use their hands, daddy's mummy uses her hands.' I've got to say that's the way some people do things, there's nothing wrong in that, just that I prefer she use a fork.

What is difficult is that I think I have become a lot less spontaneous. I used to have a very good sense of humour. People don't seem to understand my jokes, they're sort of American word jokes, and they don't do that here. I have become more reserved, more patient. When I was first here I was more volatile, you know, always wanting to sit down and write a letter to the editor about something. You don't get any thanks. The danger is — and this disturbs me — that one becomes non-reactive, apathetic, complacent. The effort of doing something is sometimes not worth it for the amount you are going to gain. I remember I was driving along one day and came across this huge tractor tyre lying in the side of the road. It was old and obviously unused and discarded. I asked this guy to help me load it, so I could take it home for the yard for the kids to play with. There was such a huge palaver, it soon seemed to be becoming a great issue. There was a full discussion, simply because nobody had thought of doing that before. I eventually got our driver to load it and take it home. As soon as my husband came in, the driver said: 'D'you know, she got me to go and pick up this tractor tyre . . . ?' All that palaver. I must say my husband didn't understand either. But it was just something on the spur of the moment that could have been fun. It was all spoiled by the palaver. So sometimes you just let experience go. That's as much Africa as any proud cultural background, and that is what my children will inherit. You sometimes want to shake them and say: 'But you're *American* too,' and you wonder if they

are going to become non-reactive and apathetic.
Maybe reminding them that they are also American
would avert that . . .

The black American wife of a Ga told me:

> In the Ga culture the wife is seen as a vehicle for bear-
> ing children for the husband's family. I think this is a
> deplorable approach to life because the children
> inevitably suffer. My children are growing up with
> certain Western ways of thinking, and this will
> probably create problems for them later on. But I
> feel that if they want to know more about the
> African way of things, they can choose to do so
> later. I don't actually feel that there could ever be
> difficulties over the custody of the children. I'd
> certainly not buckle down to the Ga way. If
> tomorrow my husband and I broke up, I would pack up
> the children, take them and go. He did say once — he
> was making his will — 'If we both died or something,
> what would happen?' I said I guess my mother wouldn't
> mind taking care of them. He started about sons and
> daughters being 'lost to Africa' — they're always
> talking like that — and saying that they ought to stay
> with his family. Then he smiled and he changed his
> mind. Now the compromise is that my mother would
> come here and bring them up here. Maybe my
> children will have problems because I'm not
> interested in bringing them up as Ghanaian. If my
> husband were interested he should do something about
> it. He would like them to know more about their
> heritage, I guess, but he doesn't do much about it.

The feeling of being alien to your own child's basic culture —
even before you encounter the usual incomprehensibility
of teenage culture — is not a distant one and is sometimes
powerful. The American wife of a Grebo in Liberia said to
me: 'My son, the African . . . even before he's got to the
stage of rock and roll or whatever the hell they'll be doing
when he's older, he's a stranger. He's pure black, and I'm
proud of that. I was engaged to a white guy in the States,
and it was the wisest thing I ever did not marrying him.

But if my boy was a half-caste or something you'd be able to see he was in some way different from you. But a different kind of black kid? That takes a lot of getting used to.'

Nearly all I spoke to talked of equally special compensations. There is, for the cynical, the matter of a social status that may well have been denied them in America. The Afro-American wife of a senior professor said: 'In the States I would probably have married a social worker.' She paused and went on, 'Or maybe a postman'.

Some talked of their relationship with their husband having been positively enhanced by the struggles they both had, in their different ways, to adjust emotionally to what was for both a strange environment. Some talked of having discovered subtleties they could not define in the character of their husbands that, few other kinds of marriage could reveal. Their marriages were different from any other kind, they said, because of the expectations and romance they, as black people in America and the West Indies, had brought to their marriage. Few other kinds of romance have to withstand the maturing process of such physical or emotional intensity. An American wife in Ghana made a further point, and what seemed to me the central one:

The whole Africa thing was romance to me. Love was also romance. I've found roots here because I love my husband and he's African. You can't love Africa, but you can love an African person. The people who have to 'adjust' to Africa will never make it all the way, because it's abstract, and it will always be that to them. But an African husband is something real, you can touch him, and know him better than you can know his own country. I'm not saying it doesn't have its heart-aches. The weather's just awful, and there's driver ants and snakes and you can't understand a half of what's going on. But I do feel I've returned to Africa, like I always knew I would, and when I see my kids, and maybe I'll see my grandchildren, then the return will be complete.

CHAPTER 7

Zion Revisited

'I would not give the enjoyment I have had since I have been
in Africa for all I have seen in America. I have set out all
kinds of fruit trees that are in Africa. We have preaching
every Sunday, and prayer meeting every night through the
week . . . My son, George Washington, is spelling in three
syllables, and reading in the new American spelling-book,
words of one syllable. I think Monrovia will become a fine
good place, in course of a few years. The people are
building every day. We have had war, since we have been
here, with the natives. The first day we started, we went
to St Paul's; the next day, we marched to King Brumley's
town and took it. We only lost one man.'

(Letter from Liberian settler to his former mistress, 1832[1])

Any visit to Liberia is, by reputation, nasty, brutish and overlong. Beloved, it seems, only by owners of oil tankers and the Firestone Rubber Company, the country has been run by a succession of people to whom nepotism is as flower-arranging is to the Japanese, and who have ground the country into the red clay until it is apparently a corrupt little backwater, effectively colonized by European and American multi-national companies, the laughing stock of the West African coast. Most white writers have found it impossible to describe modern Liberia without a good deal of ill-temper. Typical was John Gunther who, in his *Inside Africa,* talked of thieving being a national sport. He repeated the saw of being visited by the postmaster and asked for a 'loan' of one hundred dollars to ensure prompt delivery of his mail, and tells the hilarious story of the entire fingerprint collection at police headquarters being stolen. He also explained the forests of top hats at official functions; after the guests have gone, hostesses tend to find their toilet rolls missing.[2] Another more recent writer remarked: 'In most West African cities poverty is relieved by charm. Monrovia is unique in its overwhelming nastiness.' This same writer complained that it was impossible to convey the full extent of the doings of the rascally ruling class, not because of lack of evidence, but because of a group of shark lawyers who make a handsome living out of spurious libel actions.[3]

Friends of mine had told of frequent arbitrary arrest, and of being all but mugged by police officers in their hotel rooms. An English businessman based in Monrovia told me that two days before I had met him he had been driving past the presidential mansion. At dusk the national flag is raised, at dawn it is lowered. At these times passing traffic must stop. Believing he was well before time for the flag to be lowered, he was driving home. He arrived home and was taking a shower some half an hour later, when several policemen burst into his bathroom and took him naked to the police headquarters, where he was kept for five hours with, of course, no charge being preferred or access allowed to one of the host of Monrovia lawyers. His main problem was that there was nowhere about his person that he could have secreted the necessary 'dash' (bribe) and it was only when his wife arrived and paid the pathetic sum of five dollars that he was allowed to go.

A Ghanaian friend found that the evening he arrived in Monrovia he was visited by two policemen in his hotel. They first offered him a girl. He declined. They insisted. He switched to a more appropriate tack. 'How much should I pay you *not* to have a girl?' A sum was agreed. Next morning, he was again visited by the same two policemen, this time in uniform. Would he care for some pot? No. Too bad, they said, we've brought this. Once again: 'How much do I have to pay *not* to be possessing that?' That day and evening they continued to tail him 'for protection', and, entering into the spirit, my friend began buying them drinks as he jaunted from bar to bar. Finally, he said: 'How long is this going to go on? How much do I have to pay not to be protected?' One of the officers produced a notebook and with impeccable fairness, tallied the amounts my friend had spent and said: 'Thirty-seven dollars and fifty cents. That'll be all right, buddy,' and left with his colleague.

In other West African capitals one frequently finds Afro-Americans and West Indians who have naturally tried Liberia first. A West Indian I met in Freetown said: 'I have lost, lost, lost. From the moment I stepped into that country I started paying, all the time small bribes, customs, cops, everybody, until I was very nearly broke. I never even got to the point where I had built anything up to where I was paying big bribes. That was what was so stupid. As soon as I've made enough money for the fare, I'm leaving. Every day I feel I'm losing something by being away from the West Indies.' A black American in Accra remarked tartly: 'They're black Irish, with a touch of Syrian, and a whole lotta cornpone Alabammy. They'll cut your throat with a knife and fork. When they shake hands with you, man, count your arms.' But the more one read of the villainous behaviour of the Americo-Liberian elite, its criminal neglect of the interior, the grip of foreign investment on the country, the more unsavoury anecdotes one heard, the more one was amazed at how little impact the reality of conditions in Liberia had made on Imagined Africa in the United States.

One is unprepared, then, for the less easily definable flavour of Monrovia. Unlike several cities I have visited, it does not have the rancid general air of viciousness and thuggery. In many ways is it like a small hick town in Georgia, its centre six blocks by four. It is a disarmingly casual city, and the knavery at all levels is conducted behind a screen of almost self-mocking charm. You are fleeced with so many 'you're welcomes' and 'take cares' that you hand over with a smile. That dubious practice is taking place there is little question. A country with no exchange control on currency is too tempting a haven for certain elements. But it all takes place with polished self-mockery. 'The smiles fade', said an interested British businessman, 'when you realize that it is a national destiny at stake.' The slogan of the day was 'Total Involvement for Higher Heights', and inevitably one found the odd 'Total Involvement for Higher Heights' tailoring shop around Monrovia. One's suspicion as to exactly who was commanding those higher heights was somewhat lessened when one noticed sleek Cadillacs bumping and grinding along the main street, their springs totally shattered by the holes in the roads. One is also unprepared for the reactions — sometimes bordering on delirium — of Afro-Americans who have returned. These reactions are understandable when one realizes that the spectacular successes stay, and the spectacular failures leave. And there is hardly any middle ground.

I arrived on a Sunday. I was immediately reminded of Mrs Falconbridge's description of the early days of Freetown: 'I never met with, heard, or read of any set of people observing the same appearance of godliness; for I do not remember . . . my ever awaking (and I have awoke at every hour of the night), without hearing preachings from some quarter or another.'[4] The entire staff of the

broadcasting service seemed to be graduates of the
Armstrongs' Ambassador College (an impression later
dispelled: they are employees of the Ministry of
Information) and a perpetual religious 'hour' on radio
was punctuated only by an occasional announcements
of a delicious surrealism: 'It is 12.25, as I said earlier.'

Monrovia is in many ways a retreat from Africa. One
or two other capitals in West Africa have this quality,
Freetown with its late Victorian haze, Abidjan with
its garish awfulness, but none quite to the degree of
Monrovia. It is a right little, tight little island of a community,
seeming to exude not the song of the plantations, but the
aura of a small town in a 1940s American movie. It is a
bakelite radio in a motel room, a black Spencer Tracy in a
chaotic general store-cum-soda-fountain, cookies and
gingham tablecloths (fussily straightened by black Jean
Simmonses), with more than likely some whiff of
escroquerie from some black Orson Welles in the Mayor's
Parlour. For some returnees, this is exactly the lure of
Liberia. They are no longer in the stalls watching a movie of
a piece of the American Dream; they have starring roles. 'I
can look out of my office here on down Main Street, and you
would swear you weren't in Africa at all', said a black
American businessman. 'You've sometimes got to pinch
yourself. But you know, when I go to Accra or Lagos, those
really African cities, I get kind of depressed. I don't like it
one little bit.' And the gritty, self-help ethics are very real,
once you are allowed, a black man in a black country, to
participate enough to exercise them. Another businessman
told me: 'There ain't no paradise here. You gotta be
prepared to work you ass off, break your ass to get anywhere.
I been broke here. I got down to fifty dollars, but I started
again with one petrol pump, and now I got a really big
concern. But man, I'd shovel shit to stay here.'

Unlike modern independent Africa, the more recent
magnets, Liberia has generations of returnees in its
population. More than anywhere else on the coast, people
returning to Liberia in this century were moved by the pull
of mystic Africa. Meeting returnees of different generations,
one sees how steadily the beckoning flame burned, and still
burns, and how the reality of life in Liberia has only

strengthened it in most of the people who journeyed back and stayed.

The pious self-help may or may not lead directly to an assured place in the Monrovia Establishment. There is, however, certainly enough historical antecedence. Determination to emigrate in the face of staggering odds — and the odds may be violent opposition or merely apathy — is a theme that runs through most returnees' accounts. One often catches more than a hint of the Great Trek West in nineteenth-century America. The trek produced qualities not only of extraordinary heroism, but in some people pushed reverence over the edge into sanctimoniousness, humility into rich if sometimes purblind thankfulness, single-mindedness into ruthlessness, ambition into rapaciousness.

There were, to be sure, casualties, of disease, disposition, of malpractice. But three different people, from three different generations, arriving in Liberia at different times (in 1917, 1951 and 1967), working in different fields, told me striking stories that have a curious impetus in common.

The first was related by the somewhat declamatory widow of a West Indian missionary. She came from Atlanta and hers is now a prominent Liberian family.

I was reared in the church. My father was a deacon in the Baptist church, and I learned to love the church. I was always with my father, my little feet dangling off the bench, as he preached. I heard about Paul's missionary journey from some Yankee woman, and I read a great amount. Our pastor was a professor at Moorhouse, and occasionally students were invited to our church and then to Sunday dinner, which, like in all Southern homes, was something extra. My husband was one of these students, but at first he did not interest me at all. He had the call to come to Africa. He had, back in the West Indies, promised God that if he would be educated he would dedicate his life to Africa. Later, I used to say God called my husband and my husband called me. I said: 'Where is Liberia?' because in my book there were but three lines about how it came to being on the West coast, but then I thought, O.K. we'll live in a mud hut or in a coconut tree, it didn't matter to me. My husband asked me to go to Africa with him, then he asked me to marry him. I imagined Africa as a place desolate with ignorance, I thought it a continent of need that I could help to fill. There was this sense of destiny about Africa, although I don't know that I was mature enough to be all that excited. When we came the First World War was going on. We came on a neutral ship, the *St Paul,* across the Atlantic. It was a beautiful ship, painted white, all lights blazing. We stayed for a while in Liverpool, and I was so struck by the black-out. I remember a fireplace in the house we were staying in, a tea kettle and iron things around the fire, and a warming pan with coals for our bed. How could I think of Africa? It was January and very cold. We changed ships, to the *Egori* — I later heard it was sunk — and set off for Africa. I wasn't twenty yet, you understand.

I remember a terrible storm in the Bay of Biscay. The only safe place to stay was on your bed, but although you kept the window closed the water still came in. I found this little alcove with a seat in it on deck, and I used to go up there and watch the storm. The lifeboats were washed away, I swear you could even see the fish being thrown up out of the water. You couldn't go to the table to eat, even though they had little rails around them, and everybody was in their rooms praying, and I was praying too, and with the help of the Lord we came out of the storm. I remember, though, the captain on the deck shaking his head — there were all sorts of distress calls that he couldn't answer — and there was this great iron tank (I suppose it was) lashed to the side of the ship with wires, great coils of wire, and they were fighting to keep it on board. If it had gone, the ship would have overbalanced. The Lord saw us through. We got to Dakar, and we had to wait while they cleared it of mines.

Those first moments in Africa? Well, I remember my husband being very provoked by colonization. He had always felt that colonization was wrong and that the people of Africa were being mercilessly oppressed. As soon as we saw the boys crawling on the ship at Dakar, we took quite the reverse view: there they were sitting on a gold mine crying 'pour mouth' and not doing anything towards self-development. They didn't even seem to know how to wash their clothes. No, it struck us that the Africans had not really done enough for themselves. But even through the storm and those first thoughts in Dakar, I never began to think of regretting deciding to come. My husband had been posted to a mission in Grand Bassa County. We stayed three weeks in Monrovia, then took this launch — you'd tremble if you saw it — a steamer called the *John Payne,* oh, it was so broken down. The station was thirty miles from the landing place, and most of that was on foot, along these tracks through the bush. We stayed at that mission for five years. When we got to the station, there were ninety-five students, they had yaws and jiggers and the sanitation was very bad. There had been no planting. There was not one cassava, not one goat. By the time we left there were thirty-six goats, nine cows, rice farms, cassava that lasted for years, all types of vegetables, and collard greens as tall as my husband.

What has been fantastic is to see not a town, nor a city, but a whole country develop, and to be a part of it. I have had some terrible experiences here and never regretted coming. All things work if you work together in the Lord. I never tried to destroy anybody, or maim people, just go on in the faith. Soon after I came, I became very, very ill. My husband being from the West Indies knew something about bush medicine, quinine being the only 'proper' medicine, and if you took too much of that you got blackwater fever, and that was instant death. He fixed baths for me, and I sweated it out. He sent for the doctor, and the children explained that it would cost five dollars 'leading fee' — we used to have two-boy or four-boy hammocks, depending on how heavy you were — and they tried to take me to the doctor. I got worse and worse, so they had to turn back. So my husband

wrote a note saying: 'For humanity's sake come and
see my wife.' I was terribly ill, and in those days
there was nothing on the shelves of the stores except
dust. The doctor had to swim a creek on a horse and
eventually he got there. He stayed with me through
the night. He was very impressed with the mission, and
he decided to send his two boys to us. One of them,
James A.A. Pierre, is now Chief Justice of Liberia.
The malaria was terrible, and I was so ignorant of
mosquitoes.

During our first furlough, there was a family
conference. This would be in 1922. I was prone to
such sickness that the doctor advised me not to return
to Africa, and the family said that if I did go back I'd
be disinherited, counted out of the family. To this
day there are members of my family I hardly know.
My father was the only one who never worried, and
he passed. And only one brother, my favourite
brother, kept in touch, and I buried him in 1969. But
we persevered. Everything I do I do as unto the Lord.
The Africans? Many, many are sneaking, mistrustful
and accusing. This comes from slavery. When they talk
of us exploiting them, I say: 'You give us the money
you got for selling us as slaves . . .'

As we have seen, some returnees to Liberia undoubtedly set
out to harness Africans into roles they themselves had just
left. But not all. Others sacrificed a way of life, and what
they found in Liberia in no way deflected their judgments.

In Gbatala, in the interior of Liberia, a small village at
the side of a laterite road that leads to the Guinea border, I
found an elderly gentleman, Mr James Flemister, from whom
contentedness shone in a truly enviable way:

When I was a boy I knew prejudice in the South. On
those narrow roads in Georgia, I remember it was always
my father who gave way when white folks came towards
us. I remember thinking he was a coward. But when in
later life I went to Tennessee and saw it all for myself,
when I was confronted with it, why, I realized my
father was the bravest man that ever lived. Well, I

moved to Chicago as a young man, and I'd been there three Sundays when I heard this great parade and saw this flag I'd never seen before, red, green, black and heard a lot of music. I asked what was that all about? And this guy said to me: 'That's Garvey and they are going back to Africa', and I knew that was for me. I recalled all the talk of Bishop Turner when I was a boy, and here it was again. I signed on with the Garvey Movement in Chicago and signed up for a piece of land by the Cavalla River in Maryland County right here in Liberia. It had all been surveyed and they said a lot of equipment had been shipped and was waiting on the docks. Well, all that fell through, and you know, a funny thing, I've been here since 1951 and I've never even been, like out of curiosity, down to the river to see where the land was supposed to be. I didn't care that Garvey had failed, well, I did, but I never lost my desire to come. I was a janitor and dishwasher in Chicago. I had planned to go to Tuskegee but never did. My education was never too good; when the cotton had to be picked when I was a boy, why you picked it, and you didn't go to classes . . .

I was forty-seven when I came . . . all the [seven] children were trained to the idea that they were going to come home to Africa, and not one has gone back to the States. It took so long to come because, well I had this idea about travelling. I thought it was actually impossible to get here. Also I had no finance. Then there was the fear of the unknown. I realized that when you break, it means a break away from the church, and the community, and even your merchant you trade with. And it's not just a matter of yourself. There's your family to think of. But people think funny things. My brother said: 'You be sure and take a big gun.' I said: 'Why?' And he said: 'Aw, well, er, you never know.' Anyway, one day I went to see this Mrs Crockett who was vice-principal of my boys' school and said I wanted their transcripts [school records] because I was going to take them to Africa. She said: 'Whatever for?' I said: 'I'm going to Africa to seek something you can feel within but you can't see with your eye.' Without a word she gave me those transcripts. Then I saw my estate agent and said: 'I'm selling my house because I'm going to Africa.' And he said: 'Wha-a-at? All these years you been talking 'bout goin' to Africa and you really gonna do it?' Yes, I said. 'Well,' he said, 'maybe I can help you.' He came and asked me how much I wanted for my place. I said four thousand dollars. He went away and we started reckoning up our debts and how much we would need at the beginning in Africa, and we were two thousand dollars short. Yowee! So I went back and said to the agent, 'I'm sorry, I can't sell for four thousand dollars', and he said he thought that had been pretty cheap anyway. A couple of days later he came and said he would give me six thousand dollars, and he would also give me his commission, which was two hundred and fifty dollars. But, he said: 'I don't have much time.' I said: 'Nonsense. You come when we've built a house, you come and visit us in Africa.' We drove down town and signed it all. That was the Tuesday. On the Thursday he dropped down dead.

We paid off our debts and bought the tickets. The office said it would be two thousand five hundred dollars, but with that number of tickets all the stuff would go for nothing. We went down to New Orleans, and they said the furniture was going to cost one thousand two hundred dollars. I said, 'You just go ahead and throw it in the ocean. I'm not able to pay that.' In the end they made us pay eight hundred dollars. By the time we got here we had just ninety-two dollars. The nearer the ship got to Africa the more nervous I became. We got here one Saturday morning. One of my boys had come here forty days before. Well, he'd made a lot of friends but hadn't gotten us a house or anywhere to stay. He met us with his friends with two trucks and we had to set about finding a place. We went to see the Assistant Secretary of State. See, I had written from the States to the Secretary, the Honourable Gabriel Dennis, but when we got here he wasn't in Monrovia, he was in Europe. Anyway, this guy took us round and took us to an apartment house. Sure we got an apartment, they said, one hundred and fifty dollars a month, one year in advance. Sheee! Then we were told at another place, one hundred dollars a month, six months in advance. Wow! By then we were getting desperate. We went next to this lady, and this Assistant Secretary of State, he said, well this is the end. This lady, she's something of a dragon. We took it. Instead of being a dragon she was the greatest person you can imagine. She gave us a whole floor at her place, and we stayed six months.

You know, all the way coming over I was saying: 'When I get there I'm gonna kiss the ground', and my daughter, the eldest, said: 'Oh pa, don't you embarrass us', and my wife said: 'No Jim, you ain't going to do no such thing.' So I didn't, but I really felt like doing it. I still had this sense of fear of the unknown and a feeling of insufficiency, a feeling that I wasn't qualified to meet the thing I was coming to. Tubman took care of things straight away. What a man. We had an audience with him, and I knew he was suspicious because so many Americans were coming, then leaving again. I said: 'Sir, I want to become a citizen', and he said: 'Are you sure?' I said: 'Yes sir. And the only thing that's wrong with me can be cured with a little hard work.' And he said: 'Well, just you acclimate yourself and get about a bit and we'll put you to work.' He also paid our rent for the first three months. We were the largest family to have come here in thirty years, and people thought us a curiosity and kept calling by to see us. I started work with the Public Works Department, building some culverts in the street. They wouldn't let me do too much work. I did very little for six weeks, then I was sent for and they said: 'You're going to go on heavy duty work.' That was my wife's fault. When Tubman had asked what I could do, I'd thought for a while and was about to say: 'Well, nothing,' and my wife said: 'He can do heavy duty vehicle work, sir.' I choked and tried to stop her, because you see I'd never done anything of the kind. They put me to a 'dozer, and me and this boy tried to make it work, but we couldn't put it right, then they took me to this motor grader. The guy showed me how to work it, and I didn't know what he was talking about, and I operated it in second gear for three days. Then ditch-digging — I'd never done that before either — and that seemed to be all right. So I got higher and higher. I ended with quite a senior job, until my health got bad. Oh, I guess there were heartaches. My dear wife died. But there hasn't been one incident that has made me regret coming here for one minute. I am very poor, but what I have made I have made here. You know, it surpassed everything I thought it would be. I expected nothing but hard work and troubles. I found automobiles and lights that burn — sometimes — and I would *never* go back. Mostly it's what I see in the years to come. Here, I found there was nothing between me and the top but myself.

Mr Flemister remarried and spends his retirement in his vegetable patch. He also grows pineapples and citrus fruit which he sometimes sells. His neat house smells of warm scones, while around him the scrubby land, occasionally thick with rubber trees, pours out a low screech of insects. Two of his sons run a very successful electronics business in Monrovia. As I was leaving, Mr Flemister said: 'Man, ain't it *nice?*'

Of course, other people powered with such a drive are sometimes less than ecstatic when they reach Liberia, and their experience can show just how precarious ideas based on an African idyll are. A few hundred yards back down the dusty red road from Mr Flemister's to the capital is a straggling compound, formerly a road gangers' camp, now occupied by Jim Greer and his family. Greer is a Black Hebrew, one of a group of American blacks who believed they were descendants of Abraham — who, they claimed, was black — and whose ancestors were dispersed up the Nile by persecution and sold into slavery. In 1967 a group of several hundred emigrated to Liberia. Only eight or so are left. One runs an excellent ice-cream parlour in Monrovia, another is a secretary, a third is a self-defence teacher. Greer himself appears to be the sole inheritor of a pastoral ideal that was created in the streets of Chicago and collapsed in the Liberian bush.

The group of Black Hebrew fundamentalists gathered in Chicago in the early 1960s. Their original idea was to found a rural community in the United States. Then the desire for a Return took hold. There was considerable disagreement over whether this return should be to Israel or to Ethiopia. Finally the African faction prevailed. According to Greer, they believed that they would not be given visas for Ethiopia, so it was decided to emigrate to Liberia instead. In his bungalow in Gbatala, Jim Greer gave me this account:

> You might say our philosophy is similar to that of the Rastafas [sic], although we were not so much involved in doctrine. The basic concept was to live a communal type of existence, sharing everything equally. My interest arose from three articles in the *Chicago Courier* by some economist. He said that the black 'problem' was not religious, political or social, but economic. Before you solve anything else you have to solve the economic problems. I had a business dealing in freezer foods that could potentially make a hundred thousand dollars a year, but then it fell through. I went for a job at Pepsi-Cola and they told me that at thirty-five I was too old. I ended up taking a job in the building trade as a labourer. I was getting older and not accomplishing anything. At that time, in the early 'sixties, everybody was talking about integration and I couldn't see any sense in it. Forced integration is as bad as forced separation. We had kept away from white economics and politics and white women but still we hadn't gotten anywhere. They made us the laughing stock of the world, man, the laughing stock of the world. Look at the Superfly concept. The only way they make a hero of a black man is by having him as a pimp and a pusher. You realize something very simple. That the black man in America can't set up an industry in America to produce goods that will be consumed in America. One alternative is to set up an American industry in Africa to produce goods that will be consumed in Africa. Production is the key to the salvation of Africa, you understand what I mean? That

was my plan, once we had set up a community.

But more than that. The United States is a nation with plenty to repent about, how it has gained its wealth, how it has used it. It is the only nation ever to have dropped the atomic bomb on people. I would rather stay here with nothing at all than go back and share the suffering of the retribution they are going to suffer. I came here on July 26th, 1967, and I was the first of the group. We thought two hundred would come, but through the rest of the year, many more than that came, and many left. We bought* three hundred acres of land at fifty cents an acre right here in Gbatala. We also had a subsidy [of fifty dollars a month for every passport holder]. We made a lot of mistakes. We came at the wrong time of the year. We relied too much on money from the United States, charity collections and so on, and bad publicity dried that up. We mostly lived in tents but some people built small huts. The hang-ups came through the culture difference. This was the whole reason why most couldn't stay in Liberia. I myself had a lot of technical know-how, that's how I could stay and manage. I don't regret that most people went back. But American society has created a monster, a person who can't do anything for himself, or build his own house.

As soon as we moved out of Monrovia we realized we had no independence. The pioneering spirit was on too high a level, on an abstract level.

There was too much concentration on politics, and that created cliques and we had, at the same time, no programme for orienting ourselves into the culture. Nobody spoke Kpelle, of course. We came to realize something very remarkable about the true relation between the slave and the free man. We imagined we

---

* Only citizens of Liberia can buy land. Every genuine immigrant is given a grant of twenty-five acres of farm land or a town lot on which to build a house. A different arrangement appears to have been worked out for the Hebrews. They bought some land, which is now in a Liberian citizen's name, and were allowed to attempt to work it.

248

would be the free ones and we would liberate the enslaved Africans. It was quite the opposite. The Kpelle man is truly independent, a free man. He can feed himself, and build his own house, and if he is sick he can go out into the bush and easily find the right medicine. He has self-reliance, a true self-sustenance. We realized that there had been patterns of know-how that had been formed in us in the States that were wrong, that what we had been made into by acquiring this know-how was completely alien to Africa. Neither us or the Africans were able readily to change. We employed Africans to do things that they can do for themselves but we couldn't. They couldn't understand this. We created a situation whereby they wanted to gain money from us, but for things, to buy things that would make them enslaved, things they didn't need, consumer things, and we were the source of this evil influence. We knew we hadn't freed ourselves from anything the United States had made us, and unintentionally we were trying to make the Kpelles into people who were just as enslaved.

Our first death was an old man who had been ailing before we came. We hadn't been trained to deal with it. There was this dead person and we didn't know what to do. We had to resort to the Kpelles because they knew what to do. Then our first birth. It was incomplete, and we had to send the woman to hospital because we didn't have the intellectual or physical means of dealing with it. Now, of course, I know that there are midwives all around us, as well qualified and experienced as any in the West, and also people who can deal with any of those other things that go wrong with women. But we didn't know then. So our major problem was in not being able to re-pattern our minds. We should have started with short-range crops, vegetables, pineapples, pawpaw, then gone on to long-range crops. That would have been all right. But we put in cassava, sugar cane and so on. When they came up it was unexpected. I mean, we had no idea how to farm in the tropics. There was a constant flow of people going back to America. About fifty per cent went back to the States. I found that I could stay and make my home here, although I realized that it was not naturally my home, it had to be made so.

For years here I felt insecure because I didn't feel equal to what the environment might spring on me. But now, if I don't have money I know that nobody else around here has money, and if I turn out my pocket and there's nothing there, then that's no big deal. I don't have any fear about survival now. I can make a pair of pants that's as good as any they can make around here, and if I have holes in the soles of my shoes, well so does everybody else here. Your ability — your confidence in your ability — to cope with the opposition of the environment makes you secure. We accomplished something. The whole world, why we made them aware, and we were the only group actually to make a move.

The production that Jim Greer has gone into for 'Africans is that of bed frames and other furniture, wire coat hangers and ersatz African jewellery, which he sells in Monrovia. One man in Gbatala told me: 'They tried to cut the bush with machetes, twelve of them. Everybody told them, but they said they had done it in Illinois, and in a whole morning they had only done what one man could have done in five minutes. They wouldn't take jobs. One couple was running a chicken farm near here, and doing a pretty good job of it, but the leader made them give it up and go back to the camp. They didn't behave like men. They behaved like cry-babies. Like men looking for fool's gold. They were just helpless'.

Before I left Jim Greer in Gbatala, we stood for a moment by the baking road. Then he said: 'The white man, when he touched us, he touched the apple of Almighty God's eye. What did we ever do? He made us covet him. Now the retribution for the white man will be terrible. All men will go back to where they came from, there won't be any more slaves. I hear that there have been a hundred tornadoes in America this year. Garvey did say he would come back in a storm . . .'

One half of the Hebrews went back to the United States, and the other half moved on and tried to emigrate to Israel.[5]

The first party of four families arrived at Lod airport in

1969 asking to be treated as Jewish immigrants. Taken by surprise, immigration officials gave them tourist visas, and they were treated as potential immigrants and taken to Dimona, an expanding, polyglot industrial town in the Negev Desert. They were welcomed there, and given jobs in the local textile mills. When a second group arrived, they too were settled in Dimona and publicized as a counter to the Arab accusation that the Israelis were as anti-black as white colonists. But then, without warning, many more began pouring in from Liberia and the United States.

Officials began denying entry to some, but the community at Dimona grew, with local residents complaining about over-crowding in the Black Hebrews' living quarters. (There were never, on the other hand, complaints about their behaviour.) Examined by rabbis, they were found to have scant Talmudic or religious knowledge. Finally they were told that if they were to be allowed to stay in Israel, they must convert to Judaism according to the religious law of Halacha. They refused and brought a test case to the Israeli Supreme Court. It was found that they did not qualify for immigrant status under the Israeli law of return, since they did not prove they were born of Jewish mothers, or that they had been properly converted. An appeal was rejected. And thus hope for an alternative home in another Promised Land was confounded.

Migration to Liberia has, in fact, been mostly to urban areas, and in particular to the synthetic community of Monrovia. Adjustment to the tribal societies in Liberia can, as the Black Hebrews discovered, be an exceedingly difficult experience. For the black American adjusting to Monrovia, it is a matter of finding an involuted black aspiration that may count them in instead of out. It is exclusive, dominated by a number of families, such as the Tolberts, the Shermans, the Barclays, and the Dennises. The American wife of a leading Liberian said: 'I know one family that has a picnic every year so that everyone will see exactly who's in the family so that they know who they mustn't marry.' But once you are in, it is comfortable and satisfying in a materialistic way. A black American businessman in Monrovia described it to me:

> There's no language or monetary problems. A man can

adjust here more easily than anywhere else in Africa. I
married a Liberian in the States, and my idea was to just
come here and have a fling for a couple of years. I wasn't
that set on staying. But when I went back to the States I
began asking myself: 'Where do I belong? Here or there?'
The rewards here are much more tangible. And you have
the freedom of movement, there's nowhere you can't go.
Can you imagine it? Sure, it's like some little Southern
town, like hundreds of them, except that the judges are
black, the cops are black, everybody's black. You are in
the majority for the first time in your life. If someone's
going to be uncomfortable, let someone else be
uncomfortable. When I got here, the airline seemed to
reserve for Africa the lousiest, dirtiest, noisiest place in
the entire fleet. I was all shook up. It was cloudy, like
it had just been raining, although there was this red dust
everywhere. I arrived covered in this dust. Then people
were offering jobs at two thousand five hundred dollars a
year. This was 1959. I said they gotta be kidding . . . but
the point is that kids outta college these days, they take
a job at nine thousand dollars, they mortgage themselves,
get far into debt, nice big car, get a regular raise of five
hundred dollars a year, until they get to thirteen or
fifteen thousand, and then no more. They're trapped.
Here, that's just when you're taking off. When you get to
other countries in West Africa you realize how unlike
Africa it really is. Our executives coming through here
breathe a sigh of relief. 'Civilization at last', they say.
Sure, it's a small society, and they don't overly want an
outsider. I was fortunate because of my family connection.
When an Afro-American comes here he comes from a
background of being disadvantaged, so he finds it
surprising. Here the Americo-Liberians are advantaged,
so to say, in their own country. When an Americo-
Liberian studies international law, he may go on ahead
and practise it, but your feeling is that if an Afro-
American does, the best he can expect is to run a corner
store in Harlem. It takes some time to realize that you
are just like one of these people, just the same. You
may not be part of the inner group, but you are One of
Them.

So, for many, Liberia is a means of achieving solid American virtues, associated with a bourgeois calm and personal empire building. Instead of being consigned to a lower-middle-class bracket and mediocre comfort, they can be extremely comfortable as part of the ruling class in Liberia. One American wife said: 'I feel in no sense assimilated into Africa, but then you couldn't say we would be assimilated in any real way in America. We have things here, a nice house in Monrovia, a little farm up-country, and we're doing very well.' Another said: 'I'm satisfied. But what I have is my own and I will use it for myself. I could speak all twenty-six dialects and be as black as that telephone but I will still be an American to them, so . . . '

It is, then, a chance to create a black Connecticut that has brought many black Americans to Liberia. And they can be satisfied because that is precisely what they have created in one section of Monrovia. Of course, there is no blame attached to that, and many realize that the community they have entered is itself an 'outsider' to the rest of West Africa. They naturally feel more at home in a black suburb in Liberia than they would in a similar suburb in America. 'Say what you like, it's better than Chicago right now', said a black American tourist who told me he firmly intended to come back and settle.

The Liberian Government, never slow to sense an ambition that might end in a deal, recognizes that a middle-class Back-to-Africa interest would not only be profitable but, at long last, good publicity.

In November 1972, the Reverend Jesse Jackson visited Monrovia with a delegation of black Americans. His group had a series of talks with the President, William Tolbert, and a number of proposals were published. The Ministry of Information in Monrovia described the talks as 'perhaps the most significant development ever in relations between an African Government and black Americans'. It was proposed that incentives be offered to black American businessmen to invest in Liberia. In return Jackson would ensure that outlets for Liberian-manufactured goods would be created in America. Jackson said on television: 'It is high time for the nearly thirty million American blacks, who have a gross national product of some forty-two thousand million dollars, to start moving from "lip service" to "ship service" with Africa, which means black Americans buying products made in Africa, in Liberia in this case, and to exchanging a variety of skills with African countries.' The possibility of dual Liberian and American citizenship was also mooted. Even more tempting was a proposal from a group of American real estate developers to build fifty thousand houses in Liberia, to be offered as second homes for black Americans.[6]

These proposals were very well publicized at the time as a generous offer by Liberia to Afro-Americans. In fact, the free movement of currency through Liberia does have its attractions. But when I arrived in Liberia some time later, there had been few inquiries, and fewer takers. 'In fact, none, actually', said a man who had been closely concerned in the negotiations. There was no doubt, he said, about the 'compatibility' between Operation Push (Jackson's People United to Save Humanity) and the Liberian Government's Rally Time, in which every Liberian citizen was being asked to subscribe voluntarily to a ten-million-dollar Government redevelopment fund. (A number of Civil Servants were somewhat surprised to find that they had 'volunteered' one month's salary.) But one problem, said the official, was that of finding a formula on the matter of dual citizenship. The problem was to enable well-to-do black Americans to have this facility, but not white Americans (which, in any case, is probably contrary to the American Constitution) and certainly not any poverty-stricken brethren from further north in West Africa. 'It was all much too vague', he said. But he added: 'We're always interested in investment . . . ' A senior official at the Liberian State Department vouchsafed: 'I don't think it'll come to anything at all. Black Americans lack the pioneering spirit.'

But what has been the result of the initial pioneering spirit of the ill-starred repatriation from America? What are the historical consequences of the return of the lost tribes?

White American and European investment command the economy of Liberia. Apart from the rubber, there are vast quantities of iron ore, now virtually accounted for by American, Swedish and German concerns. The Swedes are sitting on what is literally an iron mountain at Nimba, near the Guinea border. Germany, with an estimated 150 million dollars invested, is second only to the United States, with more than 244 million dollars, in overall investment in Liberia. (The United Kingdom's share is around four million dollars.) Despite immense profits to be made from its resources, Liberia is still a very poor country, its under-developed hinterland (underdeveloped, that is, except for foreign-owned rubber plantations, company towns and the farms owned by rich Monrovians) is a sad monument to the true nature of the late President Tubman's much-vaunted Interior Policy. Government public relations men thrust assurances at you of increased participation by people of tribal origin in government and of energetic efforts to expand services in the interior. The sincerity of the latter claim can only be judged in later years; expenditure has certainly increased, but there is such an age-old backlog of total neglect that it is difficult to see that spending has made much discernible impression. Liberia's chief crime is indeed that it is poor and black in a rich, white world, and the country has been alternately abandoned and coveted, isolated and clamorously surrounded, disavowed by the colonial powers yet commercially colonized. The activities of the ruling cliques have not helped the reputation of Liberia in times when the world was more accustomed to believe the hypocrisies of the colonial nations. When the 'unacceptable face of capitalism' is a black face, then it appears to be doubly unacceptable.

Those who would have expected a dynamic cultural synthesis to have resulted from the meeting of the forces of New World settlers with those of Liberian tribal society are disappointed.

Liberia — and Sierra Leone for that matter — has not shared in the rich literary harvest that has been gathered since the late 1950s in West Africa, and in particular in post-Independence Ghana, Nigeria and Senegal. The only collection of Liberian *oeuvres* I could find was published in Germany in 1970.[7] It contains: *Murder in the Cassava Patch* (actually a rather fine short story by the Assistant Minister of Culture who hailed from the interior), a transcript by the same man of an oral tale, surveys of the natives' songs and stories, and a number of German

travelogues on Africa, only one of which concerns
Liberia, and that is an account of the establishment of
German interest in the ore industry in the late 1950s. In
addition, there is a poem by Beverly R. Wilson, a
nineteenth-century settler:

> Come hither, son of Afric . . . come;
> And o'er the wide and weltering sea,
> Behold thy lost yet lovely home,
> That fondly waits to welcome thee.

Yet the fact is that Americo-Liberians were confused by, and
still have an ambivalent attitude towards, the native cultures
of the interior. Americo-Liberians successfully infiltrated the
tribal secret societies, such as the Poror sect, which are
important social and religious structures, yet maintained
infinitely greater status for the Freemasons. There has been a
great deal of intermarriage and a limited amount of mingling
of traditions — enough to cause some element of culture
shock in black American arrivals — yet the step upwards for
an educated man from the interior is to adopt the quasi-
American ways of the coast.

The native culture of Liberia is as vibrant and vital as
anywhere in West Africa. (The Vei language is one of the
oldest written languages in West Africa; after Arabic, it is
possibly the oldest.[8]) The Americo-Liberian culture is still
essentially foreign. The two have considered each other, as
through a glass partition, without commitment, for 150 years.

A Mandingo who had gained entry to the inner reaches of
Monrovia society explained it to me this way: the corner-
stones of tribal society were traditional religion and morality,
traditional hierarchical authority, a practical education
culminating in initiation into a secret society and plural
marriage. Americo-Liberians had confronted this with a
form of church worship, materialism, a political system
that was foreign, an education system based on literacy and
monogamous marriage. Each culture yearned towards each
other, in much the same way as modern African and Afro-
American cultures yearn towards each other from a distance,
and the consideration Americo-Liberians gave to native
culture was much stronger, if less successful than that shown

by the Creoles to the up-country areas of Sierra Leone.

The ambivalence arose, he said, when America-Liberians realized that to *adopt* the native cultures as their own would effectively lose them the control that their economic and political system and their literacy gave them. Their power was seen to be greater than that of tribal chiefs who controlled much smaller areas. The admittedly tottering economy also gave them an access to the outside world that provided some material benefits.

On the other hand, the natives saw that to share this power, to participate in it, they would have to adopt America-Liberian culture, and in that culture they saw that the churches became increasingly concerned with arguments about the embezzlement of their funds, the political system was increasingly exploitative, the literate education was withheld or unevenly spread, and the marriage practices were only nominally monogamous. It was a culture, he said, that faced the native with a difficult choice: to gain access to this admired new culture involved a participation in that same Western corruption. For the America-Liberian to adopt the native customs means a diminution of his privileged status. Thus, over the years, developed a sort of stand-off position, with each relating to the other's culture only in a bemused way. While it is true that no direct America-Liberian descendants survive, the two cultures are utterly separate.

It is into this mostly recognizable society and culture of the America-Liberian that the Afro-American almost invariably moves.

I had a curious conversation shortly before I left Monrovia. 'The tribal people are not ready for government', said my companion. 'You sound like a Rhodesian,' I said. 'Exactly', he replied. But isn't that just what people said about Liberia before Independence in 1847? 'They were right', he said. 'Surely you can't believe that a dose of colonialism would have done you any good.' 'Absolutely', he affirmed. My companion was not one of the bilious white businessmen of the Coast, nor was he an America-Liberian. He was originally from a tribal area to the west of Monrovia. Monrovia has at least the appearance of a town for which some semblance of a plan was drawn up before work on it started. Its tiny centre is an American grid, and while it thins — or rather thickens — out to familiar slums and lean-tos, separated by sombre dusty alleys, it seems orderly, even if that is precisely what it is not. Freetown gives one the irresistible impression that somehow it began life at the top of the hills behind it and has in some way slithered down the mountains to lie in a wriggling, sweating, protesting heap at the bottom. The city began with a very strict street plan, in fact, but you feel that architectural niceties, such as horizontal or vertical lines, have been thrown to the hot clammy winds, and are replaced by more natural forms, the sag, the warp, the creaking bow. These are unsteadily held together by rotting mortar and carious fissures. The Creole buildings are usually of three storeys, with sloping corrugated iron roofs and teetering balconies of splintering wood or elaborate wrought iron running round them at first-floor level. A short flight of steps would ordinarily lead up to the wooden facade, and the house would usually be presided over by a scraggy vulture. The predominant colours of these shamblingly elegant houses are a kind of faded blood red, with browns, greens and greys mixed in with the occasional dark turquoise. Slotted into every available space between and around the larger houses are the 'adjoinins' — what Graham Greene described as 'horizontal tenements' — more or less habitable sheds added later, as if it had been decided that the grandiose lines of the larger houses were not worth bothering to afford or repeat.

It is a town in which you expect door-handles to come away in your hand and in which you seem to spend as much time extricating your foot from between floorboards as actually standing on them. The whole is crumbling in a self-regenerative way, as if it started crumbling the day it was built, and will always crumble, defying gravity as much as it ultimately defies description. Freetown has a haunting charmlessness, which makes the infrequent moments of beauty all the more weird and astonishing. Towards dusk in the rainy season a violently mauve tinge enters the air, as if a pinch of potassium permanganate has been swirled into the heavy atmosphere, spreading a bizarre cloak of unreality over the city, a land of Oz, perhaps, or a Brigadoon.

Freetown was, of course, excellently described by Graham Greene in *The Heart of the Matter*,[9] and its inhabitants sometimes tiresomely behave as if they were walking-on parts in a Greene novel. The *demi-monde* of Freetown seems propelled by nothing so grand as cupidity, but more by a helpless inability to leave, as if by leaving it would incur the final curse of invisibility. The confluence of all this, for Greene, for the old expatriate Coasters, the more raffish of Sierra Leonan professionals and the new arrival alike, was and is the City Hotel, where, if nothing else, one can at least assert one's dogged visibility. The entire town appears to pass through the peeling hotel on Saturday afternoons. For the rest of the week it is a mumble of a jovial kind of misanthropy, under the hooded, baleful gaze of the owner, Freddie Ferrari, as famous a Coaster as any. Occasionally, there is a flutter, as one of the tough, spectacularly mini-skirted Freetown lovelies, maybe wins the jackpot on the fruit machine, and the hotel is alive with hoots and crackles and pink-knickered bottoms. Or, occasionally, there is a visit from a khaki-clad figure, who strides to the bar, chalks on the floor, 'MR MUSA BOIMA OF KENEMA' and executes a series of cart-wheels all around the floor, holding the while a tray with a glass of water on it. But then the bar subsides, the yellowed faces of the expatriates burying themselves once more in their beer and muttered gossip, and the girls go back to desultory flirting.

The city, and the colony of which it was the centre, has been cruelly mocked, abused and despised down the years. It is as if travellers along the west coast have reserved one very special burst of splenetic contempt for the town and its Creole inhabitants. Sir Richard Burton, travelling there in 1862, was mortified by the 'mildewed cankered gangrened aspect of the decadent Europeo-Tropical settlements' and of all the 'darkies' he encountered, the most unspeakable were undoubtedly the Creoles, 'these spoiled children, [with] their puerile inept ways, their exceedingly bad language, their constant intoxication, and their disposition to quarrel on all occasions'.[10]

A succession of only marginally less malevolent travellers, colonial administrators and writers noted the querulous nature of Freetowners. Mary Kingsley was not free of this same contempt:

> . . . to the casual visitor at Sierra Leone the Mohammedan is a mere passing sensation. You neither feel a burning desire to laugh with, or at him, as in the case of the country folks, nor do you wish to punch his head, and split his coat up his back — things you yearn to do with that perfect flower of Sierra Leone culture, who yells your bald name across the street at you, condescendingly informs you that you can go and get letters that are waiting for you, while he smokes his cigar and lolls in the shade, or in some similar way displays his second-hand rubbishy white culture — a culture far lower and less dignified than that of the stately Mandingo or the bush chief.[11]

This reputation joined that of Sierra Leone's being the White Man's Grave, or, as the magazine *John Bull* put it, 'this costly pest-house'.[12] (Attacks such as these were more often prompted by support for the pro-slavery lobby during the campaign to abolish slavery in the West Indies than by concern for the health of the despised inhabitants of Sierra Leone.) Sierra Leone found a doughty champion in Dr James Africanus Horton. Horton was the son of an Ibo recaptive from Gloucester, behind Freetown. He became a doctor and a redoubtable man of letters. In the 1860s, he expressed the general Creole resentment at being pilloried abroad as 'the most impertinent rogues in all the coast'. Those who made such attacks did not wait for the truth, 'but they rant upon the platform seeing who can crow the loudest . . . [and] . . . forge red-hot sentences at their pens' points . . . '

Against the barrage of damaging contempt, Horton attempted to assert the dignity of the Creoles. 'We are not descendants of slaves, but of a freed people. And putting race and nationality aside, we can compare favourably with those Australians who are descendants of quondam convicts and felons . . . '[13]

There is little evidence to show that Sierra Leone was less healthy for Europeans than, say, the West Indies or Bengal. It was merely one of many malarial areas that came under

260

the sway of the British Empire, and malaria remained a threat only so long as its cause was unknown. (Evidence of the link between malaria and the Anopheles mosquito was first published by Sir Ronald Ross two weeks before the end of the nineteenth century.[14] Horton's injunctions went unheeded by those who preferred racy and factually inaccurate accounts from nineteenth-century travellers and ill-disposed colonial rulers. The reputation for unhealthiness was mostly lately perpetuated by the Sierra Leone Government itself. In 1973 it instituted an Honours List, and among the nineteen orders and medals for this gallantry or that service appeared the Medal of the Mosquito. It was, said a Government spokesman, a tribute to the little hero that had decimated the ranks of the white people and prevented Sierra Leone from becoming a West African Rhodesia. Also, before I left Ghana, a friend said to me: 'Ah, Sierra Leone. The slave touch. We sometimes tell our children that if they don't behave they'll be sent to Sierra Leone where they're really harsh, and then they'll be sorry.'

Others down the years have echoed Burton's contempt for the pretentiousness of the Creoles. Yet from the beginning the early resettlers were imbued with a self-righteous sense of their own importance by their white sponsors, as only with such an attitude could they fulfil a crucial part of the white programme, to be an example to the natives. John Clarkson, who had been sent to Nova Scotia to organize the second group of emigrants, wrote to his colleagues in London in 1791:

> I have told the men that I shall form a very unfavourable opinion of those who may show an inclination to be servants to any gentleman, when they have an opportunity of becoming their own masters, and valuable members of society if they please, and that in short, the character of the black people for ever after will depend on the manner they conduct themselves, and that the fate of millions of their complexion will partly be affected by it.[15]

Their ambiguous superiority was created by their white benefactors and remained one essential element in whites'

attitudes towards the Creoles for some time. The true
ambiguity was revealed, however, when it b :came
apparent that they might exercise this superiority over
the native peoples of the interior, but were not
encouraged to push their luck, as it were, with the white
masters. Not unnaturally anxious to be the beneficiaries
of certain civil rights they had been promised in Nova
Scotia, they pressed the directors of the Sierra Leone
Company, who remarked: 'It should be remembered that
all of them were once slaves; that, like others in the
same state, they were probably little restrained in
many branches of morals . . . they probably know little
of the true nature of civil rights.'[16]

This parallel attitude in white people, the alternate
inflation and deflation of the self-esteem of the
settlers, infuriated the Creoles, who regarded provision
of schools and medical facilities, for example, as rights
and not privileges. It is this ambiguity that is reflected in
many reactions from white people who encountered
Creoles through the nineteenth century: the Creoles
might reinforce the colonial administration, become
agents in the back-breaking interior, and usefully act as a
buffer between the white colonists, on their heights
around the Hill Station, and the troublesome natives of
what became the Protectorate. Once they became
uppity enough to display their artificial rank to whites,
they would not be slapped down, but merely scorned,
a much more damaging and lasting punishment.

Their relationship with the natives of the
Protectorate — established in 1896 — became one of
considerable strain. The natives regarded them as direct
and untrustworthy agents of the colonial administration.
The Creoles, trapped in a set of roles and assumptions
they had too eagerly accepted from the whites, were
despised by the whites with increasing vigour. They
were ridiculed for their dress, their strutting manner,
their air of leisurely privilege, and not least for their
language. It was regarded as merely a bastardization of
English — it is still mistaken for pidgin English — the
brand of the truly ignorant. Blyden noted: 'The speech
of the Sierra Leone streets cannot be called a *patois* of

262

English.' But even this great champion of the black people could not quite extinguish a note of exasperation when talking of the Creole language. He wrote: 'It is not the pigeon English of China nor the unintelligible lingo of the West Indies. It is not the dialect of the Quashee nor the humorous slang of Uncle Remus. It is a transfusion, so to say, of numerous African idioms and phrases. Words from the Timne, Eboe, Aku, Mandingo, Foulah, Soosoo, and Arabic, are blended with words from the English language, which is itself a mixture — so the proper designation of the Sierra Leone vernacular would be . . . *mixture of mixtures, all is mixture.*'[17]

The Americo-Liberians became to a great extent the tools of the Firestone Rubber Company; but while it controlled the Liberian economy, the company did not install a complete governmental administration. The Sierra Leone Creoles were *seen* to be propped up by British colonial rule. The discovery of ore and diamond deposits, and the growth of the mining industries, brought wealth to the provinces. This wealth gave the people of the Protectorate a basis from which to challenge the Creoles politically. In Liberia the wealth was concentrated in the companies concerned and in a number of pockets in Monrovia. The rise of dynamic Sierra Leone anti-colonialist movements, chief of which was that of Wallace Johnson, and the wane of colonialism in West Africa, left the Creoles on a limb, bewildered and resentful. They had made no attempt to relate as equals to the Africans of the interior, and their isolation was underlined when, on the basis of majority representation, the assembly of Independence left them in a minority.

There is nothing so vulnerable, to whites and newly independent Africans alike, as the shambling relic of a power formerly exercised and now seen as a feeble sham. The majority of the bombastic, self-deluded white blimps left West Africa with the coming of Independence to, say, Ghana and Nigeria. The remnants of this caste of Englishmen, those who might never again fit into English society, totter about, the objects of hearty ridicule. But the Creoles had no escape back to Europe, and they were condemned to remain amid the scenes of their former transitory glory. They do retain important influences in certain sections of Freetown society, and their manners are to this day scrupulously copied by some people from the interior. They still have the air of an educated, cultured class. To me, watching the legions of Creoles marching off to church on a Sunday evening in their strange Victorian garb, hearing the oddly mellifluous accent with its French guttural 'r', and meeting and talking with young Creoles, they seemed as a group to be far from objectionable. Those who had blinded themselves to loss of political power seemed simply pitiable, not unlike Distressed Gentlefolk.

The Americo-Liberians are not given to critical self-analysis, whereas there are in the Creole community astute and scholarly men who are more than able to examine their own society. But as in Liberia, the body of literature among the Creoles is slender, as if their emotional group status is even now still too sensitive to be examined. There are critics of international repute, such as Eldred Jones, yet the situation of the Creole himself has provoked little literary speculation, among a traditionally literate group. The 'twice-removed' position of the Creoles produced a social but not an artistic introspection. The most widely read piece of Creole literature is *Kossoh Town Boy,* by Robert Wellesley Cole, required-reading as an account of a Creole upbringing. It is a vivid and fascinating work, but while the author remarks that 'we were British, if not Britons' there is scant exploration of the Creole identity. This remains to Creoles a difficult and diffuse matter. Only in the early 1970s were there glimmerings of the vein being mined. One young Freetown poet writes of

> . . . the nigger who does not know
> his own genes who knows
> his Afro-Saxon name . . .[18]

But if a small number of young *literati* have started looking at the bruised result of a 150-year-long dupe, the *mores* and manners of the Creoles are still to many a curiously prized culture.

Black New Worlders in Sierra Leone are principally from

the formerly British West Indies. A substantial number are the wives of educated Creoles whose families could afford to send them to Britain or the United States to study, and some are professional people or businessmen.

There has been a slim tradition of contact and migration between the West Indies and Sierra Leone. During the early part of the nineteenth century the mortality rate among the European soldiers of the Royal African Corps, based in Freetown, was so high that it was decided to re-garrison with black troops from the West Indies. In May 1819, the headquarters and five companies of the Second West India Regiment were moved to Sierra Leone to garrison that country, the Isles of Los, and the Gambia. West Indian soldiers from the Freetown headquarters later fought in the Ashanti wars. (On the fall of Kumasi in 1896 it was a West Indian soldier who donated the first shilling towards a new Basel Mission in Kumasi.) Descendants of these soldiers are still to be found in the Cape Coast area of Ghana. Soldiers from the West Indies continued to man the Tower Hill barracks through the nineteenth century and the first part of this century. Another group of West Indians arrived in Sierra Leone during the early part of this century, to work as drivers and mechanics on the railway system — since closed down. Few of these survive today. In addition, West Indian teachers were recruited for several educational and religious establishments.

Sierra Leone is not normally a destination for those fired with ideas of mystic Africa. Its ill-gotten reputation would discourage that, and since 1800 no serious organized attempt has been made to resettle New World blacks there. But those individuals who have gone have settled in or near Freetown, so it is to that unique Freetown Creole society that they must primarily adjust.

West Indians whom I met remarked at how similar they found parts of Freetown to, say, Georgetown, and at how they were struck by the similarity in appearance of parts of the Sierra Leone coast to that of areas in the Caribbean.

Many also noted complex reactions to the Creoles themselves. They talked of the process of adjustment being almost the reverse of the experience New Worlders undergo in other parts of West Africa. Elsewhere, the immigrants

feel they are beginning from a standpoint of finding
everything strange. They are confronted with an alien
environment with which they must gradually become
familiarized. Even those who spoke of familiar details in the
landscape of Africa or the ways of Africans accepted that
black Africa was at first outlandish and strange, and only
after a while did it even begin to form a pattern to which
they could relate. On the other hand, the first impression
of a West Indian arriving in Sierra Leone and meeting
Creoles was frequently of the familiarity of the scene and
attitudes. The Creole language has elements that are
recognizable from the West Indies, attitudes appear to be
not dissimilar from fairly strict Jamaican middle-class
attitudes, and the living conditions of the middle class
do not appear to be very different. The culture shock
was therefore delayed and sometimes intensified. The
familiarity was an illusion, disguising a deeply separate
culture.

The shock of realization of these differences might
come in many different ways. It may be a mounting
irritation at Creole talk. Said one wife: 'I just got to hate
it. When I was pregnant they called me *bella woman,*
heavens! "belly woman". They'd say, *"Look na de bella
woman com."* '

But it may be a more serious matter. Another wife told
me: 'At first, I thought it was all so familiar, even talking
with my husband's family. Then after a while, when I'd met
more of them, I got this strange feeling of somehow
talking to a generation that was not just one above me,
but God knows how many, eight or nine or ten.'

A Jamaican wife said:

At first I thought the Creoles were very like
Jamaicans. Then I realized they were like one
particular group of middle-class Jamaican people,
the sort of people, oh, who would react to reggae
and say it was raw and uncouth and rebellious, and
even filthy, and they would disapprove, and condemn
it, even though the rest of the world saw it, quite
rightly, as an expression of at least a part of the
island's population. I found the atmosphere unreal and

stifling. It was only when I started learning about African cultures in the interior that I felt happier. I probably know more now about the African culture than the average Creole does.

It was, said others, almost a deception that Freetown perpetrated, and as time went by they simply became more distanced from it. It was African and yet it was not, it was solid and yet it was ephemeral, it was of the Caribbean and yet it was increasingly unrelated.

Some remarked that they had left their islands to lose the Caribbean sense of claustrophobia, only to find an even more enclosed society in Freetown. 'You do get the feeling of wide open African spaces,' said one immigrant from Jamaica, 'but you sometimes feel you are in a bottle in the middle of it.'

The son of West Indian settlers gave me an almost perfect prescription for acceptability in Creoledom. He said:

There are certain things which absolutely *must* be in a person's life or background before he'll be considered even as an honorary Creole. The first is religion. He must be a Christian, although in fact there are a number of Muslim Creoles. If you are a sidesman in church, you have a great advantage. He must speak the Creole language, which is not as easy as it sounds. For lunch on Saturday he must east cassava *fufu* and *plassas* [palaver sauce]. Without fail. He must maintain a kind of condescension towards the people of the old Protectorate, and that includes the politicians. Creoles now like to feel themselves to be above politics, and only natives go in for it. He must adopt a kind of Western culture pattern, a very special kind, like wearing a bowler hat or a top hat, adopt a Victorian culture pattern which really doesn't bear any relation to present-day Western culture. He must share a reverence for the past, and he must be acceptable on an individual level in a social circle. If somewhere along the line he can acquire a Creole name, the process is complete. I myself have the feeling that I'm only just accepted, even though my family has been here for

267

many many years. The white outsider would never expect to be integrated into Creole society, but it is very nearly possible for the black West Indian. But is is still very difficult indeed.

West Indians from somewhat more open societies are therefore shocked at how rigid, inhibited and snobbish some sections of Creole society are.

And yet, for all that, there are those who successfully merge into Freetown. A former mariner from the West Indies told me this compelling story:

My grandfather was the son of an ex-slave, so this gave me the desire to return to Africa. I remember as a child getting books from the library about explorers and campaigners against slavery, and I got very caught up by them. I think I went to sea with some feeling of looking for somewhere to belong. I first came here during the war, in 1940. We just loaded and turned around and went on. The next time I came, in February 1941, I remember being very struck indeed by places like Masimera and Marampa, at how like it was to the parts of Guyana I knew. While we were load-ing coal we stayed a month, and I remember meeting a number of people who reminded me of people back in the West Indies. In particular, I met one woman who told me a very strange thing. 'You are going to die here.' Of course, I didn't know what she was talking about. Later, we were torpedoed, and after six days in a boat, we were landed here in Freetown. There were so many survivors in Freetown at that time, a regular depot, but one little boy recognized me and remembered me, and he took me to the same woman. She looked after me, but again, as I was leaving, she told me I would die here. I had short periods here shortly after that, but then went on to routes through the United States and Europe. Finally after the war, I went home. I had seen all these places and been through the war, and for years after it was always nagging in my mind that Africa was where I belonged. I went to England then, and won

some money on three horses: Teal, Running Water and
Tulyar. With the money I signed on a ship in Liverpool
and came back to Freetown. I took a job at four
shillings and twopence a day in the fisheries, but made
my way into the tug service, where I was very successful.
If only I had come to Africa twenty years before,
thirty years. I lost thirty years of my life in the West
Indies. Rum, dancing, our own kind of permissive
society. My marriage went wrong there. Yes. The things
that never brought me any joy are in the West Indies.
I married again here. Now, my wife was in town one
day, it was 1964, when she met the woman who had
taken care of me all that time before. She was an old
woman then. But she turned out to be my wife's
sister's godmother . . .
    When I came here I felt immediately at home. There
was no misunderstanding. That depends on your
attitude and spiritual needs. But I had a peculiar feeling.
You can go into a person's house and feel uncomfortable
No reason. I often used to get this, a feeling of
tenseness. But here I have felt a complete lack of
tenseness. When I came here I only expected one thing,
and that was that I would be among my own kind. I
have never had the urge to go back, never felt one
moment's homesickness. What we have in common with
the Creoles is the lack of culture and real language. This
is something we can never get back, but it's something we
share. I wish I could live my life over again. I would
live it all in this country.

The honest admission of the sense of sharing a burglarized
cultural heritage was surprisingly strong in some West
Indians I met in Sierra Leone. Where this sense of loss or
impairment of heritage was strong enough on a personal
level, the immigrant adjusted well to the community of
Creoles who still remain hesitantly outside the frame of
Africa. A businessman from Grenada told me:

    I look at myself and say I'm African, yes. Then, no,
    I *was*. I'm like the Creole. But no again, not even like
    him, but more like him than any other group in the

world, in that I don't really *know* what I am. Quite
unlike the Africans who simply know they are Temne,
or Susu, or Mende, or whatever. Without the Creoles I
could never have stayed here. I could never live in an
African African society like Ghana or Nigeria or up-
country here. My social contacts are within the Creole
level, or among those Africans who have been
thoroughly urbanized.

John Stuart Mill gave as the basic elements of nationalism —
and by inference, of all national identity — 'identity of
political antecedents; the possession of a national history,
and a consequent community of recollections; collective
pride and humiliation, pleasure and regret, connected with
the . . . past'.[19] The destruction of this community of
recollections is the heart of the crime of slavery since, after
centuries have passed, it can never be rebuilt.

Du Bois was more optimistic. He wrote:

> My tie to Africa is strong. On this vast continent were
> born and lived a large portion of my direct ancestors
> going back a thousand years or more. But one thing is
> sure and that is the fact that since the fifteenth century
> these ancestors of mine and their other descendants
> have had a common history; have suffered a common
> disaster and have one long memory . . . the real essence
> of this kinship is its social heritage of slavery; the
> discrimination and insult; and this heritage binds
> together not simply the children of Africa, but extends
> through yellow Asia and into the South Seas. It is this
> unity that draws me to Africa.[20]

But Creole society is itself a reflection of the destruction — or
at least the partially successful destruction — of the common
heritage, as much as Afro-American society and that of the
West Indies may be held to be. Those New World black
repatriates I met who had considered this realized that to
re-enter this community of African recollection completely
was impossible. A community attitude is achieved by
absorbing its assumptions; it is an unconscious affair that

must go on despite the conscious efforts to adjust to the environment. Those direct efforts which can be made must, necessarily, be made gently.

I talked of this with a Jamaican, now retired, who had been in Sierra Leone since childhood, had been educated there, had married a Sierra Leonean, and had held an important job which entailed long periods in the Protectorate. He said that he himself had always considered it possible to graft on to himself the two or three hundred years of cultural heritage he had missed and to feel it as naturally and ordinarily as any African could. (In many ways, he seemed more attuned to Africa than most Creoles were.) The only reason he doubted it was that he had missed the 'seep' of impressions from parents and early childhood. He explained this lack:

It takes years and it comes from the Africans themselves. They are very well aware, albeit in a vague oral way, of their traditional heritage. Their history lives in them in a vital, un-selfconscious present way. They are their history, the past is not something they are divorced from in the way Westerners are divorced from theirs. If you can truly relate to them, then you are relating to their history, and thence to your own. I have returned to Africa as black as I left it — and admittedly I returned at a very early age — and I feel that if you can grow *with* people, then you can regain your past.

I have tried not to extrapolate too many generalizations from the experiences of those black Americans and West Indians I spoke to in West Africa, and from the histories of the communities of New World blacks that were transplanted back to Africa in the last century, because the Return is such an individual experience, not unakin, as one wife told me, to a form of romantic love. I met those who were highly successful, and those who had experienced bitter disaster. West Africa is a merciless environment in which to come to terms with subtle, barely understood, predispositions.

Politically, black Americans and West Indians have made a great and enduring contribution to Africa. As Jewish Zionism was a creation of the Diaspora, so Pan-Africanism was a product of the American and Caribbean exile. The literature and philosophy provoked by Africa, real and imagined, in the New World, are ample testament to a singularly talented race, afflicted as it was by the unparelleled abomination of slavery. Africa will undoubtedly continue to be a painful and enlarging inspiration to black Americans. Africa, still so much the benighted but proud continent, will continue to need the talents of its black brethren in exile.

Yet, in the light of the history of the past one hundred and eighty years or so, the physical return to Africa has never been an answer to the sufferings of the New World Negroes, and utopian dreams have crumbled. The dreams gave American Negroes new pride and determination, and revitalized a demoralized society. But in reality, the groups who returned failed to merge back into Africa, at least in Liberia and Sierra Leone. This is no doubt because they returned in groups and managed to maintain their own cultural identity in an essentially foreign land. In many ways, the return of these groups may be said not to have benefitted the Africans greatly. Just as the Palestinian people were the hapless victims of Jewish Zionism, so the Africans of the interiors of Liberia and Sierra Leone became the victims of the Back-to-Africa fantasy.

Skilled and sensitive New World black individuals, however, patently do have a future in Africa. Many I met had made a very great impact on African communities, and were serving them, and themselves, well enough. There was no gainsaying the spirit of brotherhood that existed between these Negroes and Africans. I met many brave and admirable men who had made the journey back, and many equally courageous women who had made the enormous commitment to Africa. Those who succeeded found a peace and energy they could never otherwise have found. Those who failed are, in reality, more sad victims of the viciousness of the white race.

SOURCES

In the historical sections I have mostly used secondary
sources, except where stated. The primary sources were
mainly in the Ghana National Archives in Accra, or in the
archives of Fourah Bay College, University of Sierra Leone,
Freetown. Like many other recent writers on Sierra Leone,
I vainly attempted to unearth material overlooked by
Christopher Fyfe in his massive but brilliant *A History of
Sierra Leone.* This is a truly monumental work, and I
acknowledge my enormous debt to it. Accounts of early
settlers in Freetown were in Prince Hoare's biography of
Granville Sharp and elsewhere. There are two other notable
histories of Sierra Leone: John Peterson's *Province of
Freedom, 1787-1870,* and Arthur Porter's *Creoledom.*
Other sources are acknowledged in notes to each chapter.
Richard West's *Back to Africa* —an interpretative history of
both Sierra Leone and Liberia — is full and very incisive. I
regard it as one of the finest history books dealing with
West Africa. The standard works on Liberia are J. Gus
Liebenow's *Liberia: The Evolution of Privilege,* P. J.
Staudenraus' *The African Colonization Movement 1816 -
1865,* and C. H. Huberich's dry but compendious
Political and Legislative History of Liberia. Works produced
by Liberians are eccentric but illuminating. Surprisingly
fruitful and fascinating was the obviously biased *African
Repository and Colonial Journal,* recently republished in
New York in 68 volumes. Its partiality one takes for granted,
yet it still provided a powerful evocation of the early days of
Liberia, and in particular of the experiences of the settlers. I
have drawn on the writings of W.E.B. Du Bois and Edward
Wilmot Blyden, two of the most important emigrants to Africa
from the New World, and I acknowledge them where
appropriate.

On the literary front, the most important and complete
collection of early slave songs is that edited by Allen, Ware

and Garrison. I am also indebted to critics such as St Clair Drake and Gerald Moore, and in particular to Janheinz Jahn, whose *History of Neo-African Literature* was invaluable. A tremendously interesting volume is the collection *Black Brotherhood,* edited by Okon Edet Uya, who brought together many of the neo-African texts and speeches and although it makes an uneven volume, it is nevertheless a good general treatment of the relationship of black American to Africa.

The Back-to-Africa movements of the nineteenth century and early part of the twentieth century have been dealt with separately. (My only claim to originality is to have drawn a line directly from the A.C.S. through Turner and Chief Sam to Garvey and thence to the modern Rastafarians and other mystic groups.) The best work on Bishop Turner is undoubtedly Edwin Redkey's penetrating analysis, *Black Exodus.* The comparatively little known Chief Alfred Sam was jauntily but well portrayed in *The Longest Way Home,* by Gilbert Geis and William Bittle. Garvey's own *Philosophy and Opinions* are formative — as we see in modern Africa — but tell more about his opinions than of his significance. The best biography of Garvey is, and will probably remain, *Black Moses,* by E. David Cronon. Little has so far been written of the Jamaican Rastafarians but I have drawn extensively from the report written by Smith, Augier and Nettleford of the University of the West Indies in Kingston.

A number of black Americans and West Indians have written accounts of journeys to Africa and have recorded their impressions. The first major accounts were, of course, those by Delany and Campbell in the mid-nineteenth century. More recently, there have been *Black Boy,* by Richard Wright, a sad but well-written book; *The Rise and Fall of a Proper Negro,* by L. A. Lacy, an account written by an upper-middle-class black, and a disappointing piece, *A Kind of Homecoming,* by E. R. Braithwaite. I found this a disappointing area. The finest expression of the reactions of a New World black living in Africa, though, is the poetry of Edward Brathwaite.

Those works listed in the Bibliography are central to study of Black Zionism; references given in full in the notes are incidental.

The second half of the book is substantially based on interviews I conducted in Ghana, December 1972 — May 1973, and July 1973; in Sierra Leone, May 1973, and in Liberia, June 1973.

GENERAL BIBLIOGRAPHY

African Repository and Colonial Journal (Washington 1826 etc., reprinted in 68 volumes, New York, 1967)

Allen, W.F., Ware, C.P., Garrison, L.M., Slave Songs of the United States (New York, 1867, 1929 and 1951)

Anon., Africa Redeemed (London, 1851)

Blyden, Edward Wilmot, From West Africa to Palestine (Freetown, Manchester, London 1873)

_____Christianity, Islam and the Negro Race (London, 1889)

_____A Voice from Bleeding Africa (Monrovia, 1856)

Booth, Charles, Zachary Macaulay (London, 1934)

Braithwaite, E.R., A Kind of Homecoming (London, 1963)

Buell, Raymond Leslie, Liberia: A Century of Survival (Philadelphia, 1947)

Butt-Thompson, F.W., Sierra Leone in History and Tradition (London, 1926)

Campbell, Robert, A Pilgrimage to my Motherland (London, 1861)

Camphor, Alexander Priestley, Missionary Story Sketches.

_____Folklore from Africa (Cincinatti and New York, 1909)

Clendenen, Clarence C. and Duignan, Peter, Americans in Black Africa up to 1865 (Stanford, Conn., 1964)

Clower, Robert, Dalton, George, Harwitz, Mitchell, and Walters, A.A., Growth without Development; An Economic Survey of Liberia (Evanston, 1966)

Cole, Robert Wellesley, Kossoh Town Boy (London, 1960)

Cronon, E. David, Black Moses (Wisconsin, 1955)

Crooks, J.J., A History of the Colony of Sierra Leone, Western Africa, (Dublin, 1903, London, 1972)

Dallas, R.C., The History of the Maroons (London, 1803; 1968)

Davis, Stanley A., This is Liberia (New York, 1953)

Dean, Harry and North, Sterling, Umbala; The Adventures of a Negro Sea Captain In Africa and on the Seven Seas in his Attempts to found an Ethiopian Empire (London, 1929)

Delany, Martin, Official Report of the Niger Valley Exploring Party (New York and London, 1861)

Donnan, Elizabeth, Documents Illustrative of the History of the Slave Trade to America (Washington, 1930-35)

Drake, St Clair, and others, Africa From the Point of View of American Negro Scholars (Paris, 1958)

Du Bois, W.E.B., Dusk of Dawn (New York, 1940)

_____ The Souls of Black Folk (Chicago, 1903)

_____ Selected Writings, ed. Walter Wilson (New York, 1970)

Dunbar, Ernest, The Black Expatriates (London, 1968)

Edwards, Adolph, Marcus Garvey 1887-1940 (London and Port of Spain, 1967)

Falconbridge, Anna Maria, Two Voyages to the River Sierra Leone During the Years 1791-93 (London, 1794; 1967)

Fanon, Frantz, Toward the African Revolution (Paris, 1964, London, 1970)

_____The Wretched of the Earth (Paris, 1961, London, 1965)

Foner, Philip S., W.E.B. Du Bois Speaks, Speeches and Addresses (New York, 1970)
Fox, Early Lee, The American Colonisation Society 1817-1840 (Baltimore, 1919)
Fraenkel, Merran, Tribe and Class in Monrovia (London 1964)
Fyfe, Christopher, A History of Sierra Leone (London, 1962)
———Sierra Leone Inheritance (London, 1964)
Fyfe, Christopher, and Jones, Eldred, Freetown, A Symposium (Freetown, 1968)
Garvey, Amy Jacques, Garvey and Garveyism (New York, 1963)
Garvey, Marcus M., Philosophy and Opinions, compiled by A.J. Garvey (London, 1967)
Geis, Gilbert, and Bittle, William, The Longest Way Home (Detroit, 1964)
Grant, Douglas, The Fortunate Slave (London, 1968)
Gratus, Jack, The Great White Lie (London, 1973)
Herskovits, Melville, The Myth of the Negro Past (New York and London, 1941)
Hoare, Prince, Memoirs of Granville Sharp Esq. (London 1820)
Huberich, C.H., Political and Legislative History of Liberia (New York, 1947)
Hughes, Langston, and Bontemps, Arna, The Poetry of the Negro 1746-1949 (New York, 1951)
Ingham, E.G., Sierra Leone after a Hundred Years (London, 1894; 1968)
Jahn, Janheinz, A History of Neo-African Literature (Düsseldorf,1966, London, 1968)
Jefferson, Thomas, Notes on Virginia (London, 1787)
Johnson, James, Reality versus Romance in South Central Africa (London, 1893; 1969)
July, Robert W., The Origins of Modern African Thought (London, 1968)
Lacy, Leslie Alexander, The Rise and Fall of a Proper Negro (New York, 1970))
Lanternari, Vittorio, The Religions of the Oppressed (New York and London, 1963)
Legum, Colin, Pan-Africanism (London, 1962)
Leibenow, J. Gus, Liberia: The Evolution of Privilege (Ithaca and London, 1969)
Lewis, Roy, Sierra Leone (London, 1954)
Lock, Alain L.R., The New Negro (New York, 1927)
Lynch, Hollis R., ed., Black Spokesman, Selected Published Writings of E.W. Blyden (London, 1971)
——— Edward Wilmot Blyden, Pan-Negro Patriot (London 1967)
McKay, Claude, Harlem: Negro Metropolis (New York, 1940)
———Selected Poems (New York, 1953)
McKay, Vernon, ed., Africa in the United States (New York, 1970)
Morgan, Gordan D., African Vignettes; Notes of an American Negro Family in East Africa (Jefferson City, Missouri, 1967)
Moore, Gerald, Seven African Writers (London, 1962)
Nkrumah, Kwame, Ghana (London, 1957)
Okoye, Felix N., The American Image of Africa; Myth and Reality (New York, 1971)
Oliver, Paul, Savannah Syncopators: African Retentions in the Blues (New York, 1970)
Peterson, John, Province of Freedom 1787-1870 (Evanston, 1969)
Porter, Arthur T., Creoledom (London, 1963)
Redkey, Edwin S., Black Exodus (New Haven, Conn. and London, 1969)
Richardson, Nathaniel R., Liberia's Past and Present (London, 1959)
Roberts, W.K., An African Canaan for the American Negro (Birmingham, Alabama, 1896)
Rodney, Walter, Groundings with my Brothers (London, 1969)
Rodrigues, José Honorió, Brazil and Africa (Berkeley and Los Angeles, 1965)
Rollin, Frank A., Life and Public Service of Martin R. Delany (Boston, 1883)
Sartre, Jean-Paul, 'Orphée Noir': foreword in Senghor, L.S., Anthologie de la nouvelle poésie nègre et malgache de langue française (Paris, 1948), trans. S.W. Allen (Paris, 1963)

Shepperson, George, and Price, T., Independent African (Edinburgh, 1958)
Smeathman, Henry, Plan of a Settlement to be made near Sierra Leone on the
    Grain Coast of Africa (London, 1786)
Smith, M.G., Augier, Roy, Nettleford, Rex, The Ras Tarafi Movement in Kingston,
    Jamaica (Kingston, Jamaica, 1960)
Staudenraus, P.J., The African Colonization Movement 1816-1865 (New York, 1961)
Uya, Okon Edet, ed., Black Brotherhood (Lexington, Mass., 1971)
Van Danzig, Albert, and Priddy, Barbara, A Short History of the Forts and Castles of
    Ghana (Accra, 1971)
Washington, Booker T., Up From Slavery (New York and London, 1901)
Weinstein, Brian, Eboué (New York, 1972)
West, Richard, Back to Africa (London, 1970)
Wright, Richard, Black Power (London, 1954)
Yancy, Ernest Jerome, Liberia: A 19th-20th Century Miracle (Tel Aviv, 1971)
⸺ Historical Lights of Liberia's Yesterday and Today (New York, 1934)

PERIODICALS

Daily Graphic, Accra

Ghanaian Times, Accra

Spectator, Accra

The Mirror, Accra

Legon Observer, Accra

Transition, Kampala and Accra

West Africa, London

Ovserver, London

Sunday Times, London

New York Times

Sierra Leone Weekly News

Savacou, Kingston, Jamaica

Newsweek, London

Guardian, London

Africa Report, U.S.A.

Africa, London

West African Review, London

Gold Coast Leader, Accra

Freedomways, New York

NOTES

PROLOGUE

1 Huberich, p. 18
2 Donnan, vol.III, 321
3 Marsh, J.B.T., *The Story of the Jubilee Singers, with Their Songs* (Boston, 1880) pp. 196 ff.
4 Allen *et al.,* p.95
5 Grant, pp. 65-118; p. 170
6 Gratus, p. 43
7 Jefferson, pp. 228-30; p. 240
8 Beloff, Max, *Thomas Jefferson and American Democracy* (London, 1848) p. 95; also West, p. 95
9 Staudenraus, p. 3
10 West, pp. 13 ff.
11 Butt-Thompson, p. 71
12 Huberich, p. 12
13 Hoare, p. 267
14 ibid., pp. 312-13
15 ibid., p. 320
16 ibid., p. 313
17 ibid., p. 323

CHAPTER 1

1 From *On These I Stand* (copyright 1925, Harper & Row Publishers Inc.; renewed 1953 by Ida M. Cullen)
2 *Black Power*, p. 158
3 *Black Orpheus* (trans. S.W. Allen) pp. 19-20
4 Ball, Charles, *Slavery in the United States: A Narrative of the Life and Adventures of Charles Ball, A Black Man* (Lewistown, Pennsylvania, 1836) pp. 203-5
5 Herskovits, pp. 276-9
6 Oliver, p. 68ff.
7 Frazier, E. Franklin, *The Negro in the United States* (Toronto, 1957) pp. 10-19. Much of the demographic information in this chapter is based on Frazier's work, which in turn is substantially based on official U.S. census figures. See also Frazier, *The Negro Family in the United States* (Chicago, 1939)
8 Frazier, pp. 38-9, 45-6
9 Phillips, Ulrich B., *Life and Labour in the Old South* (New York, 1929) p. 195
10 Marsh, p. 196
11 Allen *et al*, p. 7
12 ibid. p. 102
13 ibid. p. 46
14 ibid. p. 2
15 Frazier, p. 61
16 Okoye, p. 130 ff.
17 Jahn, p. 143
18 Bastide, Roger, *A poesia afro-brasiliera* (Sao Paulo, 1943) p. 47
19 Jahn, p. 125
20 Seward, Theo. F., *Preface to the Music,* in Marsh, p. 121
21 Jahn, p. 157
22 Blyden, *A Voice from Bleeding Africa*
23 ibid.
24 Frazier, p. 160
25 Woodward, C. Vann, *Tom Watson Agrarian Rebel* (New York, 1938) p.432; Frazier, p. 159
26 Frazier, pp. 190-4
27 Hughes, Langston and Bontemps, Arna, *The Poetry of the Negro 1746-1949* (New York, 1949) p. 250 ff.
28 Hughes, Langston, 'I've Known Rivers,' *Crisis*, June 1921; Hughes, *Selected Poems* (New York, 1959) p. 4
29 Fitts, Dudley, ed., *Anthology of Contemporary Latin-American Poetry* (Norfolk, Conn., and London, 1942 and 1947) p. 72
30 McKay, Claude, *Selected Poems*, p. 41

31 Declaration, Conakray, October 1969
32 Quoted in Uya, ed., p. ix
33 McKay, Vernon, ed., p. 9
34 *New York Times,* February 16th, 1961
35 Herskovits, 'The Image of Africa in the United States', paper delivered in Boston 1961; in McKay, ed., p. 40
36 *Souls of Black Folk,* p. 13
37 *Africa Report,* August 1964; McKay, ed., p. 19
38 *Dusk of Dawn,* p. 116
39 *Transition,* vol. IV, no. 15, 1964, p. 20
40 *Dusk of Dawn,* p. 116
41 Baldwin, James, *Notes of a Native Son* (Boston, 1955) p. 112
42 Williams, Denis, *Other Leopards* (London, 1963) p. 20
43 ibid, p. 27
44 *Focus* (Journal of the students of the University of Science and Technology) Kumasi, Ghana, vol.V, no. 1, 1973, p. 19

CHAPTER 2

1 Woodson, Carter G., ed., *The Mind of the Negro as reflected in Letters Written During the Crisis, 1800-1860* (Washington, 1926) pp. 30 ff.
2 Johnson, Henry W., *African Repository and Colonial Journal,* vol. XLI, p. 375
3 Sierra Leone archives, microfilm collection
4 Du Bois, 'Liberia, the League and the United States', *Foreign Affairs,* New York, July 1933
5 Falconbridge, p. 64
6 ibid., p. 125
7 Elliott, J.B., *The Lady Huntingdon's Connexion in Sierra Leone* (London, 1851) pp. 14-15
8 Falconbridge, pp. 147-8
9 Ross, George, *Diary 1800,* Ms in Sierra Leone archives
10 Falconbridge, p. 134
11 Quoted in Fyfe, *A History,* p. 52; the originals of Macaulay's journals are in the University of California at Los Angeles
12 Fyfe, *A History,* p. 87
13 Dallas, pp. 286-9

14 See Porter, pp. 20-53
15 Burton, *Wanderings in West Africa* (London, 1863); West, p. 192
16 Examples of anti-Lebanese cartoons in Senegal are reprinted from *Les Echos d'Afrique Noire,* 1954, in Rita Cruise O'Brien's splendid *White Society in Black Africa* (London, 1972) pp. 75 and 77
17 Fyfe and Jones, *Freetown,* p. 200
18 Prof. Herman von Holst of the University of Freiburg, quoted in Staudenraus, p. 1
19 Huberich, p. 45
20 Staudenraus, p. 3
21 ibid., p. 3
22 ibid., p. 18
23 Sherwood, Henry N. and Cuffee, Paul, *Journal of Negro History,* vol. VIII (Lancaster, Pennsylvania, 1923) pp. 154-9
24 Staudenraus, p. 43
25 Caldwell to Samuel A. Crozer, December 10th, 1819; Huberich, p. 96
26 Huberich, p. 77
27 *Africa Redeemed,* pp. 46-7
28 ibid., pp. 48-9
29 Staudenraus, pp. 70 ff.; West, p. 114
30 *A.R.C.J.,* vol.I, p. 29
31 Staudenraus, p. 155
32 *A.R.C.J.,* vol.I, p. 96
33 *A.R.C.J.,* vol.I, p. 219
34 *A.R.C.J.,* vol.II, p. 110
35 *A.R.C.J.,* vol.III, p. 277
36 *A.R.C.J.,* vol.III, p. 278
37 Liebenow, p. 1
38 *A.R.C.J.,* vol.V, p. 13
39 Staudenraus, p. 153
40 *A.R.C.J.,* vol.V, p. 155
41 *A.R.C.J.,* vol.V, pp. 60-61
42 *A.R.C.J.,* vol.VI, p. 178
43 *A.R.C.J.,* vol.V, p. 282
44 *A.R.C.J.,* vol.III, pp. 301-7
45 West, p. 135
46 Staudenraus, pp. 155 ff.
47 Liebenow, p. 66
48 Declaration of Independence, 1847, amended May 1955
49 Liebenow, p. 25
50 Liebenow, p. 18
51 Letter to A.C.S., dated February 15th 1910
52 The Commission appointed by the League of Nations was headed by a

Scots dentist, Dr Cuthberg Christie —
the body came to be known as the
Christie Commission, and had two
other members, a Dr Johnson, a
black American academic, and
Arthur Barclay, a former President of
Liberia. The commission reported in
September 1930
53 Liebenow, p. 143

CHAPTER 3

1 Redkey, p. 221
2 Cronon, p. 66
3 Forten,Charlotte L., *The Journal of
Charlotte L. Forten, A Free Negro in
the Slave Era,* ed. Ray Allen
Billington (New York, 1961) pp. 16-
17
4 Thomas, William Hannibal, *The
American Negro* (New York, 1901)
pp. 340-41
5 Delany, pp. 10 ff; Redkey, p. 21
6 Delany, p. 26
7 ibid., p. 27
8 Campbell, pp. 34-5
9 ibid., p. 19
10 ibid., p. 43
11 ibid., p. 11
12 Delany named his children Toussaint
L'Ouverture, Charles Lennox Remond,
Alexander Dumas, Saint Cyprian,
Faustin Souloque, Rameses Placido,
Ethiopia Amelia
13 Crummell, *Relations and Duties*
(Hartford, 1861) p. 4; Uya, ed.,
p. 65
14 Crummell to J.E. Bruce, November
26th, 1895; Redkey, p. 230
15 Du Bois, *Crisis,*(New York, July 1915)
p.132; Redkey, p. 230
16 Redkey, p. 29
17 ibid., p. 31
18 ibid., p. 32
19 ibid., p. 33
20 *Call of Providence* (New York, 1862)
21 Blyden, *The Origin and Purpose of
African Colonisation* (Wahington,
1883) p. 15, quoted in Lynch, p. 116
22 Uya, ed., p. 102; Redkey, 'Bishop
Turner's African Dream', *Journal of
American History,* p. 54(New Haven,
Connecticut, 1967)pp. 271-290
23 Redkey, p. 41

24 Turner to *A.M.E. Church Review,* I
(New York; January 1885)p. 246;
Voice of Missions, November 1895;
Uya,ed., p. 107
25 *Christian Recorder,* February 22nd,
1883; Uya,ed., p. 102
26 Letters to *A.M.E. Church Review,* 8
(New York, April 1892)pp. 446-98,
quoted in Redkey, p. 44; Uya,ed.,
p. 107
27 Uya,ed., pp. 108-9
28 Redkey, p. 241
29 Washington, pp. 221-3
30 Harlan, Louis,'Booker T. Washington
and the White Man's Burden',
American Historical Review, vol. LXXI,
p. 2 (New York, January 1966)pp.
441-67
31 ibid.
32 State Department to Rice, Washington, October 16th, 1913
(Correspondence in Ghana National
Archives)
33 Lee Cruce to British Consul, St Louis,
November 11th, 1913
34 Guess to Sir Edward Grey, Colonial
Office, December 20th, 1913
35 Colonial Office to Guess, January 6th,
1914
36 Geis and Bittle, p. 7 (See also Geis
and Bittle, 'Alfred Charles Sam and
an African Return: A Case Study in
Negro Despair', *Phylon,* Atlanta, June
1962, pp. 178-194
37 Geis and Bittle, p. 72 (Articles of
Incorporation, Akim Trading Company Ltd, Secretary of State, Pierre,
South Dakota, March 21st, 1913)
38 Geis and Bittle, p. 160
39 Secondary sources supplemented by
interviews by author in Ghana
between December 1972 and July
1973
40 *Tulsa Star,* May 1st, 1915; Geis and
Bittle, p. 192
41 'Faduma,Prof. Orishatukeh', 'The
African Movement', *Gold Coast
Leader,* July 10th, 1915
42 Geis and Bittle, p. 196
43 W.H. Hurt to Governor's Office,
Accra, August 2nd, 1920 (This
correspondence is in the Ghana
National Archives)
44 Hurt to Welman, December 19th,1921

45 Furley to Hurt, April 22nd,1922
46 Hurt to Furley, July 15th,1922
47 Geis and Bittle, p. 207
48 Garvey, *Philosophy and Opinions,*
vol.I, p. 126
49 ibid., vol.II, p. 405
50 Cronon, p. 17
51 Garvey, *Philosophy and Opinions,*
vol.I, p. 9
52 ibid., vol.II, p. 82
53 ibid., vol.I, p. 1
54 ibid., vol.II, pp. 140-41
55 Cronon, p. 65
56 ibid., p. 66
57 Garvey, *Philosophy and Opinions,*
vol.II, pp. 300-405
58 Cronon, p. 129
59 Garvey, *Philosophy and Opinions,*
vol.II, pp. 389-90
60 ibid., vol.I, p. 77
61 ibid., vol.I, pp. 5 and 6
62 Rogers, Joel A., *World's Great Men of
Colour* (New York, 1946)pp. 11 and
602; Cronon, p. 198
63 Drake, St Clair, 'Hide my Face', in
Herbert Hill, ed., *Soon One Morning*
(New York,1963) pp. 78-105; Uya,
ed., p. 209
64 Nkrumah, p. 45
65 *Daily Gleaner,* Kingston, Jamaica,
July 12th, 1964, quoted in Amy
Jacques Garvey, p. 308
66 Smith *et al,* pp. 1-15; Lanternari, p.
159. (See also, Errol Bowen, 'Rasta-
farianism and the New Society',
Savacou, June 1971, pp. 41 ff.)
67 Lanternari, p. 306
68 ibid., p. 301
69 McKay, *Harlem,* p. 176
70 Cronon, p. 163
71 Smith *et al,* pp. 18-30
72 ibid., pp. 59-60

CHAPTER 4

1 *A.R.C.J.,* vol.V, p. 95
2 *New York Times,* September 5th,
1971
3 Du Bois, *Dusk of Dawn,* pp. 117 and
125
4 *Black Power,* pp. 36-40
5 Lacy, *Rise and Fall,* p. 123
6 Blyden, *From West Africa to
Palestine,* p. 112; Lynch, p. 55

7 Brathwaite, Edward, 'The New Ships',
from *Masks* (London, 1968)

CHAPTER 5

1 Blyden, *The Call of Providence to the
Descendants of Africa in America*
(New York, 1862)
2 Agyemang, Fred M., *A Century With
Boys* (Accra, 1967) p. 20. Also un-
dated documents and letters at
Presbyterian Mission, Akropong-
Akwapim, Ghana. An account of the
establishment of the mission appeared
in *West African Review,* July 1962.
The archives of the Basel Evangelical
Missionary Society are in Basel.
Additional details were provided by
the descendants of the original West
Indian missionaries in Akropong
3 *Mirror,* Accra, August 4th,1972
4 *Daily Graphic,* Accra, August 22nd,
1972
5 *Mirror,* Accra, August 4th,1972
6 An absorbing fictional treatment of
Brazilian repatriation to West Africa
is *The Water House,* by Antonio
Olinto (London, 1970)
7 *Black Power,* p. 153
8 Legum, *Pan-Africanism,*p. 137
9 Blyden, *From West Africa to Palestine,*
pp. 104-5
10 *Daily Graphic,* Accra, July 20th, 1971
11 *Daily Graphic,* Accra, July 24th, 1971
12 *Daily Graphic,* Accra, August 4th,
1971
13 *Daily Graphic,* Accra, September 4th,
1971
14 See Isaacs, Harold R., *The New World
of Negro Americans* (New York,
1968) pp. 288-305, reprinted in Uya,
ed.; also Isaacs, 'A Reporter at
Large', *New Yorker* magazine, May
13th, 1961

CHAPTER 6

1 Ankrah, Mrs Maxine, 'The African
Connection', *Africa* magazine (Paris,
March 19th, 1973)
2 Falconbridge, p. 126; Fyfe, *A History,*
p. 53

3 Achebe, Chinua, *No Longer At Ease* (London, 1960)
4 Armah, Ayi Kwei, *Fragments*(Boston, 1970); Armah also wrote the best description by any writer of modern Ghana in *The Beautyful Ones Are Not Yet Born* (London, 1969)

CHAPTER 7

1 *A.R.C.J.*, vol. VIII, p. 282
2 Gunther, John, *Inside Africa* (London, 1955) pp. 827-31
3 West, p. 324
4 Falconbridge, p. 135
5 An account of the problems of the Black Hebrews in Israel appeared in the London *Sunday Times*, October 7th, 1973
6 Numerous newspaper accounts include that of the London *Observer*, November 19th, 1972
7 Bai T. Moore, *Murder in the Cassava Patch* (Holland, 1968); also in *Liberian Writing: Liberia as seen by her own writers as well as by German authors* (Tübingen, 1970)
8 See Koelle, S.W., *Outlines of a Grammar of the Vei Language* (London, 1854). Koelle says the language was invented in the early nineteenth century by one Momoru Doalu Bukere, 'the noble and modest originator of the only mode of native writing ever discovered among the negro race', pp. 229-40
9 Greene, Graham, *The Heart of the Matter* (London, 1948)
10 Burton, *Wanderings in West Africa*, quoted in West, p. 194
11 Kingsley, Mary, *Travels in West Africa* (London, 1897, 1965) p. 19
12 *John Bull* magazine, April 24th, 1826
13 Horton, J.A.B., *West African Countries and Peoples* (London, 1868) pp. 61-2, 89,97-100; also Fyfe, *Inheritance*, pp.206 ff.
14 Fyfe, *Inheritance*, p. 208
15 J. Clarkson to Henry Thornton, December 1st, 1791; Porter, p. 30
16 Porter, pp. 36ff.
17 Blyden, *Christianity, Islam and the Negro Race*, pp. 244-5
18 Cheyney-Coker, Syl, from 'The Masochist', in *Concerto for an Exile* (London, 1973)
19 Mill, J.S., *Representative Government* (1861); Redkey, p. 11
20 Du Bois, *Dusk of Dawn*, p. 116